An Image of My Name Enters America

Also by Lucy Ives

Life Is Everywhere

Cosmogony

The Poetics (with Matthew Connors)

Loudermilk: Or, The Real Poet; Or, The Origin of the World

Impossible Views of the World

The Hermit

Human Events

The Worldkillers

nineties

Orange Roses

Novel

Anamnesis

My Thousand Novel

As editor

The Saddest Thing Is That I Have Had to Use Words:
  A Madeline Gins Reader

An Image of My Name Enters America

Essays

Lucy Ives

GRAYWOLF PRESS

Some parts of "An Image of My Name Enters America" were published online under a different form in *Lapham's Quarterly*.

Author's note: I have tried to recreate events, locales, and conversations from my memories of them. In order to maintain their anonymity in some instances I have changed the names of individuals and places, and I may have changed some identifying characteristics and details such as physical properties, occupations, and places of residence.

Published by Graywolf Press
212 Third Avenue North, Suite 485
Minneapolis, Minnesota 55401

www.graywolfpress.org

Published in the United States of America

ISBN 978-1-64445-311-7   (paperback)
ISBN 978-1-64445-312-6   (ebook)

2 4 6 8 9 7 5 3 1
First Graywolf Printing, 2024

Library of Congress Cataloging-in-Publication Data

Names: Ives, Lucy, 1980– author.
Title: An image of my name enters America : essays / Lucy Ives.
Other titles: Image of my name enters America (Compilation)
Description: Minneapolis, Minnesota : Graywolf Press, 2024. | Includes
    bibliographical references.
Identifiers: LCCN 2024013423 (print) | LCCN 2024013424 (ebook) | ISBN
    9781644453117 (trade paperback) | ISBN 9781644453124 (epub)
Subjects: LCSH: Ives, Lucy, 1980– | LCGFT: Essays.
Classification: LCC PS3609.V48 I43 2024 (print) | LCC PS3609.V48 (ebook) |
    DDC 814/.6—dc23/eng/20240426
LC record available at https://lccn.loc.gov/2024013423
LC ebook record available at https://lccn.loc.gov/2024013424

Cover design: Kapo Ng

for Yves

Contents

An Image of My Name Enters America

Of Unicorns

> They say that this animal
> cannot be taken alive.
> —*Pliny the Elder*[1]

When I was pregnant with my son, the midwife who would attend his birth told me a strange story.

I don't remember how the conversation began—probably we were seated in her small office, all of us in masks, me on the edge of the couch with my belly between my thighs. My son was a long baby and the belly that contained him and the placenta (plus cord, fluids, sac) was a long, relatively narrow belly, one that jutted out like a rounded fin or half egg. I sometimes liked to rest a small plate or cup of coffee atop it. When I looked at this belly in profile in the mirror, so prominent was this protuberance that it appeared to be tugging my lower body gently upward, rather than weighing me down, although that was not how it felt.

I would likely have been rubbing my midsection in the midwife's office, enjoying the tautness of its simultaneously firm yet ever-shifting surface, the warmth of my skin beneath whichever garment I had managed to make fit that week, along with the occasional fetal shift or kick. We arrived at the topic of the experiences of the fetus; thence, to what the fetus can remember.

Neither my partner nor I have memories of the portion of our lives we spent enclosed in a uterus. It did not occur to me to conceive of this period, the prenatal period, as one of unfiltered bliss, although many people do think of it in such terms. Symbolically, particularly from the point of view of two of the three Abrahamic religions, it is a lived time that occurs before the possibility of sin; it is prelapsarian, everyone's Eden.

Because I am neither a believer nor prone to imagining states of ecstatic suspension (I'm afraid of heights), my personification differed. I said something like, Could the fetus experience vertigo? If he is upside down all the time and confined? Could he feel like I sometimes feel when I am on an airplane? That I am in too small a space and too large a space, both at once? That, paradoxically, I am certain to fall precisely because I cannot leave this metal tube?

Does he want to throw up? I might have asked. Does he have to keep repeating to himself an idiotic statistical mantra about relative risk in order to distract his mind? Is he worried that he will never get out of here? Is he extremely, unbearably disturbed?

The midwife laughed. She did this in a kind way. She was frequently fielding my hyperbolic anxieties and didn't seem to mind. I could swing from a state of hazy, dreamy satisfaction to one of sheer terror on a dime, an affective transit that I more than once simultaneously observed myself embarking on as from a distance—for pregnancy is a hormone-stuffed state of many, many points of view and as many moods. A cliché perhaps yet no less true: I often thought that without the high I derived from the proliferation of signaling molecules that were instructing my body to sustain my son-to-be, along with his abode, it would have been impossible to withstand the sheer alterity of current events within my abdomen. However, given this otherwise helpful physiological and mental transformation, activities like driving or public speaking presented new challenges. My mind was buoyant but obtuse, optimistic yet unconcerned with details, for example, interstate exits, accurate dates and proper nouns.

"I think," the midwife said, meanwhile, "that he will have a very interesting relationship to language."

She had an uncanny knack for reframing my assumptions.

She began to tell a story: When she was a child, she said, she had a recurring dream. In this dream, she was always touching a deliciously smooth surface. The surface was perfect in its smoothness. To feel its smoothness was to eat the richest food, smell the most delightful and calming smell. She used to hate to wake up from this dream, a source of joy. Only later did she come to suspect that the beautiful dream was not a dream, at all. Rather, it was a memory. She now believes that the recurring dream was a memory of being inside her mother's uterus, an experience defined by an intense tactile pleasure that is not available after birth. Although there are other pleasures.

I listened. I wanted to believe that there are things that most of us cannot remember but that, for some people, do figure ambiguously as memory.

I had also heard (and read), in my sundry peregrinations online and elsewhere, that people who are in the presence of a birthing person, or who are themselves giving birth, may relive their own births. This was the sort of thing I could be hopeful about.

How we get here, how smooth that portal is, how the portal is alive and unlike any other door.

My earliest memories are of my own interest in perfection. The supreme object of my interest, of my deepest intellectual and sensual love, was a product designed and manufactured with the aim of capturing the attention of very young girls.

I was hardly unusual. I was obedient, even; in some ways unimaginative. Still, I think we can learn something from my thrall:

My Little Pony, a figurine copyrighted by Hasbro, was first produced in 1982. Based on My Pretty Pony, a larger and clunkier toy with unimpressive sales, My Little Pony was, despite the singularity baked into its name, always plural.[2] There was no "pony," never a one. Only ponies—many ponies, always proliferating, mutating, reaccessorized. Earth ponies and sea ponies and winged ponies and, of course, unicorn ponies. Each pony with its distinctive not-to-be-found-in-nature shade, its shimmering corn-silk plastic mane, its rump with allegorical symbol, a.k.a. "cutie mark": ice cream, clover, seahorse, stars, flowering plants, and on and on, emojis avant la lettre. The ponies' bodies were plastic. For now, the ponies would not decay, although fire might melt them or a car wheel crush them. Their eyes were round and bedecked with long lashes, irises illustrated in such a way that each pony eye appeared perpetually brimming. Highlights, as on a meniscus of dew, were standard.[3] The ponies might weep soon. They might cry for joy. They might look in your direction.

The ponies lived in Ponyland. It is not clear where they came from nor how they reproduced. They were inside the television, part of a twenty-two-minute weekday cartoon called, fittingly enough, *My Little Pony*, and thus inhabited a visual realm, temporally constrained yet constantly available if one had a VHS system and knowledge of how to record. They were material, as stated. They were moving images, as stated. They could be purchased and held. They could be watched. They were smooth, seamless, without any roughness. One might run a hand down their necks, across their shoulders, along their backs. One might brush their plastic-scented, flower-color hair.

The myth-world of My Little Ponies was allied with other myth-worlds of the mid- to late 1980s: the land of the Care Bears; the stationery empire of Lisa Frank; the intergalactic realms of She-Ra, of Wildfire the magical horse, of the ThunderCats. These myth-worlds flowed into one another and got confused; it did not matter that they were unaffiliated IP. They had rainbows, lots of rainbows, and craggy cliffs and lush forests and desert planets with buried fortresses, and were always elsewhere, beyond the sky or solar system. You did not attain these places by walking down the street. They were like heaven, although no god was present. Devils aplenty: deranged scientists and bitter witches and space dictators and reanimated corpses with surprisingly good social skills were available to frustrate bliss. But there was no singular author of the good, no logos. There was only a puffy, sparkling spirit that cheerfully resisted death, corruption, violence—the ponies were mild imps who lived in terror of a Christian Satan. They always won out but it was by no means certain they would survive. These were the terms of the contest: femme tribe of hunter-gatherer horses versus citadel-dwelling autocracy equipped with what I now take to be early sixteenth-century levels of technology and opposable thumbs.

You collected the ponies. You displayed the ponies. You made the ponies move and speak. You had them interact with She-Ra or perhaps Panthro, your favorite ThunderCat. You watched the cartoon series and the mediocre animated movie. You sided with the good. You experimented with the struggle of the good and caused the plastic bodies to crash into one another. You brushed their tangled silky hair and sometimes cut it off with safety scissors.

My Little Pony's bodily gestalt closely resembles that of characters in Disney's *Fantasia* (1940)—specifically, a herd of infant pegasi and unicorns who make brief appearances in "Pastoral Symphony," a visual interpretation of Beethoven's Sixth. Here a highly stylized version of ancient Greece, rendered by artists who had obviously never set foot on the Peloponnesus, supports aggressively manicured flora. The rolling hills and pom-pom trees are reminiscent of Grant Wood's precisionist landscapes and therefore oddly Iowan, none too Olympian. The little mythical horses gambol in leafy zones. They are impossible pastel shades and offer relief from hetero mating games enacted by the main characters of "Pastoral Symphony," a group of nubile centaurs and "centaurettes."

Ponyland, once it appears over four decades later, is not located anywhere near fake ancient Greece. In the 1980s, visuals associated with woodlands of the European Middle Ages were all the rage and therefore the ponies do not live in a caricature of the grounds of Monticello, although they are magically connected to a well-to-do part of rural America where their human intercessor Megan makes her home.[4] The My Little Ponies inhabit a Germanic forest of pleasure, just steps from the locations of such unicorn-centered films as *The Last Unicorn* (1982) and *Legend* (1985). Swords, cauldrons, drawbridges, and magic wands are available, even as roller skates, legwarmers, tutus, boomboxes, examples of anachronistic architecture (e.g., suburban tract home), plus soft-serve ice cream, proliferate.

Why did unicorns become such a thing in 1980s America?[5] I watch a commercial for school supplies by Lisa Frank, a major proponent of unicorn imagery, and the child actor explains that the glut of stickers, binders, and the like is "impossible to keep up with." This said, "It's fun to try!"[6] "Lisa Frank: You Gotta Have It!" was the slogan. She must have it. All the rainbows and unicorns and butterflies and penguins in sunglasses and gumball dispensers and glistening hearts. All the smoothness, cuteness, perfection, palm trees. All the lozenges of light beaming from these ideal forms. Grinning orcas, infant tigers, pandas in overalls.

As if summoned by this deluge of devotional imagery, unicorns seemed to come into actual embodied existence at this time too. In or before 1980, Morning Glory and Oberon Zell, an enterprising neopagan couple, created a "Living Unicorn" by transplanting the horn buds of immature goats so that the animals' horns grew together into a single "corn" at the center of their foreheads.[7] The Zells toured Renaissance fairs, monoceros goats in tow, and signed a deal with the Ringling Bros. and Barnum & Bailey Circus in 1984. The circus took four of the Zells' specimens on a cross-country tour that kicked off in Houston, Texas.[8] It was in this way that a unicorn "attends party at disco"—as a headline in the *Park City Daily News* of Bowling Green, Kentucky, reported on April 19, 1985. Among those also on display were "Eric Douglas, son of actor Kirk Douglas," as well as "a man with white hair coiffed in a one-foot horn like the unicorn's" and "baby sharks in a tank."[9]

In one reading, the Zells' goats satisfied a collective longing for a fantastical nature religion, inflected by an uncomfortable nostalgia for pseudomedieval times. In another, the circus unicorns seem an example of the unkind lengths to which humans will go to shape that which is living into a desired image. The American Society for the Prevention of Cruelty to Animals and the US Department of Agriculture certainly took note of the Zells' innovations.[10] In the spring of 1985, as controversy swirled, the chief federal veterinarian in New York State, one Dr. Gerald Toms, announced, "There is nothing wrong with the goats, and that is a considerable relief to find."[11] A week later, the unicorn celebrated its sanity by joining Eric Douglas and the sharks at the club.

The unicorn breed or variant of My Little Pony was less real or realistic than the Zells' goats and was, therefore, an even more potent site of fantasy. Wingless (apparently turf-bound), she possessed a talent: wiggling, wriggling, twinkling her flank, she was able to disappear from one location and reappear in another. She teletransported—a magic body. She therefore underlines a peculiar quality of the time inherent to the MLP myth-world: this myth-world is not historical, although significant events (crises) in the style of history occur. The My Little Ponies seem to lack the sorts of mnemonic affordances (e.g., writing or social institutions) that would allow them to retain intergenerational memories, and, in any case, although baby My Little Ponies exist, the My Little Ponies appear to be immortal, unaffected by death. They wink in and out of an eternal present. They disappear when the show ends and reappear when it begins again, and nothing has changed. They increase in number but not one of them ages. They have little reason to believe that any day will be at all unlike the last.

In late twentieth-century Ponyland, there is no god, death,

or recorded history. And there is no erotic love.[12] The ponies might have some hermaphroditic capacity, like the velociraptors of Michael Crichton's *Jurassic Park* (1990) who are engineered from amphibian DNA, but their reproductive lives are never explained. It would be unsurprising to come across a "nest" of My Little Pony "eggs"—candy-colored and trembling and ready to hatch. Yet Ponyland, a garden of earthly delights, is ultimately chaste. In it, the unicorn's traditional association with purity has been so amplified as to become sterility. Here nature is a backdrop and is dead, despite the verdancy of the realm. Is not the world of My Little Ponies an image of postindustrial reproduction, in which images beget other images by means invisible to human eyes? It is a social space at once sexless and intently feminized. This femininity is slavishly devoted to (1) vague expressions of care, and (2) adhering to personality traits allegorically entailed by the symbols on any given pony's rump.

More enticing to me than this soulless cartoon and its anodyne landscapes were My Little Pony's mesmerizing commercials, featuring tropes strung together in more or less the same order: cartoon vignette displaying rainbow logo and frolicking characters; introduction of new plastic figurines corresponding to cartoon characters; elaboration of possibilities for play in time to jingle by live child actors. The little girls, always primped as for a pageant, animate their ponies using their hands. They cause them to walk into the Satin Slipper Sweet Shoppe or Poof 'n Puff Perfume Palace, offer them nourishment or grooming, raise them to their lips, and kiss them on their plastic muzzles.

"I'm a My Little Pony mommy," the jingle goes, "and now I'm happy as can be, because the My Little Pony Perm Shoppe beautifies my family!" The jingle extols "a beautiful place to comb their pretty hair." "My Little Pony, My Little Pony" croon soft female voices. The jingle announces, "We're My Little Pony girls!" Someone sings, "Little Pony, it's all for you!" "I love you, My Little

Pony," a girl says, briefly able to speak above the music. She murmurs, "I love the way you feel, my So Soft My Little Pony." She reverently whispers, "You dance wonderfully, my Little Pony."[13]

The commercials' live-action environments were shade-speckled playrooms and artificial gardens. Collectible enclosures—the Dream Castle or Lullabye Nursery or Baby Bonnet School of Dance—were displayed on tabletops. The heads of the child actors nodded close by, their eyes and mouths visible through the windows and doorways of various sanctuaries and salons. The girls manipulated the pastel equines. One could almost imagine that the Flutter Ponies and Secret Surprise Ponies and Fancy Mermaid Ponies and Sundae Best Ponies and Twice as Fancy Ponies and Sweetberry Ponies and Drink 'n Wet Baby Ponies and Twinkle-Eyed Ponies and Brush 'n Grow Ponies and Sparkle Ponies and Princess Ponies and Newborn Twins Baby Ponies and Baby Ponies with First Tooth and Magic Message Ponies and Dance 'n Prance Ponies and Tropical Ponies and Rockin' Beat Ponies were alive.

The unicorn is neither an American nor European invention. In the Bundahišn, a Zoroastrian book of creation probably compiled sometime between the third and seventh centuries, a gargantuan, three-legged, white ass with six eyes and nine mouths reflects the tumult of primordial matter. Its single horn "is of gold and hollow, and a thousand branches grow out of it." This encyclopedic cosmogony teaches us that the giant unicorn-ass will use its horn to "strike and shatter all corruption that comes from harmful animals," purifying the waters it stands in.[14]

Horned recluses proliferate in earlier foundational texts: in the Ramayana and Mahabharata, one encounters Risyasringa, a young man with horns who becomes a rain-bringer and is later tempted out of his hermit's retreat by love; in the Gilgamesh narrative, the wild bull-man Enkidu may be associated with Enki, a god with a horned crown who governs water and fertility.[15] Enkidu's singular concern in life is that animals be able to drink in peace.[16] In these two mythical accounts, horned beings act on behalf of nature, devoted to the essential element of water. Danish art historian Lise Gotfredsen observes that such narratives were "probably suited to communities which still remembered their hunting past."[17] In the Chinese tradition, the sacred one- or two-horned *qilin* (sometimes transliterated *ch'i-lin* or *kirin*) is a figure of justice whose powerful body may be depicted as partially on fire.[18] The *qilin* is not thought to be an ancestor of the European unicorn.

A traceable unicorn of the West first appears in 398 BCE or so, in a fanciful book on India by the Greek physician Ctesias of Cnidus. Ctesias served at the Persian court, where he was in a good position to act as an intermediary between the traditions of Iraq, Iran, and India, and the Greek empire. His *Indica* contains accounts of a wild ass about the size of a horse with a white body, dark red head, and striking blue eyes. It possesses a single, multicolored horn: white at the base, crimson at its tip, black in between.[19] Aristotle also makes brief mention of the unicorn, and subsequent Roman travelogues include descriptions. Aelian and Pliny follow Ctesias, locating these beasts in India but inventing new breeds, giving some elephant feet and black horns. One of Aelian's rhinoceros-like unicorns makes a threatening bellow. Julius Caesar, an innovator, claims that the forests of southwestern Germany contain elk-like unicorns. Some of these textual unicorns will die to avoid capture. Their priceless horns have therapeutic properties.[20]

The word *unicornis* (literally "single horn") subsequently earned a permanent place in the Old Testament by way of Saint Jerome's late fourth-century Latin translation of the Greek noun *monokeros*, itself a questionable Septuagint translation of the Assyrian *remu*, rendered in Hebrew as *re'em*, or ox.[21] But even

before this act of creation, the qualities and powers of the unicorn were broadcast throughout the Christian world by the
Physiologus, a text supposedly authored by an anonymous zoolo-
gist that began to circulate sometime between the second and
fourth centuries. Here we find the story of a fierce unicorn who
can only be tamed by a female virgin. The *Physiologus*'s tales became the basis for numerous medieval bestiaries, and it is not
hard to see how interpreters of scripture who were also conver-
sant with it, or other derivative creaturely text, might have begun
to perceive Christ as a persecuted unicorn, with his mother Mary
a maiden welcoming him into her lap.[22]

By the thirteenth century, however, with the rise of the culture of courts in Western Europe, the unicorn was popularized
as an emblem of earthly love. The alluring virgin was sometimes
shown entirely naked, leaving little mystery as to the symbolism of her unicorn's erect horn.[23] In a further trend toward the
worldly, by the fifteenth century depictions of unicorn hunts in-
corporated tropes from medieval stag hunts, including trained
dogs.[24] The unicorn, apparently male in these accounts, is lured
into a *hortus conclusus*, tamed by a girl, pursued by a force of
hounds, then slaughtered by well-armed men. His horn has powers of purification: perhaps these powers are Christian in nature,
perhaps alchemical, perhaps pharmaceutical, perhaps erotic,
perhaps an archaic green magic.

Thus, the unicorn of the Middle Ages is a walking metaphor,
capable of playing host to a variety of belief systems and customs.
Hildegard von Bingen, the "Sybil of the Rhine," a polymathic
German abbess, wrote in her twelfth-century *Physica* that beneath the horn of the unicorn lies a bone as clear as glass, a sort of
mirror in which a person may see their reflection.[25] This is one
of the wiser statements regarding this medieval beast. Even after
various sixteenth-century detractions, including the Council
of Trent's prohibition of Christ's allegorical representation as a
unicorn and André Thevet's conclusion in his 1575 *Cosmographie*

universelle that the unicorn does not exist at all, the unicorn persisted.[26] Sir John Hawkins reported in his 1564 account of voyages to North America that inhabitants of Florida wore pieces of unicorn horn as jewelry.[27] Arnoldus Montanus's 1671 *The New and Unknown World* contains Canadian unicorns who sport a "horn right out of the forehead" and frequent "the gloomiest wildernesses."[28] In the nineteenth century, in the wake of European colonization of Africa, unicorns appeared north of Mozambique:

> A single horn projects from its forehead from between two and two and a-half feet in length. This is said to be flexible when the animal is asleep, and can be curled up at pleasure, like an elephant's proboscis; but it becomes stiff and hard under the excitement of rage.

The addition of a motile horn seems necessary to persuade the reader of the existence the Mozambique-proximate unicorn—as if previous accounts of unicorns had missed a crucial physiognomic detail, one that analogizes the penis with cringe-inducing plainness. Drawn from Philip Henry Gosse's 1861 *The Romance of Natural History*, this passage proudly attests to the author's "aesthetic" distaste for "mere accuracy."[29]

The unicorn familiar to American children of the twentieth and twenty-first centuries is, meanwhile, a softening of French and English heraldic unicorns found on fourteenth- and fifteenth-century family crests and military trappings.[30] Located somewhere on an anatomical continuum between goat and horse, if more equine than hircine, this contemporary hybrid is so white as to be nearly blue, nearly silver. All the colors of the rainbow appear in its mane. It may emit a mist of sparkles. It speaks, flies, lives in the sky or in paradise. It is associated with princesses, flowers, wishes, hearts. It retains a twisted horn derived from the narwhal, the mysterious Arctic cetacean that began to contribute to the European unicorn's appearance at some point before the late Middle Ages.

Narwhals, still poorly understood by biologists, are, if male, frequently but not universally possessed of a sensitive left tooth that grows through their lips, usually in a spiral shape, forming a somewhat flexible tusk. The tusk is thought to be a secondary sex characteristic; male narwhals occasionally rub tusks but have not been observed using them aggressively. Neither male nor female narwhals have any other exposed teeth and therefore swallow their food whole.[31] Their lives play out far below heavy pack ice and, like unicorns, they do not survive in captivity.[32]

-:-

It was from My Little Ponies that I first learned of unicorns. I got the idea of an adorable outline, a particular prettiness. This unicorn had a swirled spike, a bit like a third eye. Far from terrifying me, her protuberance emphasized the soft bluntness of her muzzle. She led with her forehead, flirtily butting the air. She must hold her head up high, for the tip of her horn seems lighter than the atmosphere, attracted to rainbows and puffy clouds. The tip is tiny, dainty. Obesity is impossible for the unicorn pony. Roughness is impossible. She is sleek, infinitely sleek. She is sleeker than water, for only my eye touches her outline. She is a slip, luscious as a basking fetus, supple as a cupid.

I am ecstatic and have no idea why. I'm four years old, perhaps a year or two older.

It is not difficult to suppose that the unnatural fetish of the plasticky, pastel My Little Pony is a way of celebrating the attenuation of the senses in American culture. Our nation has repeatedly shown itself to be obsessed with pain-killing substances and institutionally managed hypnosis. Yet, the attempt to numb can coexist with other aesthetic possibilities. Indeed, it is not clear to me that the My Little Pony I hold in my lap is an opiate. She may, in fact, be something else altogether, a translating device, a vestige of alchemy.

Yes, for with My Little Pony there is always the matter of tactility. Ultimately, we are beckoned into her world through the sense of touch, although to be sure the sense of touch is so intimately tied to the sense of sight here that the two may be inextricable. The film scholar and critic Laura U. Marks has written of the way in which touch and sight become intermeshed in the new media of postmodernity in *Touch* (2002):

> The difference between haptic and optical visuality is a matter of degree.... In most processes of seeing both are involved, in a dialectical movement from far to near, from solely optical to multisensory. And obviously we need both kinds of visuality: it is hard to look closely at a lover's skin with optical vision; it is hard to drive a car with haptic vision.[33]

Although Marks has recourse to examples from IRL behavior, she is most interested in how the virtuality of cinema gives us room to feel differently—to inhabit sensory modes that are not reducible to a single sense and require that we navigate moving images in unexpected and highly specific, bodily ways.

I relate to this notion because I grew up watching television. When I write this, I do not mean that I grew up *sometimes* watching television. I mean that, from the earliest times I can remember, I sat in front of a television for any and all hours I was not in school or asleep. As I can remember a time before I attended preschool, this was often many hours per day. This period of constantly watching television, of begging its then-limited channels to teach me about the world, to interact with me in some pronounced fashion, seemed to go on forever.

What I am saying is, from an early age I had to get creative, had to do something with my mind. I sought a metaphor, one that would describe the exceptional image I wanted. For I knew I wanted an image.

I wrote that I was interested in perfection, but that is just a manner of speaking—what I was interested in was a peculiar visual liquidity, a smooth taste or malleable sound, an image I could shape and feel; an image that would be coextensive with my body and require the collaboration of multiple senses.

When I at last found this image, it was in a terrible movie. This movie was originally created in 1985 and must have been rerun on television sometime later. It is called *The Hugga Bunch*. It is about forty-eight minutes long. It is accessible on YouTube today.

A summary culled from IMDb.com, amusing in its curtness: "A girl travels through her mirror into HuggaLand to find a way to keep her grandmother, the only one who knows how to hug, young."

I had no interest in the grandmother plot, having almost no relationship with my extended family. I had no interest in the dolls, residents of HuggaLand who surveil the girl through her mirror and emerge from it to assist her. All I cared about was the possibility of this portal.

In my memory, it is a miracle that seems possible. It would be a lucky thing for such an event to take place, a mark of one's life story being a life story that defies all expectation, and it would be a form of rescue, an intervention at the last minute, the universe rousing itself to demonstrate that there is more than meets the eye.

It was my idea that I would walk through the mirror in my own room. The mirror would soften, and I would be in another land. The moment of the mirror's softening would be perfection. It would be the coalescing of image and sensation into something more and other than either of these two. It would be analogous to learning to fly or practice telekinesis. Having passed through a buoyant vertical curtain, I would find everything to surprise me. All things would be unusual and beautiful while at the same time intended for me, an infinitely complex allegory I had to decipher and continue to decipher and play with and learn from and cultivate—all of which would simultaneously be a form of food and an expression of love, whose I do not know. There would be fruit and blue skies. There might be puppets from children's television shows. There would be a purpose to my living. Animals would speak, their voices musical and profound.

This mirror-world is additionally an intermediary state, a three-dimensional decoder that helps to explain the way in which the flattish images to which I am continuously privy via the television relate to the real world of time and space, in which I interact with a limited number of other human beings. If one were to stand before the mirror and have a certain feeling, a feeling of confidence but also one of curiosity, then might the mirror not grow porous, bend, dimple, liquefy—so that a finger to its surface generates a ripple? And if this is the case, then might one not cross through? Might not that virtual realm become true? Might I not be able to cross over and experience the condition of being human as something . . . else?

A My Little Pony was a mirror, too.

-:-

The Cloisters museum in New York City was created from a collection of medieval architectural elements and artworks acquired in the early twentieth century by Illinoisan sculptor and art collector George Grey Barnard, who made his acquisitions mostly in France. John D. Rockefeller Jr. took advantage of the spendthrift Barnard's need for cash in 1925, purchasing Barnard's collection, by then consolidated in Washington Heights at Barnard's own modest medieval museum, for around $600,000.[34] Rockefeller hired Frederick Law Olmsted Jr. to design a park in the Fort Washington area, planning to site a loosely accurate recreation of a medieval monastery there, complete with gardens. In 1938, the year of Barnard's death, the Cloisters opened to the public.[35]

At this time, some of Rockefeller's own most prized possessions were on display, including the seven so-called Unicorn Tapestries.

It is due to the presence of a bulbous style of shoe sported by male figures in these tapestries that scholars have been able to date them to within a rather slender timespan: 1495–1505, also the era of Christopher Columbus, Francisco de Bobadilla, and Nicolás de Ovando y Cáceres's brutal governorships of the West Indies.[36] Similar tapestries were fabricated at workshops in Brussels, and therefore it is thought that the Unicorn Tapestries were made in Brussels, although there is no evidence to support this assumption other than that similarity. It is not known for whom the tapestries were created, although a pair of interlaced initials, A and E, worked into the landscape in each of the scenes, have proved tantalizing to scholars.

The earliest written record of the tapestries dates from nearly two hundred years after their creation. An inventory taken of the Paris town house of the recently defunct Duke François VI de La Rochefoucauld in 1680 described them as seven in number. Subsequently, they migrated to the countryside, becoming part of the decor at the de La Rochefoucauld château at Verteuil, where, in a 1728 inventory, they were listed as five in number, "almost half worn out" and hanging in the "large bedroom of the new building."[37] Two additional pieces were in storage, variously torn. Sixty-five years later, in 1793, the tapestries were liberated by revolutionaries. Because the tapestries did not contain imagery explicitly glorifying the monarchy, they were not destroyed but instead repurposed as frost-repelling coverings, taken into barns, draped over vegetables. They were extraordinarily well made, heavy, useful.

In a demonstration of the power of inherited wealth, the de La Rochefoucauld family were able to regain something of their former position by the 1850s, at which time they went about seeking looted items near their country seat. Comte Hippolyte de La Rochefoucauld and his comtesse, Elisabeth, were informed by one woman that her husband had some "old curtains" he used as tarps.[38] Perhaps these might be of interest? Investigation of this claim led to the discovery of a set of tapestries that now bear the name I have been using, the seven Unicorn Tapestries, although one is extant only as a pair of fragments displaying a distant huntsman sounding his horn in the woods, the fence of a garden, a scheming woman, a unicorn's neck and head, and another woman's arm. The tapestries were again installed at Verteuil in 1856. According to Xavier de Barbier de Montault, a nineteenth-century antiquities expert, one of the fragments was, at the time of his visit in the 1880s, employed as a door hanging.[39]

As the twentieth century dawned, the fragmentary portion disappeared. In 1905, one viewer reported seeing only six tapestries displayed, and just six tapestries arrived in New York City in 1922, where they were viewed at the Anderson Galleries by John D. Rockefeller Jr., who purchased them in February of 1923.[40] Rockefeller exhibited his goods in a Middle Ages–themed room at his New York residence for nearly a decade and a half, until, as noted, in 1937, he transferred them to the Cloisters, which after a restoration process displayed them the following year.

The fragmentary tapestry was, meanwhile, rediscovered by Metropolitan Museum of Art curator and medievalist William H. Forsyth in 1936, the year of Hitler's Olympics. Fishing for purchasable artworks during a visit to Paris, Forsyth learned from one Gabriel de La Rochefoucauld that pieces of a threadbare seventh tapestry had been retained by his father as a "souvenir."[41] Forsyth jumped at the upcycling opportunity, finally acquiring the textile for the Cloisters' collection in 1938.

This complex provenance notwithstanding, for most of the rest of the twentieth century the seven tapestries at the Cloisters were understood to form a single narrative, even as it was known that they had been obtained from a barn in a state of disrepair after the French Revolution and—what should have been obvious to anyone looking at them in more than a cursory way—they are so stylistically different that it seems unlikely they were produced as a singular work. All the same, Margaret Freeman, then curator emerita of the Cloisters, constructed a cohesive tale in a 1976 catalog. In her account, the unicorn is chased and abused and perforated and then, for some reason, briefly tamed. Next, it is taken away and slaughtered. It dies and is subsequently resurrected to sit, perhaps eternally, in its garden enclosure. It is, incoherently, an image of hope.[42]

I go to see the Unicorn Tapestries. I'm a very young person. I do not recall exactly how old I am in this memory, but I do know that my obsession with My Little Ponies precedes this visit and has prepared me.

Perhaps I've heard that we will see unicorns in this location. Perhaps I am with a class from school. I do remember my first reaction to that unicorn.

I think: That unicorn is vile.

I am desperate in my disappointment, as the story of the unicorn's capture is further simplified for us by a docent. I think: This unicorn has a beard and thick square teeth. This unicorn grimaces and rolls his eyes as he is stabbed and pierced, as his pale fur parts to reveal that he is composed not of moonbeams and sparkles but of quivering rosy flesh. Beady-eyed dogs, reeking of sweat and famine, snap at his whitish back. Translucent ichor seeps from his unpleasant wounds. It is thin juice, this blood. It is entirely unlike the bright fake blood we see on television and appears somehow lesser, resentful, staining. In these landscapes, there is no such thing as ketchup splattering a camera lens. Nothing here is so absolute as a highly pigmented American food product. Here things drip pinkly and gleam; there is no sudden death. Nothing is as definite as that—save for the unicorn's gender. No one must tell me that he is male. I know that the unicorn is male.

I am crushed and enraged that the unicorn is a boy. I cannot love this representation.

I can't comb this in my mind's eye, can't cuddle or pet it. I do not bask in searing beauty. I do not taste transcendent mystery. I do not handle something smoother than smooth, brighter than bright, warmer than heat.

I had been promised something full of charm, an image that would be a friend. I don't get that, don't see that here.

I am not transported out of my body, not even for a second.

I know enough to perceive that this is a garbled scene of carnage, despite the docent's confident description. Metal plunges into the panting flank of a greatly outnumbered, terrified animal. His lips curl in agony. He is not yet dead, but he dies.

Later, he sits like a toy inside a fence obviously too low to contain him. Why does he stay there?

The humans encircling him have spiteful eyes. They are convinced that they should not examine their surroundings too closely. They should not acknowledge the collective rape they've organized. Their looks are limited, cultivated, stupid, and so inward. It scares me to think that this is all that being alive could amount to.

It is a thought that will return to me again and again throughout my childhood: Don't fall into that trap, I'll think. Don't become old and stiff and cruel and forget that you are living. Remain vulnerable, I'll tell myself.

Today, as we visit the tapestries, while it is 1986 or '87, I'm convinced we're being lied to in multiple ways. Worst of all, no unicorns are pictured here.

-:-

In 1998, Adolfo Salvatore Cavallo, a curator of textiles first at the Boston Museum of Fine Arts and then the Met, published a novel account, showing, contra Freeman, that there are at least two different narratives present in the seven Cloisters tapestries, if not three, if we accept that the very worn, fragmentary tapestry belongs to a third and larger, once-independent work.[43] There are two tapestries depicting a hunt of the unicorn as a secular allegory for the quest of the lover. Four tapestries—the most skillfully illustrated scenes, a realistic narrative of a hunt with many dogs—portray the unicorn as Christ undergoing the Passion. The fragmentary sections depict what Cavallo calls a "Mystic Hunt of the Unicorn," in which a woman stills the powerful beast without use of force. Cavallo compels us to attend to the stylistic heterogeneity of the tapestries. There are significant differences in the representations of plants and faces in the three hunts; you don't need to be an expert to perceive them.[44] He suggests that the tapestries were part of a larger collection, belonging to a single unicorn-obsessed collector (or, family of collectors), whose household expended enormous sums to see a beloved mythical beast made manifest on multiple occasions, by way of one of the period's most technically complex art forms.

Despite Cavallo's persuasive analysis, it is not unusual to see Freeman's way of looking at the tapestries unquestioningly reproduced.[45] One must agree that it is convenient, from a present-day point of view. It's pleasant and satisfying to embark on one's own hunt for an elusive narrative, standing in the Cloisters' gallery, particularly given that such a tale (a unicorn in its own way) can exist only in the beholder's grasping eye.

I'm among those who do not think it is possible to discern a singular story in these textiles. Yet, I draw a strong and specific reading of the role of the unicorn in the commissioner's milieu: In summary, the unicorn is to be killed. The unicorn is to be captured. It's to be claimed. For the unicorn's horn is a powerful medium. It is a status object, a talisman and drug.[46] Therefore, the unicorn's sacrifice has salutary effects. The unicorn is an animal, sure, but it is also a technology.

It would be too crude to show the spiral horn being removed from the unicorn's corpse by a pair of hacksaw-equipped

nincompoops from the awkward castle in the four tapestries
of "The Hunt of the Unicorn as an Allegory of the Passion"
(Cavallo's title), but we do understand, viewing the supposedly
final tapestry in this ultraviolet quartet, that such a gruesome
event takes place. You, a royal counselor and sometime diplo-
mat, sit in your drafty abode. It is the early sixteenth century.
Outside, wars fueled by gunpowder and large artillery rage,
and pandemics decimate cities. Within your residence, you are
mostly safe from cruder forms of aggression, but not from in-
trigue and bacteria. You do not prepare your own meals, and
here is your point of greatest weakness: you are vulnerable to
poisoning, as well as to more innocent but no less deadly lapses
in culinary hygiene.

However, place a unicorn horn, or alicorn, on your table,
and you are preserved from toxins and decay, for this tusk not
only neutralizes poisons but will visibly sweat if such noxious
things are near. (You set it beside your *languier*, a miniature
decorative tree hung with serpents' tongues.)[47] Grind the alicorn into fine powder, and you have a potent restoring medicine. You believe that unicorns really exist, because everybody
does. You have read the literature. Someone once brought you a
snow-white goat with a thing tied to its head, but you saw right
through that scheme, had the charlatan thrown in the Seine.
Nevertheless, you hold out for a genuine encounter. Because
the problem of evil must have a solution. Many celebrate the
unicorn's fierceness, cleverness, and independence. Others
say that it died out in the biblical flood.[48] All the legends seem,
somehow, only to increase the power of its horn. This precious
alexipharmic item exists and therefore must be within your
reach. You are boundlessly rich. You want it.

Odell Shepard, author of *The Lore of the Unicorn* of 1930, a
surprisingly entertaining book, was brought to his subject by
the question of how people attempted to survive a craze for poisoning that apparently took hold of Western Europe in tandem

with the rise of the apothecary.[49] In the unicorn's horn, Shepard notes, one found protection

> from the arrow that flieth by day and the pestilence that walketh in darkness, from the craft of the poisoner, from epilepsy, and from several less dignified ills of the flesh not to be named in so distinguished a connection. In short, it was an amulet, a talisman, a weapon, and a medicine-chest all in one.[50]

Thus, while we might read the death of the unicorn in the four tapestries depicting a stag-hunt-like killing as purely symbolic of the well-known martyrdom of Jesus Christ, it is possible that the realism of these panels serves a more expedient purpose. The panels allow the artwork's commissioner to experience events that could not transpire in real life. By way of images, the commissioner has "proof" of the general authenticity of unicorn horn, for hunters end the life of an animal before "his" eyes—which is to say, before the eyes of a woven avatar. The tapestries are a virtual aid to a viewer who would like to believe that the exquisite alicorn he recently acquired at great cost to protect himself from botulism and dishes laced with arsenic, in fact comes from a beast that dwells—fierce yet available; invisible yet indubitably present; snorting and stomping, steam rising from its gray coat—in the forest just beyond the edges of local habitation.

The unicorn, nickering behind bluish trees, is so natural, so much a part of what is natural, which is to say so much *not* a part of what is human, that it does not exist. It fades into the mist of a human fantasy about the natural world. (In this fantasy nature exists to serve mankind.) Other animals, in contrast to the unicorn, are far more human, given they are numerous, relatively easy to capture, and sometimes even dwell with people. So, yes, we kill the unicorn for its incomparable horn, but we also kill it because it is a part of nature that we aim to seize. We aim to seize the unicorn's ability to restore nature, to undo our own technologies and pollutions. We offer the unicorn to the category of nature because we must hide that we have invented it, and, meanwhile, its death leads to our safety and our purification. It dies and has something to offer.

This narrative of the unicorn's artificial naturalness, its naturalness in service of humanity, is further complicated by the myth of its relationship to the maiden, whom, of course, it likes to sniff and lie down with. In a Syriac version of the *Physiologus*, for example, the unicorn gives itself over to more intense fleshly pleasures than in other versions of the text, beginning to "suck the breasts of the maiden and to conduct himself familiarly with her."[51] We recall that it is the maiden's grasp of the unicorn's horn that ultimately pacifies it. Without her participation, the unicorn cannot be killed. She grasps its horn until it "dies." It, he, is her lover. And there is at least one rare sensual female unicorn of the Middle Ages.[52] In the anonymous late fourteenth- or early fifteenth-century Arthurian romance, *Le chevalier du papegau*, a dwarf tells of a fierce female unicorn who breastfed both him and his infant son when they were starving. The son has become a giant able to uproot trees with his bare hands; the unicorn seems now to be the dwarf's wife.[53]

The unicorn's intertwined roles as intensely erotic semi-human and magical, nonhuman life giver may suggest another analogy. The unicorn is human in a confused and confusing, contradictory way.[54] Therefore, it, he, she (?) is a human in disguise. The unicorn is a human in a suit made of animal hide—perhaps this is a white goat-hair suit, but, on another level (given that unicorns are fictive), the species whose skin composes the suit is irrelevant. This unicorn, or "unicorn," could be a person in a garment made from the fur of wolves. In this case, the unicorn would be a werewolf, someone who exists in an uncertain relationship to society, metamorphosing, sprouting a shaggy pelt, throwing his constricting garments away in disgust, living in caves, howling at the moon, gnawing on raw meat, abandoning language—yet inexorably called back to the human community on certain nights.

I am not the first to see a parallel between the figure of the werewolf—here, broadly defined to include unicorns as additional nonlupine *wer-*, from the Old English for "man," animals— and that of another figure of uncertain status, where culture is concerned. The unicorn could be considered a scapegoat, a sacrificial being who exists both within and outside the city.

René Girard, a devoutly Catholic twentieth-century theorist whose investigations of the origins of collective violence inhabit a zone somewhere between structuralist anthropology and comparative literature, dilated quite a bit on scapegoats. In Girard's conception, we derive our desires mimetically, establishing our motivations by way of that which seems to motivate those with power.[55] We get our arbitrary wants from others rather than from innate need, and the mass result of this substitutive logic is to invest certain objects or people with irrational forms of villainy and, subsequently, sacredness. These entities—whom Girard terms "scapegoats"—become mechanisms by means of which competition, resentment, and other negative dynamics within the mimetically desiring human sphere are purged, making social cohesion possible.[56] Violence is concentrated against the scapegoat. By demonizing and subsequently eliminating the scapegoat, the community renews its faith. The scapegoat is at once powerful in its bad action and, once expunged, wonderful. The scapegoat is a sin-eater and, like the unicorn, participates in a fantastical form of purification.

The scapegoat may also solve for what the philosopher Dominique Lestel has called an "ontological hatred" toward animals on the part of Western societies, a nonsensical hatred, given that humans are animals.[57] A scapegoat makes possible a paradoxical site of division where there is no division, an abomination of other where there is only self. The scapegoat's suit of bedraggled—or gleaming and immaculate, otherworldly—fur disguises a will to violence. This violence does not belong to the scapegoat, yet the scapegoat is charged with it in perpetuity. Witch hunts, genocides: Girard claims that the scapegoat mechanism explains these crimes.[58] By means of collective brutality, human culture obscures a peculiar uncertainty that comes to define it, which is to say, us.

To return to an earlier unicorn, the monumental three-legged ass in the Bundahišn, whose multiple mouths are each as large as cottages and who stands in the ocean: this marvelous and petrifying creature reminds me of a moment in a cartoon very different in style and import from *My Little Pony*, despite the influence of Japanese media of the 1980s on coeval American toys, cartoons, and graphic design:[59] I think of the appearance of the metamorphic Great Forest Spirit in Hayao Miyazaki's *Princess Mononoke* (1997). Although this spirit, a resident of Muromachi-era Japan, has no single, determined shape, at times it takes the form of a horned, elk-like entity with the enigmatic face of an intelligent cat. In this guise, it recalls Caesar's German unicorn. Like the scapegoat, it will die to restore balance to the interrelated natural and human worlds. It offers up its own life.

Despite Miyazaki's global sway, it is unusual to see positive representations of sacrificial beings in secular pop culture. In the United States, such figures are usually relegated to the horror genre.[60] Consider *The Blair Witch Project* (1999). Few would draw comparisons between it and a coeval Studio Ghibli production, yet sacrifice related to cyclical time is *Blair Witch*'s central concern. Its simple premise—film student ghost hunters make a documentary and get caught up in the horror—is rendered more fascinating through use of supposed found footage. The would-be filmmakers of *Blair Witch* are not merely metaphorical victims of their expensive liberal arts educations but are about to perish within the very document they are shooting. The film plays on multiple cyclical times and types of repetition: the academic year and the film-school assignment, certainly, but also genuine human-sacrifice rituals (tortures and executions) associated with witch trials of the eighteenth century in Maryland, speaking of scapegoats. Incongruously, unexpectedly, *Blair Witch* brings these heterogeneous narratives together, generating an unstable amalgam, a bit like a unicorn tapestry.

These, then, are our unicorns: the boy documentarian whose tongue is cut from his mouth, the basement murderer and those whom the murderer destroys, the girl who goes mad in the woods, opening a sacrificial package of flesh and bone. Their enclosure, their *hortus conclusus*, is a boiler room, camping tent, or, perhaps, the lens itself. They are sewn into the skin of an animal we cannot see and slaughtered. They are simultaneously hunters and the hunted. They hold the horn of the camera out before their heads. Their deaths on- and off-screen are cathartic. The audience gasps, applauds. Hundreds of millions of dollars rain from the skies.

-¦-

I'm at the Cloisters. I'm in the gallery containing the Unicorn Tapestries. I seem to be the only person who has come here alone today, although perhaps I'm being melodramatic. It's a hot Saturday in late June 2023. The A train wasn't running, had to hike in from the 1. My feet hurt. Perversely, I wore heels.

Families with one, two, or three children enter the room. The adults point to a yellowish narwhal tusk displayed upright, then approach the textiles.

Without exception, the first thing each child says on seeing these images is: "Why are they hurting the unicorn?"

"Why are they killing the unicorn?"

"Is the unicorn dying?"

"Is that blood?"

Yes, a parent replies nervously, glancing across the room. And they're going to take his horn. See?

The children want to leave. The grown-ups attempt to beguile them, call their attention to various details, the realistic greyhounds and elaborate vegetation.

I'm amazed by these interactions. The gulf between the world of the young and the world of the old rises uncannily out of the floor. It can be perceived.

The unicorn I adore today remains a creature of the senses. She is not the victim of the Cloisters tapestries, nor is she a My Little Pony. She is a liminal and syncretic figure, a prismatic reflection of reflections, memory of memories. She is polymorphous and consecrated to pleasure. She may be more plausibly figured by a different set of textiles and a different unicorn, one that appears in tapestries currently housed at the Cluny Museum in Paris. Here, a goat- or dog-size unicorn, along with a similarly scaled lion, attends a series of allegorical representations of the five senses. The red background of each of these pieces is crowded with plants in bloom and tame animals (leopards, monkeys, rabbits, lambs, foxes, various birds). In the foreground, on bluish floral turf, elegant women stand or sit. A final dedicatory image, which could portray a mysterious sixth sense or the sense of understanding itself, bears the legend, *A MON SEUL DESIR I.*

To my one desire I.

The meaning of this sixth image, along with its mysterious numeral "I," often glossed over by interpreters, has been lost in the transformation of human society across time. It is not clear to us who the speaker of the dedication is, nor what the meaning of the noun *desir* may be. It is also notable, to me, that although these tapestries are sometimes referred to as "unicorn tapestries," like those at the Cloisters, their true subject is not the unicorn at all, but rather the impeccable blonds atop navy daises

(*La Dame à la licorne* is the tapestries' more official title). Their subject is allegory, that is, speaking otherwise; these woven pictures tell us that the senses offer a form of transport. For the senses are vegetal, flowering, vital. The senses extend. They do more. They are associated with femininity, itself an ambivalent figure for otherworldliness, animality, embodiment.

The philosopher Michel Serres writes, a bit incoherently, I think, but nevertheless suggestively, that the tapestries at the Cluny reveal the meaning of the ancient riddle of the unicorn, which he sees as a cypher for the silent-but-everywhere-understood influence of the sense of touch that, like a thread, enters, mixes with, and holds together other senses. Touch is, in his reading, a governing sensual metaphor and the basic sensual language that provides the "language" that the other senses "speak," so to speak,[61] somewhat along the lines of Laura U. Marks's vision of synesthetic media. The unicorn reminds us of a truth about our bodies. We are fundamentally a tissue, a mingled amalgam of weavings and crossings. We are each plural within our own soma, the soul a sort of conscious vapor that clings to select corporeal sites. We have forgotten this multifariously sensate textile that is us. The unicorn, a remarkable accessory and mascot, tells us so. The unicorn reminds us—of ourselves.

Rainer Maria Rilke, for his part, offers a reading of the Cluny tapestries as a vision of otherworldly peace. In his sole novel, *The Notebooks of Malte Laurids Brigge*, the narrator exclaims, "Look, there is always that oval, blue island, floating on the subdued red background, which is covered with flowers and inhabited by little animals busy with their own affairs." The animals and women pictured are extraordinary because they are so piquantly and convincingly posed, vibrating with some serene power, sealed off from secular time. These visions are hermetic yet lack for nothing. "Everything is here. Everything forever," the narrator begins to whisper at the close of this passage.[62]

This other world glimpsed by Rilke, a spherical realm of

absolute satiety—rich with the deep pleasure of a presence that knows no hurry—makes me think of the late psychoanalyst and philosopher Anne Dufourmantelle's conception of a vibrant "uterine body." After birth, this ecstatic corporeal memory of non-lack, non-separation, non-sacrifice, and collaborative being is "effaced upon contact with the real," although not lost. According to Dufourmantelle, it

> lingers to watch over your dreams, your fears, your night-mares; it is lodged within the scents you love; it is suddenly exacerbated as you brush against a passerby; it is volatil-ized. We spend our lives dismantling this body and try-ing to recapture it, to rediscover its scent, the miraculous draught of an elixir of lost life. We know intimately that it exists, but no longer dare to believe in it.[63]

It's the unicorn, this unrememberable memory of fetal time before chronology, personality, or want. It is woven into the six textiles hanging in a circle in a dim blue room in the Hôtel des Abbés de Cluny. An intimation of uncanny joy wobbles—intensified, brief as a word—on the surface of a mirror held by the female figure in the allegory of vision, *Voir*. The glass catches the beguiling smile of an entranced animal, along with an eerily truncated view of space and time beyond the tapestry.

These, then, are our unicorns: white and pink and purple ponies, soft and smooth and collectible, immature and American. They are images on stationery, backpacks; shapes in cereal. They trot through the internet, infusing start-ups with magic and investor capital. These ponies dip their heads, blink, wink. Their alicorns glisten. We feel that their cuteness purifies us, or whitens us, or grants us sparkles that will help us survive. We watch and ca-ress and believe, not in the terrible power of the wilderness or human desire—for these unicorns are extremely unnatural and live in an ahistorical present—but in a form of ecstatic affect irreducible to the binary of nature vs. law, in which the senses of vision, touch, smell, hearing, and taste are united (my one desire!) for the brief instant of a terrible and gorgeous, amniotic twinkle on-screen.

I'm not sure, by the way, that this synthetic affect is ever real, fully realized. It may merely be indicated, aspired to. Indeed, this might be what the endless multiform My Little Pony props (green, cloud-shaped record player with moon arm, yellow I LUV YOU barrette, pink irremovable earring, bathtub with Seapony shower curtain, felt tooth with smiley face, blue oval mirror reading "majesty" on the base, etc.)[64] were about: shoring up a spiritual, intellectual, and sensual nonevent, a failed transcendence.

Given the inability of My Little Ponies either to serve as properly ecstatic werewolves or to properly inspire ecstasy in us (are *we* the intended scapegoats?)—their limited power to return us, fleetingly, to something like our original sensuous natures—we might be tempted to side with Friedrich Nietzsche, modernity's most famous depressive, who has the nature spirit Silenus inform humankind that it would be better "not to have been born" in his preface to *The Birth of Tragedy*.[65]

Silenus offers to liberate us—at last, after millennia of apparent waffling. He will free us from our twin unicorns: the unicorn made to contain the category of nature and the unicorn that inoculates against anything natural—each of them always unstably other, only incompletely other, because these toys are us.

Silenus tells us to put down our ponies. It's time, he mutters, resinous wine on his breath, to accept that living is something we lack the imagination to do.

It's a dramatic proposition, one I wonder if we will or can accept.

Personally, I prefer to linger at the threshold.

See how I embroider my souvenir:

I don't have a memory of a sensation of intense smoothness associated with life before birth. I do have a memory of standing before a mirror, silently willing it to soften so that I might pass through it, into an allegedly more natural, unicorn-inhabited world.

An Image of My Name Enters America

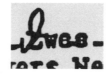

*Fig. 1, The author's surname
in early 1921*

The poet and novelist Robert Glück has a curious and useful definition of fundamentalism. As he writes in an essay published in the year 2000, "My Margery, Margery's Bob," a meditation on his own novel of 1994, *Margery Kempe*, fundamentalism is a symptom of "the yearning to be authentic, to be part of a recognizable order." According to Glück, fundamentalism has to do with history and how we regard it. It is an attempt to "'restore' a period as one would restore a house."[1] I understand this to mean that fundamentalism aims at reproducing and rendering permanent that which has already been lost. It's grasping after thin air or maybe building a castle from it. Or building a castle where there is nothing more than air.

Nothing obstructs your project, your tower of accuracy.

"It is a postmodern desire," Glück writes.[2] He means the desire to be authentic, in this sense. Only a person of our intensely and unevenly mediated era, an epoch equipped with seemingly infinite and ubiquitously accessible external memory, could want this, as we do.

Funny how access to scads of information has made many of us wish to be trapped in another moment in which what can be known by a human is far more limited.

What it was like to live there. What it was like, then, in that place, to believe that your own beliefs constituted a relatively useful image of the world.

When I was in college, I became briefly locked into what I might describe as unknowing self-voyeurism. This happened, strangely or perhaps predictably, during a freshman comp course. I needed to compose an essay on "vividness." The instructor of the comp course was a sympathetic older man who later told the class that he liked to brew his own beer in a closet. He lived on campus with his family and seemed drawn to coziness and silence. He had a beard and was one of the most helpful teachers I have ever had, although I was only imperfectly aware of this at the time.

When I told the teacher of the comp course, call him Dr. G., that I did not know what sort of vivid topic I should write about, G. said, "Well, how about something you saw or read and that you liked?"

G. smiled gently through his beard, as if to acknowledge that we both knew that this was probably the lowest bar anyone could set.

That didn't mean it would be easy for me to follow through. I went away and mostly pondered what seemed important to other people. This was in 1999, when the Kevin Spacey vehicle *American Beauty* had famously dramatized protomillennial aesthetics by way of a scene in which a teenager reverently screens miniDV footage of a plastic bag dancing in the wind. Someone I knew who hated this trite movie exclaimed, "But you can't *love* a plastic bag!"

I wasn't sure I agreed.

I just didn't know, was the thing. So many lifeless objects did seem to have the potential to speak.

At the college literary magazine, we received a sonnet that concerned the Armenian genocide. In the sonnet, which today I read with my stomach in a knot, the author relates how his girlfriend, who is Armenian American, describes a 1915 pogrom: "the ring of dancing girls, how strung / from little hand to little hand, gold beads / of gasoline bejeweled their skin. How freed / from tempo with a torch the naked brides still swung / and danced."

Please bear with me. Stay with me through this part—the part where I am an extremely confused person:

So, yes, we read this sonnet that contained children immolated and then a scene in which the poet "halved you like a peach / beneath me with my bare, bonesetting hands / and found the architecture set in me, the spark / of abattoirs, of blood arbors."[3] It's a little difficult to parse but I think the idea is that the poet discovers the same violence in himself as he has sex, the violence of the genocide. It's hyperbolic and sentimental and maybe trivializing and definitely bizarre. On the one hand, the poet shows advanced control of literary language. On the other, What the fuck?

We were eighteen or nineteen, then. Teenagers.

In the way of teenagers, I decided that I would write my vividness essay on this problematic poem, plus other materials I had come across that addressed the genocide. I saw myself as taking on grand themes, big feelings. The essay I composed was titled "Responding to Bloody Letters: A Note on Vividness." It was not really a very good essay—I recently obtained a PDF and am dismayed by the number of non sequiturs, the deadness and discomfort of the prose.

This essay nevertheless appeared in the composition program's yearly magazine of the best undergraduate essays of the year, an honor G. told me candidly he'd had to fight tooth and nail for. (The other instructors did not, apparently, find the essay to be among the year's finest.) And, in fact, I have never understood why G. took such an interest. At the award dinner, I had some sort of honorable mention status. I thought I would hear something about my writing. Instead, G. said that the beginning of my college email address was "lives at," which he pronounced to rhyme with *gives*, not *chives*. He said that he had never in his life met anyone so alive to the present. He left things there.

I later would have read a sidebar in the magazine, probably composed by G.; I find it now in the file emailed to me by a generous librarian:

> The assignment for Lucy's last Expos essay was to define and explore "vividness." Lucy began by analyzing a few of her favorite passages, to figure out why they seemed to her so vivid and what that might say about the nature of vividness itself. As she was working on the essay, though, she read [call him J.]'s poem, "After Siamanto, A Poet of the Armenian Genocide" as a submission to the [undergraduate literary magazine] and she became interested in the Armenian tragedy. By sheer coincidence, she also encountered Les Murray's book-length poem, *Fredy Neptune*, which includes a translation of Siamanto's "The Dance"— the poem describing the scene that haunts [J.]. This coincidence began to preoccupy Lucy; she abandoned her earlier examples and "decided to try to come up with some way to discuss the popularity of this particular poem by Siamanto." She says, [prepare to cringe!] "I was a little puzzled since the language itself didn't really turn me on so much. My paper is basically me trying to figure out why we (adding myself to the troop now) are so fascinated by the German woman [more on her later on]'s story." Lucy, who is a Literature concentrator from New York City, wrote this essay for [Dr. G.]'s "Style and Styles in Prose."[4]

God, I was so cavalier. "My paper is basically me trying to figure out . . ." It's the nattering voice of a dilettante. Why "basically"? And why, oh why, do I write, "I was a little puzzled since the language itself didn't really turn me on so much"? Is it possible that I am demanding to be "turn[ed] on" by the verbal description of atrocities? What sort of person am I? Am I like J. in my own way, using my "bonesetting hands" to carelessly arrange naive sentences?

I should say here that J., the author of the sonnet, was at least a year older and possibly alarmed that I had chosen his poem as my object of intense analysis. I think there was a whiff of appropriation of others' experiences he himself could sense and was embarrassed by, after the poem's fact. I remember an awkward encounter at a party, him wearing what looked like an expensive sweater. I believe he quickly moved away from me, although who really knows.

I subsequently came to understand J. better when we attended the same midwestern writing program. There is a photo of us standing together near a low wall he'd constructed outside the basement apartment I rented. An older relative of his had taught him how to build stone walls by hand and he made the structure for my landlady—a single mom who taught children's art classes upstairs in her living room—for free and, as he said, "for fun." He was a generous person, French in his family if I am remembering correctly. He showed me how to drink Calvados, never once hit on me, and worked on convincing me that life was basically good.

I do recall saying to him one night, "Why do you keep on trying?"

"How do you mean?"

"I mean," I said, "not letting things fall apart. Doing well. Being a success. I mean, what keeps you from going away and living alone in a cave somewhere and never speaking to anyone again?"

"I don't want to live in a cave," J. said, frowning. "Do you?"

It is an odd thing to remember, but I can call this moment up with arid precision. Not what was said, but what it was like in there, in my mind. No one had ever asked me if I wanted to live alone in a cave, perhaps because everyone assumed that I could not possibly want to live alone in a cave and never see another human being again, but I did. How I wanted this. I turned toward myself and saw a desperate wish to be cut off. I desired, with the ardor of a fanatic, to be lost, to become unreachable.

In truth, the belief that this might be possible sustained me. I *was* a fanatic, the core of me beyond reason.

It did not, I should clarify, make me happy to know that this was what I wanted. This was a fact that sat in my brain like an extremely expensive overdue bill.

Something was wrong yet it made no sense. My life was fine. My life was uneventful. My life was safe and good. Still, here I was, ineluctably going insane.

I haven't communicated with J. in years. I should write him an email. How strange it is that there may be people with whom we seem to share only a brief and casual friendship, who, in the end and perhaps unintentionally, confer on us the most precious clues.

There are whole years I have difficulty remembering. I would sometimes black out in the late afternoon, but not from drinking. If anything, drinking might have helped me, I sometimes think, but I didn't really drink much in college; that all came later. I didn't drink or take other substances, but I lost consciousness all the same, and the worst of it was that I did things. I went around and did things. Not much, but there were times when I later found the emails I had written. There was a time when I told a professor to "go fuck" himself when he offered me a place in his cherished seminar. I, formerly a straight-A student, my body now gone rogue, typed these words out in Telnet,[5] hit "send."

go fuck yourself

He let it slide, for some reason. He was always kind.

I was always afraid, although almost nothing had happened.

I remember once standing in a Gap that used to be on Mass Avenue near Porter Square. I was touching items on a sale rack. I was already feeling pretty bad, but then it hit me full force:

My limbs began to lock up. I could feel my face contorting

into a rictus. I was floating near the ceiling even as I begged myself, DO NOT DO THIS.

Time ballooned. It imploded with a silent bang, drugging me with its languorous punch to the face, charring the canals of my ears, choking me. Other people seemed to look over in alarm.

Don't scream, I told myself. Don't burst into tears or begin clinging to garments you do not own.

DO NOT SCREAM.

NO SCREAMING.

With a monumental act of will, I directed my body out of the store.

In the cold, on the street, I was bathed in shame. I could not calm down.

Who did I think I was?

I was a Literature concentrator. I was from New York.

I wrote in my essay on vividness:

> Some texts are vivid by virtue of skillful descriptive writing that draws us into a momentary dream. When we read a certain Virginia Woolf passage, the room that Woolf describes—because she has given just the right details and chosen brilliant verbs to incite us to recreate the scene from our own experience—replaces any awareness we had of the room in which we are actually reading. And just as the scene feels aesthetically complete, so we feel emotionally complete. But the vividness of violent texts seems to work differently. Such texts supplant our immediate reality more by virtue of what they describe than by how they describe it. And rather than putting us in a satisfying dream space, the fact that our minds participate in the creation of the scene brings restlessness and upset—incomprehension mixed with strange feelings of involvement and responsibility.[6]

My eye lights on the phrase "replaces any awareness we had of the room in which we are actually reading." "Replaces," I wrote. I wrote, "Such texts supplant our immediate reality." I also wrote, of scenes of violence, of "restlessness and upset—incomprehension mixed with strange feelings of involvement and responsibility."

This paragraph, with its thematization of otherness and elsewhere, is perhaps the best and most thoughtful in the essay. I haven't yet started telling half-truths. I'm still progressing via small steps, edging out into the bright words.

-:-

I have never been one to believe everything I read, but I have never so agreed with literature as in late 2014, when, at the age of thirty-four, I experienced what I took to be the end of my life. *Ché la diritta via era smarrita.*[7] Where the right way was—one barely needs to translate Dante's adjective, the sound itself offers so much. *Smarrita.* This gorgeous adjective, an offspring of the verb *smarrire*, "to lose or become faded," has survived in modern Italian. It is used to mean missing, mislaid, astray, stray, bewildered, nonplussed. Synonyms include *vagabondo, perduto, disperso.* Doesn't it even sound wiped away? Swept into a mess, a dusty pile subject to the frivolities of the wind; meaningful traces covered with material, smeared and eroded, disordered and glommed, cluttered, lost. *Smarrita.* That *s* and *m*: you feel and see the soil of the road, rub your palm in it. At least I do. The trail gets harder to make out then, as you touch it, attempting to convince yourself that it is real, this is real. I wasn't even thirty-five yet.

Was it the middle of my life? I don't know. Was it the end of my life, as I feared? No, it was not the end. In a certain way, it was the beginning. It was a time when what had formerly been hidden was abruptly laid bare. It felt, strangest of all, like a return to something far earlier, a rehearsal of a vulnerability I had hoped to escape by ceasing to be a child.

In the middle of my life's journey, I came to myself in a dark wood where the right way was lost. It is a hard thing to speak of, how wild, harsh, and impenetrable that wood was. Indeed, thinking of it recreates the fear.[8]

Everything happens for a reason. Or, rather, things don't just happen by accident. Or: only accidents happen by accident. That is why we call them accidents. (Etymologically, the term is related to falling. Accidents are what befall us; they slide out of the sky, somehow.)

I have a peculiar way of progressing through life as far as knowledge of myself is concerned. It is not that I know what I know, learn what I learn, by accident. Yet I can convince myself that this is so. I do follow my own desires, along with something I think of as my "interest": it's like a little ball I toss. It flies from my hand, soft yet determined; knocks against some surface at a distance, *plunk*. Information is communicated.

In 2014, I chucked my little ball and it struck the notion of the period room. Perhaps it sailed through the crystal globe of a rococo revival chandelier with a sweet crash. That would have been enough to attract me, had there been such a tempting, brief sound.

I was drawn to what a curator might call the immersive quality of these spaces, the way they purport to show you how things *were*, with a careful, doctored accuracy. Walk inside, the claim goes, and you stand in the shoes of a resident of the late eighteenth or early nineteenth century. Such a person would have been slighter and shorter than you, given nutritional differences, and thus you will know what it would have been to be a smaller version of the being you are today, daintier and subject to wasting diseases.

And you will know, as I thought then and still often think, of the ease that arises from colonial plunder and the presence of servants and the enslaved. Walls covered in papers and silks, fires that must be tended beneath elaborate drippy mantels, the pallid painted faces of cavorting his and hers harlequin figurines. Claw-footed chairs, settees supported by gilded, bare-breasted sphinxes, bloodred table lamps in figured crystal, landscapes displaying ships with strange trapezoidal sails. You may imagine what it might have been to grow accustomed to such objects, to live with them and take them for granted.

Period rooms are an innovation of the end of the nineteenth century. They are products of the rising popularity of national histories just before the first century of global wars, and they are signs of pressure on interior decor to act as a site for the expression of beliefs and aspirations of those who live in its embrace.[9]

But not just expression: also, screen.

These interiors, which are pictures in three dimensions, contain pictures, in miniature, everywhere, on every—any—available surface. They are, in this sense, hypnotic, nearly blinding.

Detail covers my eyes.

-:-

I need to pause, because even as I keep attempting to go forward with this account, I find myself unconsciously sucked back into the PDF of my freshman essay. I behave as I normally do, seeking distraction while writing, bopping around among various applications, then, dazed, I come to, my eyes in that old document, even though I hadn't meant to put them there.

The more I read it, knowing what I know now, the more I feel strangely calm, or perhaps a better term is *sympathetic*. I feel sympathy toward myself. It feels less humiliating to me now than tragic, this writing.

Early in the piece I introduce a block quote:

A German who witnessed the events at Aleppo, "reported corpses of violated women, lying about naked in heaps on the railway embankment at Tell-Abiad and Ras-el-Ain. Many of them had clubs pushed up their anus. Another . . . had seen Turks tie Armenian men together, fire several volleys of small shot into the human mass with fowling pieces and go off laughing while their victims perished in frightful convulsions. Other men had their hands tied behind their backs and were rolled down steep cliffs. Women were standing below, and they slashed at those who had rolled down with knives until they were dead. The German consul from Mosul related that . . . in many places on the road from Mosul to Aleppo, he had seen children's hands lying hacked off in such numbers that one could have paved the road with them. At the German hospital at Urfa there was a little girl who had had both her hands hacked off." Other groups were herded into caves, having been soaked in petrol. This was then ignited. Children today still search in these caves, hoping to find gold, either wedding rings or teeth. These witnesses spared their readers and listeners details of the worst atrocities.[10]

This will be my first example of a piece of writing that is vivid without being "brilliant." Although stylistically unremarkable (as I observe), it has "an extra charge of vividness."

Again, what a strange girl I am. I want to travel back in time and help her.

-¦-

So yes, it was 2014 and I had begun thinking about period rooms. I kept going to see them. My rooms of choice were at the Metropolitan Museum of Art. They are American rooms.

I think we can agree that, although basically scaled for occupation by an adult human, a period room can feel like a miniature. We tend to see such spaces as at a distance, even when we are standing right in them or next to them (cordoned off by a velvet rope or plastic partition). We are apparently up close, yet so very far.

The seduction of the miniature, which is the seduction of the period room, is accomplished not merely through miniaturization or enclosure. The smallness of the miniature, when we consider it more intimately, turns out to be a red herring, at least where fascination is concerned. Gaston Bachelard, the French philosopher, describes the miniature as analogizing the moment between dream and waking, when the world seems at a distance but we are still conscious of it—a moment when we may contemplate the world without wanting or needing to act upon or within it. This is the world of "full and radiant liberty," a vibrant toy we do not need to touch to comprehend.[11] Or, as Virginia Woolf describes a similar orientation to phenomena that is one of plenitude and relief, a "moment of being": she feels as if she is "lying in a grape and seeing through a film of semi-transparent yellow."[12]

It is a moment of satiety, this "lying in a grape." It is one of Woolf's earliest memories, a night in the nursery at her parents' summer home in St. Ives. Woolf vividly recollects how the blinds move in the wind; light enters; the sea rumbles and crashes rhythmically.

The satiety a period room produces is tied to its plenitude of detail, its bringing near of that which is or appeared distant. This has something to do not only with the pastness of the period room, but with its fundamentally didactic nature. In the United States, the first historical house museums were a consequence of mid-nineteenth-century nostalgia for the colonial era: this period's purported peerless piety, cultural homogeneity, and unsullied excellence. Curators, activists, tastemakers, historians, and others began touting the material culture of early America in the 1840s, when the implementation of "universal" white manhood suffrage meant that home ownership no longer conferred the right to vote. At this time of nominally expanding civil rights and increased social heterogeneity, the home began to take on

new symbolic meaning as an identity-giving space. There came
to be a cult of the hearth—what Colleen McDannell has termed
a "domestic religion."[13] Whereas in Europe great formality was
observed in the development of the period room as a container of
museological knowledge at the close of the nineteenth century,
in the United States things were more mixed. Here, decor was
directed toward social control in the present.

Some of the first American period rooms, completed in 1904,
are located at the Rhode Island School of Design, where an artificial Georgian-style home for antiquarian Charles Leonard
Pendleton's collection of American antiques was constructed
from the ground up. Subsequently, in 1907, the Essex Institute in
Salem, Massachusetts, built three colonial rooms.[14] Curiously,
the Metropolitan Museum of Art's period rooms, among the
most opulent in the country, were inspired not by the completist
efforts at RISD or the Essex Institute's careful historicism, but by
the 1900 Tenement House Exhibition, organized by the Charity
Organization Society. This show made use of photographs, charts,
and maps to explain unsafe conditions in tenements. The exhibition convinced its sponsor, Robert de Forest, later president of the
Metropolitan Museum of Art, of the possibility of conveying recommendations for improvement of built environment as well as
social life by means of museum displays.[15]

However, de Forest's idea of reform was reactionary at best.
In 1924, the Metropolitan Museum of Art opened its American
Wing with an impressive series of floors of period rooms located
behind a transplanted marble Wall Street bank facade, originally
erected a century earlier. As de Forest explained in a 1924 address, the purpose of such feats of spatial reproduction, massive
dioramas into which the public could step and stroll from century to century, was "to test out the question whether American
domestic art was worthy of a place in an art museum, and to test
it out not theoretically but visually."[16] The experiment would
now be permanent, as the Met contained the first major fixed

installation of the arts of colonial and early federal America in an urban art museum, in a purpose-built wing of rooms with original paneling, ceilings, and beams, staged lighting, and painted skies visible beyond built-in windows.

The wing was the personal project not only of de Forest but also of Henry Watson Kent, an influential librarian and administrator; and R. T. H. Halsey, an Anglophile stockbroker, collector, chairman of the museum's Committee on Decorative Arts, and trustee. The three gentlemen worked autonomously, bypassing bureaucracy. De Forest personally purchased the facade of the former Assay Office Building from Wall Street in 1915, and other acquisitions arrived through familiar channels,[17] such as de Forest's wife, Emily, who gave the Met its first period-room element, a Long Island fireplace, in 1910.[18] It was not a foregone conclusion that American decorative arts were canonically significant, despite the nation's growing wealth and World War I victory. The rooms therefore had the function—perhaps not even secondarily—of increasing the value of the objects they contained. Many of those affiliated with the Met were themselves colonial-revival enthusiasts who stood to gain from the boom in antiques and Americana during the 1910s and 1920s. The rooms detailed a conservative, antimodern vision of the nation, eliding the influence of late nineteenth-century waves of immigration from Southern and Eastern Europe and the Middle East, along with the increasing importance of German, Jewish, and Catholic culture, as well as Victorian innovations in design. They presented American culture as one in which rococo revival and neoclassical styles reigned supreme and home decor was all but exclusively authored by males. At the time of the 1924 opening, the Met's period-room galleries proclaimed that great innovation and beauty in American furnishings commenced just before 1700 and ceased around 1830.[19]

Maybe one of the reasons I had become so interested in these three-dimensional images of historical homes in 2014 was that I was married. I was living a life in a house with another person and was interested in domesticity. *What is domesticity?* I asked myself on an almost daily basis. *What is this thing we do? Is there a history of domesticity?* For, of course, there was. It was a history of possession: a story of belonging and belongings; discomfort and comfort; hidden or ignored labor; institutions; stuffs.

The person I was married to was a mistake, unfortunately. Yet, as is so often the case, our errors come with hints and messages.

My husband was a supremely suspicious person, particularly, although not exclusively, where I was concerned. This proclivity could be mistaken for a sort of interest, even for caring. It would have been better had I not mistaken it in this way, but I did. I was always misunderstanding him. I underestimated him, to boot.

However, this person I was married to also helped me—as no one I had known before had done. He was good at finding. One night it turned out he had found something on the internet in a database of records related to immigration into the United States. It had begun as a hunch, he told me, offering me a print-out of a ship's manifest.

"Do you ever think about your last name?" he wanted to know.

Something loose and heavy wobbled in the air. It made an abstract noise, as if it desired to fall into place.

¦

In 1966, a British scholar of occult practices, Frances Yates, published a book titled *The Art of Memory*. Although somewhat factually flawed, *The Art of Memory* is one of the most moving works of art history I have ever read. It could additionally be categorized under media or literary studies. It is hard to pin down.

The Art of Memory is also famous. However, I didn't know that when I found the book accidentally while walking through library stacks as an undergraduate. It was one of those chance meetings that can lead a person to believe that a certain book is "for" you, has been written for you, and only you, to read. I carried the book away and pored over its instructive pages. Yates describes the Western development of techniques of artificial memory by means of which large amounts of linguistic information may be stored in the human brain without the use of external props.

It is important to emphasize that Yates never sets out to discuss personal memory, per se, memories from one's own lived life, but I nevertheless insisted on understanding her narrative as having particular significance on this point. If I can reconstruct my thoughts at the time of my first reading, I was convinced that I could use this book and the techniques it details to become not just a better writer, but a more vivid writer (my most fervent hope). I believed that there was a key to something like style in it. Or, if not style, then indelibility, along with a transmissive or viral magic. I could learn to make something out of words that wouldn't smudge—and not only this: that there was a way to manipulate words such that they would have no drag, no physical resistance. That they might be all energy, all light, all vector. That their meaning might rush into a person's head to create a crystalline image there, a hologram. A reader would see a picture. It would be as if it had not come from words at all, that picture. It would be clear, crisp, piercing, permanent, upright, still.

Yates begins with an old story. There are some people at a party. They've hired a poet to entertain them, and although he is a good poet they are crap people. This is happening in Greece, sometime around 500 BCE. Simonides of Ceos, the good poet, keeps praising the twin demigods Castor and Pollux in his victory ode. Scopas, his host, finds it a bit much. He tells Simonides that that was an OK poem, but he can forget about half his fee. Since Simonides likes Castor and Pollux so well, perhaps they will pay, haha.

Just then Simonides is summoned outside to speak with some

people in the street, a pair of young men, apparently. As the poet exits, he turns around in time to see the banquet hall collapse, killing everyone inside instantly. Meanwhile, there is no one waiting for him in the empty road.

Simonides, the last to see the guests at Scopas's party alive, is asked to make identifications for the grieving families. As Roman legend has it, Simonides, who has for a long time spoken his poetry from memory, is able to recall the exact seating arrangement, even though the rubble has disfigured the attendees beyond recognition. He will later draw on this experience to create the famous "memory palace" mnemonic system, a technique helpful in the primarily oral culture of Europe. It will be widely used until the Renaissance.

According to Yates, Quintilian, a Roman grammarian, gives one of the fullest descriptions of the memory palace. Yates paraphrases:

> In order to form a series of places in memory, he says, a building is to be remembered, as spacious and varied a one as possible, the forecourt, the living room, bedrooms, and parlours, not omitting statues and other ornaments with which the rooms are decorated. The images by which the speech is to be remembered—as an example of these Quintilian says one may use an anchor or a weapon—are then placed in imagination on the places which have been memorised in the building. This done, as soon as the memory of the facts requires to be revived, all these places are visited in turn and the various deposits demanded of their custodians.[20]

You were meant to use a real building, one that was, if possible, largely empty. And the images one chose to represent the facts to be memorized should be as odd and vivid as possible. Grotesques splashed with paint or pornographic figures would be the right idea, as other experts tell us.[21]

I had always been good at memorizing long passages—perhaps because I would see the text I was memorizing in my mind's eye, as if the letters were constructed from carved wood or painted metal, and I might hover above them, floating lazily through the center of a small *o*, alighting momentarily on the lower hump of a *B*. Now, reading Yates, I began to think of the written page as an architectural space. I thought of my reader as a sort of poet or speechmaker, someone wandering through this arrangement of rooms and alcoves hoping to be held in place by some impressive sight, stopped in their tracks, their vision gently and absolutely captured.

A harmonica made of glass. The buzzing green rectangle of a lake. A cake of translucent ash-blue jelly flecked with black.

These were the sort of beautiful and useless word-pictures I collected from the poetry of others. I kept them in a notebook, reviewing them from time to time, hoping to train myself, as I saw it, to speak and see at once. To write a phrase that was neither a threat nor a claim but that could not be forgotten or ignored. To be vivid. To write with vivacity. To construct a piece of light.

Right before my relationship with the person I was married to came to an end, I developed a habit of making audio recordings of him. The strange thing was, after I made these recordings, ostensibly related to memory, I almost immediately forgot about them, so that it was not until several months after our break, once it had become very clear we were not getting back together (I'd sent him a separation agreement and then divorce papers), that I found them in "Voice Memos" on my iPhone and began to listen to them with something like equanimity. I was surprised at my former self, who seemed to have been in some significant sense split in two: there was the me who lived and of whom I was aware, and then there was the me who made these recordings so that I could listen to them later on, so that I would have some additional information regarding what had happened.

I don't mean to imply that I now know everything about that

relationship or that former self. I only have some clues. And, in the peculiar style of my former divided self, I have erased the recordings in question, so that I no longer have access to them. I don't remember when I erased them or why. Perhaps I got a new phone and made a quick decision to let them go; I don't remember. All I have now are some early bits of things he said in a long diatribe one night when he was very drunk. For some reason, I transcribed the beginning of this conversation. I chose this one and I do not know why. I also don't know what I said, because I didn't write that down. I'm not sure I said very much. The phone would have been sitting on the table in our former kitchen/dining room. I must have opened the application that night and left it recording while he went off. It was true that I was interviewing people from time to time then in my capacity as an editor and perhaps I was in the habit. As I've said, I was at least two people then.

The transcript, which is extremely embarrassing to me although it is not me speaking, reads as follows:

I love you and I'm going to love you to the end of time but like I'm done being an afterthought

That was just a perfect example

But no, this is not, you're not

Right. You're going to like play this game

One of the smartest women I have ever met is now like pretending to be like a little pauper girl who's like I don't know how anything works

You're being very manipulative right now

Can you look at me as like one of the smartest women in the world, because that's what you are

Yeah, you're being so manipulative right now, I don't even want to like deal with you. Here was the thing, you asked me

Here's the—you want to know the—issue? And also why you're like manipulating me? Here's the deal, dude. You're like, Hey, let's have dinner together. Like, hey, that sounds awesome, cause I would love to have a night with you, especially after like hanging out with David and Rose and I thought we were just like really happy with each other like hey let's do it, and I pick up a red onion, I pick up a green pepper, I pick up some olives, I come home, you're talking to somebody in the front room. That's not—I was tired. I needed to like take a nap. I took a nap for about twenty minutes. You came by, touched my penis, my balls, actually, and I was very unhappy, because my balls don't like to be touched, and then you went back into the room and you were like Hey, twenty more minutes and then we are good to go

Here the mysterious transcript ends.

They were more and more frequent, these times he accused me of manipulating him, and yet I could not understand what he meant.

We had looked together at the ship's manifest.

My husband pointed to an entry for a boy, nine years old.[22] His first name was John, his last name a series of illegible letters: *Ewas, Iwas, Ivas?* We were not sure, could not make them out. The boy was from "Urmiath, Persia." It was 1921. He was headed to Yonkers, New York, the home of my paternal grandfather, John Ives, at the time of the 1940 census.[23]

When Virginia Woolf has her memory of feeling as if she is inside a grape, she is remembering being a sleepy child in her nursery at St. Ives. St. Ives is a seaside town on the tip of Cornwall. It is apparently named for Saint Ia, Iia, or Hia,[24] an Irish nun of the fifth or sixth century, who wished to flee her native land but arrived at the coast too late to accompany other fugitives. A small leaf bobbing in the surf miraculously enlarged itself to the size of a boat. Ia embarked on it and was carried across the Irish Sea.[25]

Ia was later martyred (drowned) for her faith and buried in St. Ives. A church was erected over her grave, giving the place its name.[26]

Ives, as a surname, is from the Old French *Ive*, which has Germanic origins, handed down from various compound names containing the root, *iv-*, *īwa*, meaning "yew tree." *Ive* is also a predecessor of the more familiar French first name *Yves*.[27] It is unclear if the "Ives" of St. Ives, meanwhile, has any intrinsic association with this etymology—and, therefore, means "yew"—or is rather an assimilation of Ia's name.

The yew—*l'if* in modern French—is one of the oldest tree species in the world.[28] Its leaves, roots, and bark are all toxic to humans; only the red flesh that surrounds its poisonous seed may be safely consumed. Yet it is the source of two cancer-fighting drugs, Taxol and paclitaxel. The yew is therefore paradoxical: deadly, helpful.[29] In some interpretations of Norse myth, the tree of the world named Yggdrasil, or "Odin's Horse," is a yew.[30] Odin, a god-king, hangs from Yggdrasil for nine nights. During this time, he sacrifices an eye to one of the wells below Yggdrasil's roots, receiving runic knowledge in exchange.[31]

The yew is a gate. Its door swings.

The yew holds power but is two-faced, ambivalent, a potential killer. It is like the world. The yew is the world writ in miniature, an archetype.

Woolf's family began visiting St. Ives in the early 1880s, when Virginia was still a baby.[32] When Woolf was thirteen, her mother, Julia Prinsep Stephen, née Jackson, died.[33] Woolf's 1927 novel, *To the Lighthouse*, is based on Woolf's memories of the time before her mother's death and set at a fictional version of the real Talland House belonging to her family at St. Ives.[34]

I first read *To the Lighthouse* in high school, after an English teacher told me that he would never teach the book again because of how upsetting the things students said about it were to him. I never found out what those students said.

Meanwhile, St. Ives, the mass-market bath products brand, is currently owned by Unilever. It was created in 1980, the year of my birth, by two American businessmen, Gary H. Worth and Robert Van Dine.[35] Its original identity and goals are a bit murky, but it seems to have been envisioned as a very inexpensive line of soaps and lotions that would compete in a crowded market through packaging and messaging that addressed consumers' susceptibility to so-called impulse purchases. The tubes and bottles touted a "Swiss Formula" and featured bucolic, herbal scenes. Health and simplicity. Not Cornwall, but the pointy Alps. In the 2010s, St. Ives became infamous as a purveyor of exfoliating gels containing plastic "microbeads"; a FAQ on the company's website now highlights their consciousness of the environmental harm these largely useless additives caused.[36]

When I was in middle school, I was sometimes called "St. Ives." Or maybe "Saint Ives." I don't really know what the girls were saying or how it was spelled. Perhaps I was a calming lotion or dirt-cheap exfoliant. In the 1990s, everyone used St. Ives's apricot face scrub (Swiss Formula!). Even now I recall its swampy smell. It was nothing like apricots. I'm sure by now that's been updated, changed.

Henri Bergson, the French nineteenth- and twentieth-century theorizer of the interrelations of the body, images, and mind who is sometimes called a philosopher but whom I see as a sort of psychologist and mystic, seems to believe that it is not things that we remember. We cannot remember things, according to Bergson. Our "pure memory" of events disappears from our bodies, leaving in its place an entity Bergson calls a "memory image." The past is, for Bergson, "essentially virtual"—it is unreachable yet causally and nearly physically connected to the images we see when we think of what we have lived. Again, we don't remember *things*. But a semiphysical trace of them exists within us, as if inscribed in the folds of the material of the mind:

> Essentially virtual, [the past] cannot be known as something past unless we follow and adopt the movement by which it expands into a present image, thus emerging from obscurity into the light of day. In vain do we seek its trace in anything actual and already realized: we might as well look for darkness beneath the light.[37]

The past is a paradox: although we have dwelled in it when it used to be the present, now it can no longer admit our bodies. If we search for it in the place where our bodies are (i.e., the present), we will not find it. Searching for it in this way is, again, like looking for the darkness within or underneath a beam of light. The past and the present, although they seem connected and necessary to each other, do not belong to the same perceptual category. Memory images, a strange sort of naturally occurring psychic media, are generated by the inexorable movement of the arrow of time, as what was once the inhabited present becomes the permanently foreclosed past.

Bergson writes of the survival of images. Memory images are what carry on. "Memory actualized in an image differs, then, profoundly from pure memory. The image is a present state, and its sole share in the past is the memory whence it arose."[38] Yet he is going to surprise us: we may have believed that our body is an unchanging container, a storehouse for a variety of images of the past, but, in fact, our body is not of a different order from the images that occur to us as memories. According to Bergson, the body is an image, too. According to Bergson, when we inhabit the present, we are always creating an image. We *are* an image. This is what our sensations and our comprehension of our body's liveliness in each moment ultimately amount to. It is lucid, trembling. A bright point of perception in the infinity of unseeing space.

-:-

When I was a little girl there must have been a time when I asked about our family. There must have been a time when I wanted to know. I recall something about a day on which we were supposed to bring a food to our class. The food was meant be typical of our ethnic background. We should share it. My mother got very angry at me that week, as I recall. I don't remember what I brought.

My mother, who was a curator at the Metropolitan Museum, home to period rooms, would sometimes take me to view the ancient, winged bull gods of Assyria installed on the museum's second floor. She liked to say things about my father while standing in front of them. She taught me this word from the past[39] but (typical of her) never explained it. I did not really know who or what was Assyrian.

As an adult, wandering the Met's American period rooms, I would sometimes play with the various touchscreen displays, installed in the late aughts. In the depths of one, I discovered a single digital card on Halsey's goals in "Educating New Americans." It was seemingly randomly placed at the end of the series in the Powel Room, 1765–66. As the card explained, R. T. H. Halsey, chairman of the museum's Committee on Decorative Arts and a trustee, hoped that the 1924 displays would "teach newly arrived immigrants about American history and values, so that they might assimilate more easily."

-:-

When did I finally google it? In my memory, it is morning. I'm in the apartment in Ridgewood, Queens, where I've begun to live alone. Light veers off cheap laminate floors.

It's incredible to me that it has never occurred to me to dare this, to enter these words into a search engine. I type *assyrian*. Add *urmia*, a word I've learned from my ex-husband's research. Press enter. I'm not sure how many links I need to pass through. How many pages is it before the word *genocide* appears? Perhaps it is there on the very first page.

I am thirty-four years old.

There are so many things we could not talk about. I recall my father throwing the cat against the wall. I was four. It was the weekend. A Saturday. She struck the wall high up, around seven feet. She was nimble, loud in that moment.

She lived to be twenty-four years old, that cat.

I must be on Wikipedia. I read sentences. I travel to YouTube. Data seizes my face. It assumes the shape of figures and symbols recognizable to me and my face imitates these, the screen, nodding, reading. It is as if a presence rises from the past, now reanimated. As if there truly is something infernal within the internet. Charred bodies in photographs you strain to make out, sure, but also something larger and more amorphous, like a hideous angel.

I go outside and feel the sidewalk pushing up against my feet. I seem to hang from it as if upside down. There is a flapping of wings.

Here is why. Here is the why. I want to laugh. I never tried to look at this.

-+-

1,000 ASSYRIANS COMING IN SMALL SAILING SHIPS

Some of the Survivors of 75,000 Who Fled From Persia Now on Their Way Here.

WASHINGTON, Aug. 5.—More than a thousand Assyrian Christians, fleeing from persecutions by Mohammedans, are on their way to the United States on small sailing vessels, Secretary Davis said today. According to information reaching the Department of Labor, he added, they are part of a party of 75,000 who started to march from the interior of Persia to ports, 25,000 of whom died on the way.

Those who survived boarded available vessels that were leaving for Japan and the countries of Europe and America. The thousand coming here, the Secretary said, will be far in excess of the quota for Persia, against which country they should be charged under the percentage immigration law, but he added that no decision had been reached as to what would be done with them.

Fig. 2, New York Times *article, August 5, 1921*

As Halsey confided to de Forest in a personal letter, "We should endeavor to show in the rooms things which have class. The furnishings should be restrained and no semblance of crowding permitted"[40]—personifications that may indicate fear of excessive crowding by unwanted, unfit, "un-American" groups.

Halsey's celebration of ancestral homes took place less than half a year after the passage of the 1924 Immigration Act, signed into law on May 24 by President Calvin Coolidge in order to "limit the immigration of aliens into the United States, and for other purposes" by means of annual quotas of "two per centum of the number of foreign-born individuals of such nationality resident in continental United States as determined by the United States census of 1890." This law made permanent even more stringent quotas than those set in place temporarily three years earlier, in 1921, by the then-unprecedented Emergency Quota Act.[41]

The restrictions of the 1924 act unpleasantly echo the aesthetic logic of the antiques collector, returning the nation by means of "informed" selection to a bygone time of supposed greater order and homogeneity. The federal government's decision to turn to 1890 census data to create immigration legislation in the 1920s emerged from eugenicist theories that emphasized the hereditary dangers of miscegenation as well as problems caused by alleged weak-minded members of the white working class, who were bound to reproduce in excessive numbers.[42] There was also the perceived danger of the spread of communism. While Germany was given a quota of 25,957 and "Great Britain and Northern Ireland" was given a quota of 65,721, Italy received a quota of 5,802. A colonial construct called "South West Africa (mandate of Union of South Africa)" received the minimum quota of 100 persons.[43] African Americans who came to the United States as slaves were considered irrelevant to the act. Other nations receiving the minimum designation included India, China, and Persia. The act additionally "excluded from immigration all persons ineligible to citizenship, a euphemism for Japanese exclusion," as Mae M. Ngai writes.[44]

The nativist shift that culminated in the 1924 act wasn't limited to the hushed discourse of collectors of decorative things, of course. "Nordic Victory Is Seen in Drastic Restrictions" read a *Los Angeles Times* headline on April 13, 1924, citing the coming act as well as Madison Grant's best-selling *The Passing of the Great Race, or The Racial Basis of European History*, first published in 1916, with new editions in 1918, 1920, and 1921. Grant, an inveterate phrenologist, outlined a three-tiered system by which whites might be identified as "Mediterraneans," "Alpines," and "Nordics," with the final category the supreme designation. He traced these dubious types to prehistoric migrations across the continents of Asia and Europe, publishing a short article and series of color maps in the November 1916 issue of the *Geographical Review* that purported to illustrate the origination of "Continental Nordics" and "Nordics of Scandinavia" in "southern Russia."[45] In this article, Grant attributed the conflict of the First World War to the "continued expansion" of the "backward race" of the Alpines into Nordic territory,[46] and, in his book, he warned against an analogous corruption of American society by immigration from Southern and Eastern Europe, as well as from economic empowerment of African Americans.[47] He predicted a dissolution of the United States into a fragmented, corrupt nation of mongrels[48] if absolute control were not maintained by individuals of Scandinavian, English, Scottish, northern German, northern French, northern Polish, northern Russian, and Dutch descent, a.k.a. the "master race,"[49] a coinage derived from nineteenth-century American apologists of racial slavery.[50] Grant's book was minutely studied by Adolf Hitler, who proclaimed it "my Bible" in fan mail to the author.[51]

Grant's theories seemed to condone ethnically and economically motivated attacks, such as the West Frankfort, Illinois, mob beating and arson carried out on August 5, 1920, against Italian Americans, who were perceived by local white Protestants to be colluding with the Mafia—"Mob Seizes West Frankfort in War on Foreigners," the *New York Times* wrote in a contemporary headline.[52] Of course, it wasn't just Grant's pseudoscientific narrative of human prehistory driving such violence. D. W. Griffith's 1915 adaptation of Thomas Dixon Jr.'s novel *The Clansman* into *The Birth of a Nation*, the first feature-length motion picture, inspired former evangelist William Simmons to revive the then-defunct Ku Klux Klan as a merchandising and life-insurance-sales opportunity that also traded in brutality.[53] The July 1924 Democratic

National Convention in New York City (the "Klanbake") saw Klan sympathizers reject both an anti-Klan plank in the party's platform and the nomination of Governor Alfred E. Smith of New York, a second-generation Irish American and Catholic.[54] A year later, in August 1925, 50,000–60,000 Klansmen marched in Washington, DC, to demonstrate their white-robed numbers and fundamentalist determination.[55]

Beyond serving as an inflammatory ideology, whiteness was a legal concept. In 1925, an Oregon court heard testimony from anthropologist Franz Boas that "it would be utterly impossible to classify" Tatos O. Cartozian and other Armenians "as not belonging to the white race" and ruled in *U.S. v. Cartozian* that they were European "Alpines." That same year, the state of Michigan successfully sued to revoke the US citizenship of John Mohammad Ali, a traveling lecturer and wholesale importer born in India, arguing that race and nationality were inextricable. When Ali became a naturalized citizen in 1921, "high caste" Hindus were considered "white" and therefore eligible for naturalization. But the 1923 case *U.S. v. Bhagat Singh Thind* had created new precedent that Indians were not white. Ali attempted to defend himself by arguing that he was, in fact, of Arabian descent, even employing testimony from a University of Michigan eugenicist who argued that Ali was white due to his Middle Eastern ancestry as well as the shape and size of his head. The judge ruled against Ali, stating that Ali's skin was not light enough for naturalized citizenship under current law.[56]

When my grandfather left England in 1921, he was labeled "brown" by the authorities of the ship carrying him.[57] In 1940, he identified himself to a census taker as "white."[58]

If you have ever been ill or sustained an injury, then perhaps you have found that certain smells will bring back the time you spent recovering from sickness or wounds with ferocious vividness.

The smell of a certain medicine or disinfectant, received by the nose in the present, may, for example, cause a near out-of-body experience, as one is whisked back to a particular time, place, and mental state. Although smell is generally acknowledged to have a powerful capacity to relocate us temporally, it is, in my own experience, most potent when linked to memories of bodily incontinence or vulnerability, not to mention pain.

A smell might be a sort of three-dimensional image.[59] We interact with so many digital and other two-dimensional pictures on a daily basis that we have a tendency to understand the term *image* as automatically denoting an entity that lacks the dimension of depth. Our images are poor, but we are always looking to them, always looking for new ones. Yet, *image* has not always meant in this way. From the Latin *imago*, *image* may indicate a three-dimensional representation, such as a sculpture; above all, it has to do with *imitation*, a word with a related root—with doubling effected in order to transfer spatially mapped information from one location to another. Images are not exclusively ocular. Much as memory is not exclusively ocular. The mnemonic potency of smell will remind us of this.

When Bergson calls the body "an image," he seems to mean that the spatial and narrative sense of the body depends on memory images, and that memory images can be carried out by *any or all* of the senses. Yates's histories of memory palaces, on the other hand, suggest that images require three-dimensional space to function correctly in relation to trained memory. Although the rhetoricians she consults never mention environmental variables such as the coldness of a floor or the sound of a bird heard through a portal, presumably there is something to the specificity of the experience of real space that contributes to the vividness of the mental images generated and stored by the ancient architect of a memory palace.

Indeed, when I think today about vividness in its relationship to memory, I am apt to go beyond the visual, to think of olfaction and the sense of touch, as well as hearing. Meanwhile, the internet is structured neither like a Bergsonian body nor a Yatesian memory palace. It is not even, properly speaking, an archive.

As the German scholar and historian of media Wolfgang Ernst has written, somewhat cryptically,

> The octopus of electronically transmittable storage is the meaning of the Internet and the promise of digital archaeology: in an era when all information may be stored, its paradoxically anarchival signature is on display: "Cyberspace has your memory."[60]

Traditionally, in the predigital era, there was a categorical difference between a given storage system, its protocols for naming and arrangement, and what it contained. Within the World Wide Web, however, there are no *lieux de mémoire*, no period rooms, no particular stopping places marked out by a unique qualitative vividness. Here there are *only* addresses. To describe the World Wide Web as an archive is mistaken; yet it is not so much that its objects are *not* archived, either. Rather, what it means to hold or lose information has changed.

Ernst signals this transformation with the neologism *anarchival*: by using this adjective he indicates the possibility that an archive may not just store information but also destroy it. "Cyberspace has your memory" because now many forms of memory cannot exist outside of the concrete technomathematical operations that materialize time in digital processes.[61] While it is obvious to everyone that digital photography, social media, and photo-sharing applications have altered the nature of memory in our era, it is probably less clear to each or any of us how human forgetting has been affected, or how personhood itself has been re-formed by the particular proximities made possible by the internet and World Wide Web.

It is very weird, in my opinion, that major events in my immediate family history remained obscure for over thirty years of my life—but that I had only to enter three words into Google to watch a veil fall. The ease of access was stunning.

We have heard about the "right to be forgotten,"[62] but what about a wish to forget? What about wishes to forget in times other than our own? I want to remember. Yet, what I want to know even more, what I retain an insatiable hunger for, is knowledge of my relations' lack of desire for memory. It is not history that they have thrown away, for they do not have that power, but rather key parts of their own most intimate experience.

However, I can barely conceive of this sort of loss, given my own formation in a style of time generated by computing;[63] that is, I "came of age" with the internet. For disposability itself has been transformed by our technologies.

In a famous passage from "A Sketch of the Past," Virginia Woolf writes,

> So without stopping to choose my way, in the sure and certain knowledge that it will find itself—or if not it will not matter—I begin: the first memory.

> This was of red and purple flowers on a black ground—my mother's dress; and she was sitting either in a train or in an omnibus, and I was on her lap. I therefore saw the flowers she was wearing very close; and can still see purple and red and blue, I think, against the black; they must have been anemones, I suppose. Perhaps we were going to St. Ives; more probably, for from the light it must have been evening, we were coming back to London. But it is more convenient artistically to suppose that we were going to St. Ives, for that will lead to my other memory, which also seems to be my first memory, and in fact it is the most important of all my memories. If life has a base that it stands upon, if it is a bowl that one fills and fills and fills—then my bowl

without a doubt stands upon this memory. It is of lying half
asleep, half awake, in bed in the nursery at St. Ives. It is of
hearing the waves breaking, one, two, one, two, and send-
ing a splash of water over the beach; and then breaking,
one, two, one, two, behind a yellow blind. It is of hearing
the blind draw its little acorn across the floor as the wind
blew the blind out. It is of lying and hearing this splash
and seeing this light, and feeling, it is almost impossible
that I should be here; of feeling the purest ecstasy I can
conceive.[64]

It is this memory that Woolf will, in a subsequent paragraph, describe as "the feeling . . . of lying in a grape and seeing through a
film of semi-transparent yellow." Her "bowl" of life "stands upon
this memory."

If I were a psychoanalyst, and I am not, I would probably
have something to say about the incomplete maternal body that
appears in the hubbub of transit of the first part of the memory,
a headless body covered with eyelike flowers (anemones, with
their rich, dark centers). I might relate this Argos-like figure to
the mimicking watchfulness of the child's own body—a body that
seems later to swell to encompass the world beyond the bed, itself a kind of giant eyeball or grape that grows until it brushes the
very horizon. The child appears to strive to complete a sensory
task on her mother's behalf; to be a heroic synthesis of seeing
and feeling. A perfect witness. Indeed, if Woolf's memory is to
be believed, the child succeeds. What was formerly an anemone
printed on fabric becomes three-dimensional; in the child's fantasy, her eye recognizes the world in full, recreating the world,
entering the world, becoming inseparable from the world, such
that there is no longer a clear difference between child and anything else. The spirit flies out and covers the landscape. She experiences a state of ecstatic communion, attachment, continuity,
mixture. She is colossal yet minute; neither entirely of the world

nor entirely of herself. She is everything: ample, granular, in no way scarce. Therefore, she is free.

I suppose this passage, set in St. Ives, must be a prototypical example of vividness in writing in contemporary English. When I composed my freshman essay, I merely name-checked Woolf, perhaps because, even as a teenager, I understood that her writing had for more than half a century been considered the hallmark in visually effective style. Woolf's patrician ways, coupled with her idiosyncratic and often earthy, plain choices—she is a lover of heaps and bowls, grapes and local flowers—result in a literary scenery at once deep, translucent, and attainable. I think of a passage in Elaine Scarry's *Dreaming by the Book*, published in 1999, a year before Robert Glück's very interesting essay. Here Scarry diagnoses the basic mechanism of vividness in what now reads to me as a bizarrely blunt gambit: that which can be grasped by the mind's eye will be vivid. Anything about the size of a flower or a fist fits well inside a brain.[65]

Although Scarry's book was widely praised when it first appeared, her theory has not found many adherents. Maybe this has something to do with the fact that vividness, vivacity, liveliness, whatever you want to call it, cannot be reduced to the static material qualities of entities described in language. No, that is not it at all. The quandary reminds me a little of the riddle about "I," who was going to St. Ives and met a man with seven wives, and every wife had seven sacks, and every sack had seven cats, and every cat had seven kittens.

How many were going to St. Ives?

Only "I" is in motion here. The extended description of the polygamist and his cat-fancying retinue is not really vivid, just visually detailed—nor, of course, is the I. One merely distracts us from the other. (You must know the trick to recognize that only "I" is going to St. Ives.)

Vividness does not arise from one's having grasped a given description. It is not due to clear writing alone. It isn't about passive consumption or perfect one-to-one reproduction on the part of the reader. It is not a synonym for *ornate*. Vividness, perhaps strangely, is not just or exclusively a visual quality, a thing on a screen, although most of us use our eyes to read.

Consider, for example, that recording I made: Is it vivid when a person says, "Can you look at me as like one of the smartest women in the world, because that's what you are"? Is that sentence like a flower about the size of a fist that one can fit inside one's head? No, that sentence is nothing like a flower, although it is a little like a fist. If that sentence is vivid, it is vivid mainly because it is insane. It plays on hyperbole and scale and is fast and erratic. "One" means singular. "Smartest" means superlative. "Women" means a limiting category that does not include men.

Can you please act as if you fit this description?

I find the words strange, violent, and not really, in this sense, lacking in vividness.

Here I want to quote from my freshman essay—at length. I do so because suddenly, reading it, I feel less shame. I despise myself less for having written it. I must take advantage of this narrow opening in my heart. I will show you.

I wrote:

> It is apparent . . . how quickly violence in a text becomes vivid: physical pain and acts which cause physical pain translate immediately from written words into our own discomfort and sadness. Whereas it seems that most acts described in texts—say in a history text—exist only in that text, only in the account, descriptions of horrible violence have an extra charge of vividness, making the past or the imagined more convincingly present in our minds because they threaten us with the reminder that our bodies can suffer too.[66]

I will spare you a lengthy and somewhat factually faulty description of the terms of the Armenian genocide, which I, in 1999, understood as exclusively affecting ethnic Armenians. I do mention Adolf Hitler's famous August 22, 1939, rhetorical question about this genocide—"Wer redet denn heute noch von der Vernichtung der Armenier?"[67] *Who has anything to say today regarding the wiping out of the Armenians?*—although in my essay I quote the sentence incorrectly, probably because of an error in another written source. Regarding my other omissions and confusions: today I wonder what it can mean to a nineteen-year-old girl to try to explain a mass killing. They did it because of money. They did it because of religion. They did it because of politics. They did it because of hatred. They were afraid and they were angry and they did it. Because they were men. Because weakness exists. Because there has to be a reason why.

I forgive myself now. Perhaps in previous days I've been angry. I've thought things like: *If only I'd made fewer mistakes in this essay, perhaps it would have been awarded a prize. And if it had been awarded a prize, perhaps I would somehow have been protected from all the challenges I was going to face over the ensuing decades. Perhaps I could have avoided certain relationships, certain harms. Perhaps school could have saved me.*

I know now that nothing I could have done could have saved me, but all the same I can't stop wishing. It's in all my dreams.

The essay continues:

One victim of this genocide was the poet Atom [Yarchanian], who wrote about the genocide in Turkey under the pen name Siamanto, when it was nearly impossible to get news out, when a message like this had to be smuggled out by a woman in her shoe:

I seize this opportunity of bringing to your ears the cry of agony which goes out from the survivors of the terrible crisis through which we are passing. They are exterminating our nation. Perhaps this will be the last cry from Armenia that you will hear.

A friend of Siamanto's, a doctor living in the city of Adana, Diran Balakian, began writing him letters that described the killings. Possessed by the vividness of these accounts, Siamanto was driven to transcribe the letters loosely into poems (until he was executed by the Turkish government in 1915) in order to make the world see and feel what was happening—to transmit his own sense of horror, disturbing though he knew it would be to his readers' sense of humanity:

> "Don't be afraid. I must tell you what I saw, / so people will understand / the crimes men do to men."

Siamanto understood that, because violence is readily vivid, the way in which people respond to reading about violence is very similar to the way a first-hand witness responds to it—especially if that violence is recounted first-hand. Many of Siamanto's poems not only force the reader to become witness to the act of violence taking place, but are written from the point of view of one who witnesses violence, thus thrusting himself into the horrors and providing a model for how one might respond to seeing "the crimes men do to men."[68]

Here, then, finally, is one of Siamanto's poems. It is titled "The Dance." It is written from the point of view of a German woman staying in a house with an Armenian girl who has just been stabbed to death. The German woman sits with the corpse and describes what she sees occurring in the field outside her window:

> "Twenty graceful brides collapsed
> 'Get up,' the crowd screamed,
> Brandishing their swords.

"Then someone brought a jug of kerosene.
Human justice, I spit in your face.
The brides were anointed.
'Dance,' they thundered—
'here's a fragrance you can't get in Arabia.'

"With a torch, they set
the naked brides on fire.
And the charred bodies rolled
and tumbled to their deaths . . .

"I slammed my shutters,
sat down next to my dead girl
and asked, 'How can I dig out my eyes?'"[69]

Vivid. This is vivid.

The German woman wants to go blind.

I still have a lot of difficulty doing any proper research on this topic and on days when I read scholarly PDFs about the history of the Assyrian population in northern Iran, who practiced Christianity and sometimes intermarried with Armenians, who lived near the now heavily polluted and receding Lake Urmia, a place I hope, in that diasporic cliché, to one of these days return to, I usually start crying at a random point in the evening, over something seemingly unrelated.

According to one account I read in an article ("The Ottoman Genocide of the Assyrians in Persia," by Anahit Khosroeva)[70] collected into a 2018 anthology by the academic publisher Routledge, in Urmia children were butchered alive and cooked in the fire. The mothers were then forced to consume this flesh.

I almost laugh writing these words; the hyperbole of it is like a 4chan meme. This is just one of the tortures detailed. It sits in a stack of them, each more grotesque than the last. It is beyond comprehending and it is simultaneously entirely comprehensible.

I have a son. There is nothing in the world I can think of that would be worse than this. And yet I think: in such a horror, I would bear witness and I would pray while consuming the body of my child. I would swallow, the ultimate sacrilege. I would pray to die but not until after his death, even as he had already died. I would pray to somehow be a hiding place, a protector, even in the pointlessness of this. Even as I could expect my own corpse to soon be torn limb from limb and discarded.

I never know what to say about my grandfather's story, but then again, how could I? He died mostly a stranger to me when I was fifteen and never told me anything himself, and when later in life I had the wherewithal to ask my father what he knew about what had happened, I got no answer. My father was, in fact, annoyed. "I have very little information and even less interest in this," he once told me over email before curtly signing off. This message dates from five years ago. It is one of a handful of one- or two-line emails I received from my father over the decade and a half when either of us used email and when I still spoke to him. He was not, as a rule, communicative.

My father did once tell me that he thought his dad was an inveterate liar. He said his father used to refer to Iran as "the land of milk and honey" and that he would constantly extoll Tehran as being "more beautiful than Paris." According to my father, my grandfather had never visited either city. And he had been too young to judge the place where he was born, as my father saw it. My grandfather engaged in insipid swagger. He would never shut up.

Yet, there is fact buried in there, a grain. I have often wondered if my grandfather was indeed born in Urmia. Given that he left England in 1921, aged nine, he would have been extremely young at the time of the genocide, a thought that makes my stomach turn, for what do you do with a three-year-old during a massacre? And I have sometimes wondered if there is another secret, hiding under the secret of our name and the genocide itself: who is my grandfather? Was he really the son of the woman whom he accompanied into America? Was he the biological child of the man with an illegible name already living in Yonkers who was listed as his father?[71] How did these things happen? How did a woman and child travel from northern Iran to the island of Britain in the early decades of the twentieth century, possibly during the First World War? What did that cost? Which language or languages were spoken along the way? How did one not die?

There is one other thing: my father once explained to me that he knew his grandparents. He said nothing of his grandfather but described his grandmother to me as a woman who "always wore black." He said, "I remember her." He may have told me he remembered her "vividly." My father said his grandmother did not speak English. He told me he communicated with her exclusively in her language.[72]

"What?" I said, uncertain if I had heard him correctly.

"I've forgotten it," my father replied, not without anger. "I guess that's pretty embarrassing." He abruptly left the room.

Whenever I tried to turn to this topic again, my father would tell me that I had misheard him or that he had been joking, that he enjoyed playing on my sentimental eagerness.

"There were so many people on that ship's manifest," he once said. "How can we know if anything written there was true?"

In the end, he did not want to help me. Or he regarded my peripatetic search as a fool's errand. Which, in some sense, it was.

One last thing I will tell you is that around the time I met my husband, I got a tattoo. I'm not sure what it means today to say that I was not the sort of person who would get a tattoo, given so many people have them, but I wasn't. I'm not. I have no idea why I did it. I was reading a book of poetry by the Egyptian-Jewish and later Parisian poet, Edmond Jabès. The book ends with two sentences I took it upon myself to lineate and translate as follows in a notebook (they are not in stanza form in the original):

Don't worry
          about the trace
You are alone
in that you cannot erase it

I followed this up with a second, more accurate translation:

Don't worry
          about the trace
Only you
cannot erase it[73]

The tattoo was done by an amateur, in the original French, and it did not turn out very well. It is nearly illegible, in gunmetal blue on my left wrist. I've never tried to have it cleaned up.

At the time, I liked what I took to be a double meaning in the ultimate sentence, this idea of being set apart both quantitatively and qualitatively through a relation to something one cannot erase. This sentence suggests that our humanity is tied to a longer-standing resistance to forgetting, a resistance that is at once constitutive of self and impersonal. We have, Jabès suggests, a responsibility to contend with the site where our personal selves begin to disappear into a deeper, collective inscription. It can be tempting to wish to be forgotten in full, to leave no trace—even as, or possibly because, we live in constant relation to forms of loss and oblivion we may be unable to control, such as violence. It may yet be that there is something beautiful about this paradoxical quality of human ethics, the fugitive and lopsided agency we seem to have been granted in relation to history, an agency at times so minor that it can seem like a flaw. On my first reading, I probably thought little of the fact that in Jabès's lyric narrative, this pair of sentences is written by a rabbi who seeks to pay homage to and possibly console another rabbi "who, in order to be forgotten, had under an assumed name taken refuge in a village at the edge of the desert, where nobody would have dreamed to look for him."[74]

When I started going to therapy, my analyst told me one day that she had had a premonition, a sort of vision about what I could expect from treatment. She said that she felt odd seeming to promise me anything, but that nevertheless she wanted to share her guess. She sent me a link to an article in the *New York Times*, a piece written by another psychoanalyst about one of her clients, a man who was obsessed with mourning and who felt the presence of someone he could not see. The man subsequently discovered that he had had an older brother who had died before his birth and with whom he shared both a last and a first name.

The man made plans to visit his deceased brother's grave, the resting place of his namesake. His older brother was a baby, and he was now an adult. In my reading, the man was cured.[75]

I had less hope for myself, but, by the same token, I wasn't sure that I wanted to be emotionally transformed.

I was less like the man in the *New York Times* article than a character I touch on in my freshman essay. I resembled Fredy Boettcher, the sailor-protagonist of contemporary Australian poet Les Murray's epic *Fredy Neptune*, who becomes physically insensible for years after attending a genocide. But I wasn't a witness, really. Unless, somehow, I was?

In 1999, I wrote:

> Murray creates a narrator, Fredy Boettcher, an Australian sailor of German descent—that is, Murray himself plus the German woman—who travels in Europe during the First World War and witnesses this very burning in Turkey:
>
> > They were huddling, terrified, crying,
> > crossing themselves, in the middle of men all yelling.

Their big loose dresses were sopping. Kerosene, you could
    smell it.
The men were prancing, feeling them, poking at them
    to dance—
then pouf! They were alight, the women, dark wicks to
    great orange flames,
whooping and shrieking.

Fredy is first horrified by the burning, but then understands it in a strange, subconscious act of sympathy with
the girls who have died. He spends five years in the world
feeling no physical sensation anywhere in his body. Rather
than putting out his eyes, he "puts out" his ability to feel
the world, in memorial to the terrible pain that the burning
brides felt.[76]

I write, in this part of my freshman essay, that I have concluded
that Murray creates a "parallel lyric." I call this parallel lyric "another body." This other body, made of words, is a place that exists
to house the memory of atrocity. It is a shadow body, an other.
It does not comfort that memory, because how can it? Instead, it
gives it a place, small recompense and yet an act that allows the
inconsolable memory to be found—by future others, by readers
like myself.

I keep trying to figure out why it matters, if it matters, that I
tell this story. I often think to myself that I am not particularly
Assyrian. I look only a little Assyrian. An American expat living
in Beijing, who, like me, had grown up in New York, once told me
that I have "Eurasian" features, whatever that meant. Anyway, I
am mostly of European descent, if we are going by percentages.
I do not speak or read Syriac and have almost no understanding
of the group's culture or beliefs. Yet I think daily about the never-
discussed genocide. Or I do now, having found out about its

existence. "Now" encompasses my mid- to late thirties, my for-
ties, and shall persist for the rest of my life. It will continue, because this is an elaboration of that pat expression, that a person
cannot "unknow" things. "Thanks," someone says in a sitcom.
"Now I can never unknow that."

It's not easy to determine what goes into an essay like this
and what doesn't. Likely, the challenge is more on the side of
"what doesn't" than "what does." I make a list of topics, of places,
spots, to write about. These are just stopping places, not *lieux
de mémoire* in Yates's sense. Or, no, perhaps I polish them, clean
them, and they do get somewhat brighter, more vivid:

- The story of my college essay
- Glück on fundamentalism
- The phenomenological character of images (as opposed to
  pictures)
- Wolfgang Ernst (so hard to write about!)
- Story of genocide
- Period rooms (what would a phenomenological period
  room look like?)
- The story of my life falling apart
- Finding out
- Memories
- My tattoo
- Therapist's NYT anecdote

As an adult, living two decades out from my freshman essay
on vividness, I realize the writing that presented itself to me
as a stylistic curiosity—or, that I described to myself as notable
precisely for its simultaneous lack of stylistic remarkableness
and extraordinary urgency—still exists. I can read it anytime.
Although I'm less apt to turn to J.'s poem or my own essay, I can
read Siamanto. I can read Les Murray.

Yet I don't understand the size of this stopping place, why I
linger here. Or why exactly I was driven to write that essay in

the first place, as ignorant as I was then. It's a level in me, a sort of register. Events in my present life can rhyme with it, but, in the end, it remains veiled, like a lake covered with an enormous piece of fabric, some artist's action. I'll never know what happened, even as I know exactly what happened. I know very little, yet I can't stop trying to formulate versions (visions) of events.

One of the small changes I have made in the past five years is an occasional practice of mentioning that my last name was transformed during the early twentieth century. I don't say this to everyone, of course. I don't tell the librarian who asks me what my name is when I mention that I have a book on hold. I don't tell people I meet. I just note it sometimes, if, for example, family history comes up in conversation. And when I begin teaching a new class, I like to play a short self-introductory game that I learned from the artist Malik Gaines, who says that he derived it from Augusto Boal's theater exercises. In the game, we go around and each tell a story about our name, any story. That's it. That's the whole game. The first time I tried it, which was in a group with Malik, I stuck to my first name. All I managed to say was that it has four letters and seemed to have no symbolic meaning for my parents, although I know it means *light*.

The thing about this game is that you never forget someone's name once they have told you a story about it. I always know my students' names by heart after the first hour of class together. Which is, in a roundabout way, an answer to my earlier question, the question about what this story can possibly mean to me and why it matters that I tell it. The story of a name is a sort of rehearsal, a chance to walk backward, to engage in a pantomime the gestures of which you may only understand a little or much later. You tell a story about a name not in order to remember everything anyone has ever known about it but in order not to entirely forget.

For memory is partial. This is its form.

I feel that I can at last write my theory of literary vividness.

Here it is: the image that affects you most may be the one (*perduta,*
smarrita) in shadow. The vivacity or strange, muffled darkness
of that which lies under erasure—buried, crossed out, immolated, bathed (paradoxically) in too much light—should never be
underestimated.

Anyway, this is just a story of something that preceded my
birth and refused to be lost, hardly an uncommon sort of tale
where humans are concerned. Chances are you, too, could tell
me something like it.*

---

* This essay is dedicated, with immense gratitude, to Gordon Harvey.

Earliness, or Romance

Love is the enemy of memory.
—Lauren Berlant[1]

There is a certain cursed object by means of which I came to my first understanding of the nature of America, as well as the nature of romantic love. This object is the 1954 musical film *Seven Brides for Seven Brothers*, acquired by my parents on VHS before my birth.

A summary: the year is 1850; the location, the Oregon Territory. "Backwoodsman" Adam Pontipee lives with his six brothers on a mountain homestead. A now-deceased mother named her seven offspring in alphabetical order, employing biblical heroes: Adam (the first man), Benjamin, Caleb, Daniel, Ephraim, until she arrived at the letter *F*. Thus was Frankincense, "Frank," christened. Last came Gideon, a blond baby. Their mother's relationship to the Great Text is matched by the simplicity and optimism of her children. Their father is long gone, too, and they are adults, living in manly squalor, rich in livestock, wheat, fresh air. They are solitary, hunky, and slowly becoming ingrown and deformed.

Adam, eldest and arguably hunkiest of all, portrayed by Howard Keel in a fanciful ginger beard, decides to sacrifice himself. On everyone's behalf, he will marry. He rolls down to the frontier town where he plans to exchange some of the fruits of his labor for manufactured items and an eligible woman. Asked at Fred Bixby's general store what "brand" of bride he seeks, Adam replies, "I'd like best a widow woman that ain't afraid to work."

As it turns out, Adam will not have to settle for used goods. In a matter of moments, he encounters Milly (Jane Powell), a bodacious bondswoman who toils as cook and general dogsbody at the local inn. He spies her chopping wood, her diminutive frame encased in a wasp-waisted floor-length gown of indigo-dyed cloth, the skirt attractively patched with a star. Milly heaves a giant axe over her head, somewhat believably applying herself to the trunk of a young pine (soft wood). She gathers logs at her sponsor's request. The film passes over her indentured status. Adam does not buy her from the owner of the inn. However, at the local minister's house, where they go to wed, it seems there are claims on Milly's person. We learn that she has been "like a daughter to us," as the black-clad man of religion announces, either ignoring her temporary enslavement or, more likely, analogizing it with his own daughter's status. He resists Milly's marriage. Milly reminds him that he himself has told her that "a girl had no right to stay single," not when the land needed to be "settled," as she describes married sex and reproduction.

The film absolves itself of the matter of women-as-chattel-in-permanence through the first of what are to be many swoons. Repurposing the minister's words, Milly claims a useful non-right: she has no right to stay single and so, although she has no right to marry, either, she does have a duty. Bizarrely, she turns next to something resembling a psychoanalytic anamnesis. She declares that when local men asked her to marry in the past, she always had a "sinking feeling." However, when Adam proposed, she "waited" for this irrational sensation of impending doom and did not feel it. Milly's affect becomes rosy, iridescent. She exclaims, "I feel just fine. I feel so good I could cry!"

Although (1950s) mores have already variously impinged on this historical comedy, Milly's revelation of her experience of true love is a particularly significant anachronism. Abruptly, 1954's most popular tropes spring into action. Adam and Milly must absolutely be married without further objection or delay. Love is exceptional. Love is the exception. God, slavery, patriarchy retreat to the shadows. Milly's face shines. She has found

the escape hatch, the drug—call it what you will. She has autonomy and value. No one reminds her that by marrying Adam she
is playing into the riskiest exigencies of Manifest Destiny with
even more zeal than anyone currently dwelling in the (already
"settled") pioneer town. No one reminds her that true love is
causing her to do exactly what North American Protestantism
and the federal government ordain. No one reminds her that she
is about to become Adam's property.

Alice, the minister's daughter, white-blond and cinched into
a petal-pink getup, swoons, too. "Oh, I think it's wonderful!" she
trills. Her mother chides her. We understand that the mother
is reacting to some intimation of sexual pleasure. Alice must
be silenced lest solidarity develop between the two virgins, for
it's but a quick logical leap from fantasies of autonomy and self-
realization to collaborative reflection on the nature of autonomy
and the best routes to self-realization, after all.

What ensues is at once a riposte to and confirmation of this
double swoon. Milly is disillusioned regarding her liaison with
Adam; he's told her nothing of his large and needy family, whom
she is to serve. These masters, Adam's goofy, horny brothers, subsequently decide, to Milly's horror, to kidnap six additional young
women from the town to marry them, too. Given these events,
some might argue that the film presents a critique of gender-
based exploitation. This is not the case. Yes, Milly will realize
that she has bought herself a one-way ticket to eternal cleaning-
woman status at the Pontipees' foul ranch. Yes, she can articulate,
regarding Adam's advantage, "You knew I was young and strong
and there was lots of work in me." However, Adam's harsh prag-
matism, which will itself be chastened by the film's conclusion,
is basically OK; it just needs some adjusting (this is Milly's work).
The younger brothers' psychotic conception of romance is OK,
too; it just needs some adjusting (also Milly's work). Conveniently,
everyone's victims fall in love with them!

The film's position is the rather predictable one that men and women, as such, have entirely distinct roles and abilities. Milly manages the cooking, maintenance of the cabin, and hygiene of the brothers with such aplomb that she seems assisted by invisible machines, talking animals (cf. Disney), or, perhaps, demons. But *Seven Brides for Seven Brothers* is not actually very interested in the miraculous "work in [her]," possibly because mechanization has already arrived in Cold War homes. Rather, it lingers over Milly's instruction of the brothers in etiquette (see the musical number "Goin' Courtin'") and thrills to Milly's transformation of the log cabin into a cozy ski lodge. At the fateful denouement, Milly has traded in her girlish bleu de travail for a Queen of Hearts ensemble: a mostly white gown with voluminous puffed sleeves and multicolored inset quilting dominated by bright red passages like blood mixed with water. While we may be supposed to think that the ever-resourceful Milly has confected this masterpiece of #cottagecore avant la lettre from shabby bedding, the effect is of flawless couture. Milly is triumphant. She has domesticated the formerly bearded brothers, along with the fractious and nubile abductees—who have, only a few scenes earlier, acted out a uni-sex group wedding in their corsets and underwear ("June Bride"), a not-so-subtle versioning of the flourishing "Women in Prison" genre. Adam is repentant, given the presence of his newborn daughter, and the townspeople will momentarily be appeased as the six remaining brothers become married men.

Milly's body exudes domestic space. It flows from her like a massive skirt or torrent of amniotic fluid. Her person is "settled" yet fertile, inexhaustible, totally natural. While it is imperative that the seven brothers recover their humanity and increase the (white) nation, we are less certain about Milly's needs. Yes, she faced harassment and assault in her position as an indentured servant. Yes, she had to admit disappointment and refuse past offers of marriage because she did not feel an authentic frisson. She was hardly one to marry simply to put herself out of the way of rape, although she does later tell Adam, "I can stand some loneliness after the inn." Milly was never desperate, nor did she die from the amount of work she had to do in inappropriate garments. Over a dozen people with infantile wants turn to Milly, render her indispensable. Surely nothing could make a woman happier!

It is easy, from a contemporary point of view, to identify *Seven Brides for Seven Brothers* as a cursed work. Yet there is a subtlety to its investment in bad acts and worse ideas. Its hysterical obsession with gender and supposedly civilized behavior (quilting and courting) is distracting. We may be tempted to overlook its two deepest commitments. The first of these I have already touched on, the notion that "true love" preserves the subject or citizen from oppression and exploitation absolutely—that true love is a guarantor of autonomy because it is a means of both "feel[ing] so good I could cry" and securing property. I will return to this idea. The film's other cherished notion is that it is OK to do violent, criminal things if one does them as part of a group. OK to abduct people, OK to organize a lynching party, OK to "settle" the West, OK to marry the nominally willing, OK to produce families of seven or more children, OK to do it because a mob does it, OK to do it because a nation does so.

-‡-

Released in 1954, *Seven Brides for Seven Brothers* is almost exactly a century away from the historical moment it depicts. It forgets certain things.

One of the things it forgets is a bit nearer to hand: In 1926, poet and short-story writer Stephen Vincent Benét published "The Sobbin' Women" in *The Country Gentleman*. Benét's role in the cultural present is mostly limited to his authorship of this brief story, even as few are aware of its existence.[2] It is this story that husband-and-wife screenwriting team, Albert Hackett and Frances Goodrich, along with Dorothy Kingsley, revised to generate the plot of *Seven Brides for Seven Brothers*, first titled *A Bride for Seven Brothers* (a phrase subsequently judged obscene by a studio censor).[3]

In "The Sobbin' Women," Milly, "a bound girl, as they had in those days," is selected for marriage on short notice by an eldest backwoodsman brother named Harry Pontipee. (In Benét's story, all the brothers' names begin with *H* and there is no biblical connection.) "Next door to a slave she was, for all she'd come of good stock and had some education," Benét's winsome narrator observes. Harry "buy[s] out her time from the innkeeper for twelve beaver pelts and a hunting knife," then it's off to the crowded ranch.[4]

This Milly, the original Milly, surely inflected by the cultural politics of the 1920s, is canny and historically minded. She loves money, not men, and has read a history book that is likely the *Life of Romulus*, Plutarch's account of the founding of Rome. She knows the legend of the Rape of the Sabine Women—who were coerced into sex with the supposedly ragtag Romans and later made peace between enraged patriarchs and less-than-chosen partners.[5] In Benét's tale, it is Milly who devises the plan to take the girls of the town by force and Milly who uses her wiles to manipulate the girls into believing that they freely marry the strapping backwoodsmen; Milly who appeases the lynch mob; Milly who grows rich by means of her own private schemes. As Benét's narrator remarks, "Here's where her education came in that I've made such a point of."[6]

Benét is not unenchanted by the historical color of pioneer life and its DIY ethic, but his writing is keenest where Milly's guile is concerned. While his Pontipees are interchangeable lugs with only mild physical appeal, Benét thrills to the question of how, exactly, a "young and thin"[7] girl without family might survive indentured servitude in a mostly lawless territory and even find a way to thrive. It amuses him to contemplate her lack of consideration of the gender-related exigencies of Christian America. It is as if she were, dare we say it, *liberated* by the level of threat facing her. Benét's Milly is a trickster, a relatively beneficent little witch.

So "The Sobbin' Women" is not exactly feminist, but it does turn its attention to the question of Milly's ingenuity, choosing to believe in the impossibility of her situation, as well as her ability to use her interrelated skills as a reader and a storyteller (again, "her education") to paint herself out of a corner and, in the process, found a mini-nation in Pontipee Valley.

Milly is the truest Roman: "She knew what she wanted and how she was going to get it—and she waited her chance."[8] Benét suggests, albeit softly, in a folksy tone, that there is something out there in America that can push its inhabitants—for remember that in the mid-nineteenth century Milly is not a full citizen—beyond the limits of good and evil. Anyone is susceptible to this thing, even those who are the targets of a sentimentalist popular culture that may seek to keep them in ignorance, especially regarding marriage and sex. Anyone can be a capitalist. Anyone can win.

And there is much else *Seven Brides for Seven Brothers* forgets, beyond the cunning of Benét's Milly. In Benét's story, we do not know the exact year of events. "It was in the early days of the settlement," Benét tells us, that the Pontipee family "came over the Pass one day in one big wagon" before moving on from the town to a nearby valley.[9] It is possible, then, that the Pontipees arrived in the Oregon Country well before the formation of the provisional government that in 1843 established organic laws permitting any "white male settler" to claim at no cost 640 acres, or a square mile, for his personal use and the use of his heirs.[10] These laws also banned slavery, suggesting that Milly's arrangement with the innkeeper is consensual and distinct from absolute ownership—or, in any case, has no basis in Milly's race. Despite the territory's opposition to the presence of enslaved persons, its white settlers were hardly abolitionists; they displayed racist and paranoid views in public discussions, and in

1844 passed an amendment to the 1843 law that would subject any free Black person living in Oregon to a whipping every six months until that person's departure.[11] Neither Benét nor the screenwriters of the 1954 film are interested in representing this foundational text of the state that "flies with her own wings."

This said, if we mix narratives, we can guess that in 1850, the year when *Seven Brides for Seven Brothers* is supposed to take place, Adam Pontipee is approximately thirty years old, and, if we use Harry's age at the time of his arrival in the territory (given as nine years in Benét's story) as a counterpoint, it would seem that the Pontipees were among the earliest white settlers, arriving in or around 1830, cutting some of the first wheel tracks in the Oregon Trail.

We don't know whence the Pontipees come. They precede and prophesy the waves of midwestern settlers of the 1840s and '50s that would flow out of the so-called oldlands of the Ohio and Mississippi River Valleys. Perhaps the Pontipees have been unmoored by the first of the many antebellum busts, the Panic of 1819. This three-year financial crisis, which inaugurated what is now an American tradition, led to a spate of mortgage foreclosures and economic depression. Farmers and other laboring people moved west to escape failing economies and recoup losses; by 1830, for example, some twelve thousand US citizens had relocated to the Mexican state of Coahuila y Tejas, later the Republic of Texas.[12] The Pontipees have, perhaps, something of an avant-garde streak. They go west and go far. They are hard to kill, wild by nature. To expand a bit on one of Benét's similes, they are like a family of raccoons, omnivorous and dexterous.[13]

Like raccoons—or, really, like humans—they multiply. They are then the harbingers of what scholar Daniel Immerwahr has called a "supernova" of North American population increase. To give a quick comparison via Immerwahr, the population of France in 1776 was approximately thirty million people. The United States in 1776 held between three and four million people.

By 1900, the population of France was forty million. By 1900, the US population was, incredibly, seventy-six million. Immigration alone does not account for this change; "the bulk of it was handled the old-fashioned way, a firehose of fecundity spraying settlers up and down the North American continent."[14] Strangely, at least one of the founding fathers, Benjamin Franklin, was entirely unsurprised by this world-historical anomaly, predicting it as early as 1749, based on a census he took of the population of Philadelphia.

"Bless yore beautiful hide!" bellows Howard Keel as Adam Pontipee. He beams, his symmetrical face like statuary, like the face of an impossibly youthful Santa Claus, the face of a Roman god or Yahweh himself, unshakable in its burnished, kooky optimism.

Meanwhile, in the film, Milly marries Adam not because she is particularly eager to marry (surely, she is not living in terror at the inn!) but because something unique, irreplaceable, and autonomous in her recognizes his apparent authenticity—which is to say, his kooky, flawed optimism. Their liaison is, for some reason, true. It lacks contingency.

I'm not sure when I first became aware of romantic love. It must have been around the same time I found out about money, as well as the existence of a nation, with a name, in which I was already living. It would have been an experience related to screens. When I was three years old, my mother tried to take me to a revival of the Disney animation *Snow White and the Seven Dwarfs* (1937)—this was in the early 1980s, when films returned periodically to the theater—but I became so terrified during Snow White's flight into the clutching, ogling trees of the haunted forest that I had to be removed before the advent of the love plot.

I try to move back into that old life, that early life, of which I have relatively clear memories. (I resided in a seedy Manhattan and watched a lot of TV.) Before the narrative of romantic love comes the narrative, and the figure, of the hero. It's in every cartoon. I was impressed by the hero and the sacrifices of the hero before I understood anything about the reciprocity and transcendence of romantic love. I thrilled to the notion of the hero's calling. The hero walked forward into fire, eyes open and melting. The hero was alone and certain. The hero had to. Although I knew nothing about Joan of Arc until I was a tween, some intimation of a child's version of her story was, long before that, my unspoken ideal, both psychologically and sartorially. This was the key to making life make sense: a mission. Cross-dressing, I intuited, could help.

I will do it, I thought. *I will do what no one else will. Nobody must ask me. I am already ready.*

There is quite a lot to unpack in such silent vows. What interests me in this context is my own comprehension, even at this time, let's say the age of five if not earlier—at four, even—that the human project is totally incoherent. Yes, I'm definitely gearing up for the repetition of something fatal, something I can't avoid, but there is this *lag* that puzzles me. And it is so damn funny and absurd: People could choose to behave otherwise, yet they never do. It astounds me. People never stop to consider their own beliefs.

I therefore like the hero's ardent and hermetic style, because the hero has taken the ultimate fungibility of human norms to a space of originality. The hero is certain. Only me! I alone will fashion a unique belief and act upon it, the hero swears. I will be inconvincible. I'll be isolated and driven. I will go totally crazy—in an intriguing way. Others will remember me.

Sadly, or perhaps happily, it is difficult to say, I don't have time to live out this fantasy of ethical exceptionalism and almost certain self-destruction. I never become a hero. Likely, it has to do with the fact that I am not a boy. Instead of living this pat fantasy, I elect a different one. Alas.

-:-

Summaries of the history of romantic love in the West usually begin with Plato's *Symposium*. In this text, elite friends at a drinking party decide to have a contest to see who can give the finest speech praising Eros, god of love. Here we learn at least two significant stories explaining love's origins and its future, which is to say, love's purpose. (No one, with the possible exceptions of John Cameron Mitchell and Stephen Trask in their song "The Origin of Love" in *Hedwig and the Angry Inch*,[15] has tried to tell either of these stories to American children, as far as I am aware.)

Aristophanes, a comic playwright, delivers a tale[16] that seeks to account for that well-known feeling associated with falling in love of a return to a formerly lost wholeness—what I believe Milly is referring to when she speaks of "feel[ing] so good I could cry," and what has also been called *cathexis*, which is to say, a form of intense emotional investment in an object. Aristophanes maintains that in primordial times human beings had double bodies. Three sexes existed: the all-male, the all-female, and the androgyne, a being half female and half male. Zeus, for political reasons, decides to split these double humans in two, generating a race that is, haha, compelled to seek its other half.

Diotima, Socrates's teacher in amorous matters, is the source of a subsequent and less humorous story. Socrates explains that Diotima taught him that Eros is the child of Ingenuity and Poverty, and that love is not an inherent quality of the beloved but rather a guiding force that impels the lover to seek beauty. Diotima instructs Socrates in a mode of love in light of which another human is a mere starting point and not an end: by loving the beauty of the beloved, a lover comprehends an intangible quality that leads to contemplation of (Platonic) forms and spiritual development.[17]

European humanity will have to wait another millennium or more for another theory of love as convincing and, apparently, socially expedient as the Platonic account. Courtly love, sometimes known as *Minne*, or "loving remembrance" in Middle High

German, appears, according to the American philosopher Irving Singer, at some time in the eleventh or twelfth centuries, somewhere (and, subsequently, everywhere) in the courts of southern France, Spain, or North Africa.[18] This was at first a profane love. As Marina Warner writes, for the promoters of this important feeling, the early troubadours, "the idea that chastity comes from love, that true love denies its own goal, would have been nonsense." Yet courtly love, like the Platonic appreciation of forms, eventually becomes a practice of nonfulfillment. Warner explains:

> The notion that true courtliness and true nobility demand that a man—like the "bold lover" on Keats' Grecian urn— pursue his lady for a kiss forever, and that a virtuous woman always refuse is a perversion of the troubadour ideal, and an accurate reflection of the returned authority of the Church and the ascetic tradition of the fathers.[19]

Or, as Singer puts it, inverting Warner's account of cause and effect:

> The two major approaches to ideal erotic love—medieval courtliness and modern romanticism—both consist of attempts to humanize the love that Christian mystics had generally reserved for man in relation to God.[20]

In either case, we see that the West's relationship to love is troubled: the body is a problem, of course, but love is more generally worrisome in its potential to challenge other sources of authority.

The "modern romanticism" Singer names is, arguably, a republican and postindustrial condition. It finds its first stirrings in sixteenth-century reimaginings of marriage as the culmination of romantic love, as in the plays of William Shakespeare,[21] and, after the revolutions of the late eighteenth century, is widely popularized via the so-called love marriage and a feminized field of cultural endeavor associated with—and perhaps produced by—ideas regarding biological determinism and separate spheres of life for women and men. Sigmund Freud's Greek-influenced stories about the projection of a spectral phallus (everyone wants it and no one has it!) will, in the early twentieth century, begin to complicate narratives regarding a biologically determined course of human life in which women have a monopoly on private caregiving while men are best suited for public action.[22] All the same, the myth of the separate spheres has been extraordinarily durable. Jean-Jacques Rousseau, in *Émile, or On Education* (1762), summarizes succinctly: "A woman's education must . . . be planned in relation to man."[23]

Propping up this myth of two worlds are quite a number of supplementary products and practices, many of which have survived to make their way into the twenty-first century. One of the best satirizers of these products and practices remains Gustave Flaubert, who in *Madame Bovary* (1856) described how Emma Bovary was, as a girl, pulled into a woozy world of detailed steel-plate engravings contained in sentimental "keepsake" albums, where she obtained a strange and ultimately deadly understanding of herself, as the vague subject of a romantic plot.[24] This is also to say that modern romanticism is tied up with everyday life and the production of families in a way that Platonic and courtly love were not. It is also tied up with citizenship.

Before I descend further into an exploration of the murky ties between the apparently unkillable myth of romantic love and contemporary citizenship, I need to spend some time on that other fraught matter, the question of the family. This territory is relatively well known or, should I say, familiar. From Freud we have the story of Oedipus's bind. Whether or not you find Freud's account of real genitals and their spectral effects useful, Freud's innovative observation that love is a compensatory strategy only incompletely based in genuine qualities possessed by the beloved is, in my opinion, very useful.[25] In Freud's account, "Love becomes a *problem*, rather than the celebrated answer to our problems," as Robert C. Solomon and Kathleen M. Higgins observe,[26] and I love this. In the psychoanalytic view, love is worthy of suspicion. As one of Freud's trickiest inheritors, Jacques Lacan, puts it, "Love is giving something one doesn't have to someone who doesn't want it."[27] (Adam Phillips rewrites this sentence: "Love is giving something you haven't got to someone who doesn't exist.")[28] Love is an error and it is an error we can't help committing.

The reason that we commit the error of love is, simply, that we are born and, meanwhile, we seem to have forgotten this. What one might call the "earliness" of human birth is a major issue. Unlike the adults who are crucial to its survival, the neonate cannot walk, stand, or lift its head. According to Freud, the infant experiences itself as continuous with the body of a caregiver and it is only through its experience of need that it develops psychosexual independence, progressing through the infamous oral, anal, phallic, latent, and genital phases by means of which it comes to recognize its (at times enraging) autonomy.[29] For Lacan, the ensuing compensatory fantasy is analogous to what happens when a child propelling itself in a walker catches sight of itself in a mirror.[30] The self is formed in an attempt, on the part of the child, to believe that it is a whole being rather than a scrap broken off from a nurturing matrix. Because the image reflected by the mirror is two-dimensional, this image can never match up to the full self the child wishes to see. The child must subsequently use fantasy to negotiate and disguise its apparently inferior personhood, risking its self as a token in later libidinal games in hopes of transcending this devastating and foundational early disappointment.

Whether we are convinced by the metaphors selected by Freud and Lacan, a general effect of these psychoanalytic accounts, celebrated by literary critics perhaps more than clinicians, is to foreground the ways in which behavior associated with a time when we could not survive on our own determines whom we love as adults and how. Indeed, it is the famous mechanism of repetition you've surely heard about: the treatment you receive at the hands of a caregiver becomes the action you associate with someone who loves you. Thus, in this account, do parents win for their children their future partners. If a parent physically abuses their child, that child will seek a lover who will do the same, even if that child is able to recognize that physical abuse is, in the abstract and rationally speaking, harmful and in no way loving. Because a child is compelled to understand an abusive parent's behavior as loving, because to survive a child must view a caregiver as loving.[31]

Contemporary psychoanalytic approaches, even if circumspect about Freud and Lacan, often privilege a sort of practical suspicion designed to help the patient explore self-defeating narratives adopted as a protective veil during childhood. To undergo treatment, then, is a bit like stopping where one is on the path of life and turning to face something that one has for so long kept at one's back. It's the thing you think is going to kill you. *That* thing. That unspeakable thing. That one thing that lacks contingency and seems fated and is therefore "yours." In a way, you're not wrong. In the past, it could have killed you, when you were small and vulnerable, but it cannot harm you anymore. What is harmful is that you run from it—and that you run, uncannily, toward it, as in a waking dream. What is harmful is that when you find another person you believe figures this thing for you, you fall deeply in love with them. And the whole world falls away.

So, psychoanalysis suggests that it is an ambiguous truism to claim that we cannot live without love. This said, quite a number of people will disagree. And American English's own persistent ambiguity shores up my point, for what is meant by *cannot*? This weird verb suggests that we are not able to live without love and we are not *permitted*. You are not allowed. No love, no living. Live as a human and you will be obligated to love. You cannot survive without loving. You will shrivel up and die and die and die. Et cetera.

Here I'd like to pause and hop into a world slightly less beset by ghosts and projection. I am fascinated by a lecture given in the summer of 1969 by German sociologist Niklas Luhmann. In this lecture, Luhmann begins to develop a description of love as a code or symbolic medium of communication.[32] Love is less a thing-in-itself than a standard of expression; it functions in literature and society as a translator between self and other(s), past and present.[33] Love is cybernetic, a governing language with respect to other languages and concepts; it determines not only what can be expressed but who may express it.

In later work, Luhmann shows the vacillating importance of love in the West. Passion only ceases being a heinous condition associated with disease—to become a world-altering heterosexual semantics—during the seventeenth century. Passionate love is unstable during this century and won't be bundled with marriage until later, but it does have the interesting effect of nurturing individualism. It seems to encourage people to choose their partners, rather than letting social stratification determine matters. Leap forward two hundred years and love is not only a facet of the institution of marriage but also key to the individuality that characterizes increasingly modern nineteenth-century humans who have egos and dwell in industrialized society. Love confirms individuals' inner experiences (feelings, thoughts) because, according to Luhmann, interiority is the source of one's love; intimacy with another is, therefore, a way of proving one's own existence.[34]

But love arrives at an impasse as of the Cold War. Whereas individuality once stood as "one of the most concrete characteristics of man," a notion that explained the location of the soul in relation to larger systems, it is now, paradoxically, only "the most general" condition of being.[35] Everyone is an individual, and we can no longer turn to our identities as such when we seek to draw distinctions between our roles as private lovers and our roles as economic consumers, since in late postmodernity the same "I" is implicated in both contexts. Individuality prevails as both the ends of personal existence and the ends of public existence. Whether this lack of distinction on the basis of individuality may also come with certain progressive boons (in that it can seem to collapse hierarchies), it troubles love, that conservative and persistent cultural term.

It is odd, because as much as Luhmann attempts to explain the social success of love by recourse to rational means, he simultaneously remystifies it. Love is a good in two senses: it is an excellent medium and it's a product of society. It exists, quite simply, because we haven't come up with anything to replace it—a better way to externalize the hidden reaches of the self. It is an organizing force but more importantly it is a preeminent technology for seeing and knowing. Would we even bother with one another without it?

At this point in our story, romantic love is double: freeing and constraining, personal and general. Luhmann's love-as-proto-internet is only simplistically psychoanalytic, yet it does touch on the classical dynamic that interests Freud and his inheritors as well—that romantic love is a force associated with personal impoverishment and personal ingenuity, the child, as Diotima claims, of the spirit of ways and the spirit of the lack of means.

Let me add my own spin: Love is what we do to get out of situations characterized by what we experience as a bad (limiting, painful) form of certainty, and it is what we do to get *into* situations characterized by what we experience as a good (enlivening, pleasurable) form of certainty. We use it to disentangle ourselves from uncomfortable familial relationships that seem to possess too little contingency (i.e., "Can these inconsiderate people really be my parents?!"), and it is something that gives us a relationship outside the family that lacks contingency in a way that makes us jubilant and hopeful, that may seem fated, a destiny. "I was made to love you," and so on.

Some of the best critics of contemporary romantic love propose that we reread the myth of romantic love in tandem with other social structures in order to better understand its alchemy of scarcity and abundance. Feminist readers of the middle of the last century, for example, identify a problematic asymmetry. As Simone de Beauvoir writes, "The single word love in fact signifies two different things for man and woman." In Beauvoir's critique in *The Second Sex* (1949), the role of a woman in a heterosexual relationship is inescapably secondary with respect to public life; while men in love "remain sovereign subjects," women must define themselves as women, as such, through total self-abnegation, so that it is "agonizing for a woman to assume responsibility for her life."[36] (The Milly of *Seven Brides* comes to mind.) Shulamith Firestone updates and historicizes this argument in *The Dialectic of Sex* (1970), discussing the Roman etymology of the term *family*, "first used . . . to denote a social unit the head of which ruled over wife, children, and slaves . . . *famulus* means domestic slave, and *familia* is the total number of slaves belonging to one man."[37] For Firestone, modern Western heterosexuality is only nominally more liberal, as a system of patronage. In other words, love is a job, and sex determines how we enter this profession and whom we serve.

In the same year as the publication of Firestone's still-influential text, the now little-known sociologist Philip Slater provided a critical reading of love in *The Pursuit of Loneliness: American Culture at the Breaking Point*, arguing that romantic love is not merely a technology for recognition—or, *if* it is a technology for recognition, this is a style of recognition that comes at a high price. Slater focuses on the origins of romantic love in detached households and the ways in which children's emotions are "bound up in a single person, and the process of spreading this involvement over other people as he grows up is more problematic." According to Slater, modern Westerners, particularly Americans, learn as children that love should be exclusive, which results in a dynamic of sexual scarcity: "Most of us learn early that there is one relationship that is more vital than all the others put together, and we tend both to reproduce this framework in later life and to retain, in fantasy, the original loyalty."[38] Slater compares romantic lovers of the late twentieth century to donkeys, who toil to reproduce lifestyles in which a fantastical attachment to a parent or other caregiver is, in light of the prohibition of incest, both central to life and impossible to fulfill.[39]

In these accounts, romantic love is a format, a means of control. Love is a prize that dangles ever out of reach. It continues to promise to make life more perfect, even as it leads us into ever-greater states of confusion. Yet love is infernally synthetic. Even these criticisms read as clichés. They bounce right off love, which is rubber, and stick to the unworthy and probably, we think, bitter philosopher, who is glue. You are unlikely to win against love by means of even a watertight argument for the simple reason that love can always retreat to that place of fear and never-ever-to-be-abandoned, hoped-and-longed-for possibility of redemption: an early attachment to a caregiver. Few people want to look at this shadow site, and the reason few people want to look at it is that to contemplate it is to see how much in this world is willful aversion, a series of shields against past vulnerabilities. It doesn't, apparently, need to be this way, but, honestly, who cares about that when you can text that person who makes you feel like your bones are on fire and made of ice, both at the same time?

The late Lauren Berlant was one of the best readers of the impasse of contemporary romantic love in recent memory. Their texts go straight to the heart of attachment's shadow realm (that hazy, mirrored region) and linger, gazing with patience and appreciation at unclear dynamics. At the time of their 2021 death, aged sixty-three, from leiomyosarcoma, a rare form of soft-tissue cancer, they were widely eulogized as the originator of the critical term "cruel optimism," an "attachment to compromised conditions of possibility whose realization is discovered either to be impossible, sheer fantasy, or *too* possible, and toxic."[40] Cruel optimism engenders bad hope. Many people read the term as particular to the uncertain economic and emotional futures created by the 2008 financial crisis; it proved a popular catchall. However, Berlant's career as a scholar of American culture encompassed a broader purview.

Berlant took love seriously. They saw it not as a feeling, per se, but a national ritual.[41] Central to the American story Berlant explores is the female person, a body and psyche that "provided a major mystic writing pad for national identity as it emerged"[42] and has long acted as a metaphorical (and sometimes literal) screen for the projection of various representations of collective identity. In the "cultural struggle over the material and symbolic conditions of U.S. citizenship," women, as domestic workers and late recipients of suffrage, generate an unstable private sphere in which "an intricate set of relations between economic, racial, and sexual processes" plays out with the aid of popular texts and images.[43] Debates over the nature of citizenship, its protections and limits, are thus less distant from questions related to the nature of love than we may at first believe, given that American romantic love was at one point the particular responsibility of individuals whose lives were defined by their inability to vote.

Transformed between the world wars by the Nineteenth Amendment ("The right of citizens of the United States to vote shall not be denied or abridged by the United States or by any State on account of sex"), contemporary romance, a romance newly practiced by two opposite-sex enfranchised citizens, becomes an ideology that retains some of its Victorian qualities, even as its circular routes and obfuscations are repurposed for

new ends. Loving has much to do with cruel optimism; it also
has to do with forgetting, as Berlant writes:

> In the modern ideology of normal love, lovers learn to as-
> pire to forget the stories they already know about the self-
> amputation, vulnerability, and social coercion so frequently
> and so intimately linked with what love's institutions iden-
> tify as mature happiness.[44]

Because heterosexual romance developed along with the sacrificial logic of the postindustrial separate spheres (i.e., women's
agency must be curtailed in order to increase men's, a topic
notably neglected by Luhmann), it makes sense that "self-
amputation" and "coercion" would be aspects of its future, even
in a somewhat more egalitarian society. It is also far from clear
that men would ever have been spared love's cruelty, even or especially in their attempts to differentiate themselves from women
legally, physically, economically, emotionally, visually, cultur-
ally, philosophically, medically, name your adverb. We can see
how capitalist societies stand to benefit by enshrining a principle that demands that humans strive without hope of tan-
gible reward in order to, supposedly, realize themselves fully—a
phrase that makes no sense.

Philip Slater compared the romantic to a donkey ("We have
found our donkey," is his full sentence).[45] But it is also the case
that romantic love remains, experientially speaking, a very
mixed bag, and Berlant's accounts do not shy away from its pleasures and mysteries. In one particularly moving description of
the romance plot, Berlant ponders its genre as an eerie negotia-
tion regarding what we are willing to know and what we believe
we must do. They write:

> If we think of romance as a genre of action film, in which
> an intensity of the need to survive is played out by a se-
> ries of dramatic pursuits, actions, and pacifications, then

the romance plot's setting for fantasy can be seen as less
merely conventional and more about the plotting of intensities that hold up a world that the unconscious deems worth
living in.[46]

"The plotting of intensities that hold up a world . . . worth living in": I read Berlant here as cautioning the reader against a
too hasty dismissal of sentimental tropes, since these perform a
representational service for our most volatile, inadmissible, and
despised memories and desires. The romance plot sets up a series of tents or scrims within or behind which the unconscious
may temporarily draw nearer, visiting us in narrative time, even
as the unconscious is—although we really do not like to think
about this—most at home outside sequential time.

It is not, by the way, as if we can avoid making concessions for
the unconscious. The unconscious is, in fact, an important source
of power that, unlike money, didn't need to be invented. That it
is "unconscious" is, of course, key to its incredible strength. The
unconscious is, additionally, extremely elusive, even as it is undeniable. We can attempt and fail and live with wanting to honor
or make love to our unconscious, but we can never enshrine, en-
case, or control it, for the unconscious is not a thing; it is an act.

The question I think Berlant is posing throughout their work
is how we can overcome a very common, very empty relationship to fantasy in the United States, one in which we undervalue
and misread the unconscious. This is another way of saying that
we should take seriously the need to make space and time for the
movements of our psyches so that these do not happen at such
a distance from what we take to be our beliefs. This matters for
politics because these movements of the psyche are about affiliation and attachment; they constitute the way in which the results
of past attachment take place in the present, are rehearsed in the
present. Indeed, these movements concern how we identify and
recognize ourselves. They are how we *are* ourselves, how we cre-

ate the thing we call individuality. They are also the fundamental materials of history.

And: We cannot but rehearse these past attachments.

I think about the writing of bell hooks in relation to Berlant's descriptions. hooks calls the family the "primary" and perhaps exclusive "school for love."[47] What blinds people to the harmful dynamics of romance is a wish not to see one's family of origin as harmful. hooks writes, "For most folks it is just too threatening to embrace a definition of love that would no longer enable us to see love as present in our families."[48] hooks recommends staying with that bond that is, in fact, an unhealing wound. hooks says that the wound is an angel. This is why the Bible contains a story of a man named Jacob (too far down the alphabet to be a Pontipee) who wrestles with an angel. We must, hooks observes, embrace our woundedness. This is what salvation looks like. It looks like push and pull—an embodiment of both plenitude and scarcity, Ingenuity and Poverty. In this encounter, we acknowledge our losses and unmet needs yet do not give up. "As long as we are afraid to risk," hooks reflects, "we cannot know love."[49]

It can be so difficult to live out what we can perceive intellectually by way of theory and criticism. But for some reason this image of the angel, a figure for risk, makes a special kind of sense to me, given the agonizing errands I've gone on as a lover. I don't entirely know how to avoid being cruelly optimistic about cursed objects that present themselves to me as candidates for love, but I do know how not to run from the angel's terrible embrace. Intuitively, I know this angel.

My maternal great-grandfather was a minor yet tireless public person. He was an evangelical Presbyterian minister, choir leader, and composer who married three times and fathered at least five children. His name was Benjamin Franklin Butts.

My great-grandmother, Onna, was the Reverend's third wife and managed to outlive him. She was thirty years younger than Benjamin Franklin Butts—she was born in 1896, the year of the invention of the X-ray; he in 1866 or 1867, just after the close of the American Civil War. They married somewhere in New Jersey in 1919,[50] fast on the heels of a significant funeral. Reverend Benjamin Franklin Butts's second wife, Mary Emma Rawlings Butts, died the same year, age forty-nine. Born in Kentucky, Mary Emma died in Nyack, New York. She and the Reverend did not have children. Benjamin Franklin Butts's first marriage, to Eva Grace Lambright Butts, ended under unknown circumstances sometime after the turn of the century.[51] He seems to have abandoned her and their daughter, Bessie Aileen, and son, Chester, in Philadelphia.[52]

The Reverend was a well-known evangelist and musician. He never stayed long in one place. I like to stalk him online via historical newspaper databases. In 1901, 1902, 1903, and 1904, for example, Butts sings in Pittsburgh and leads a chorus. He and Mary Emma, who wed in 1906 in Iowa, move to New York City, where they reside at West 178th Street by the time of the 1910 census.[53] The same year, Butts "goes south," as the *New York Observer and Chronicle* reports in its "Christian Activities" section:

> Benjamin Franklin Butts, one of the best known leaders of evangelistic singing, is now in Chicago, assisting in the Chapman-Alexander campaign; after six weeks in that city he will be associated with the Rev. William B. Holmes, D.D., of Lebanon, Tenn., in an extended evangelistic tour.
>
> Professor Butts is well known here through his connection for the last five years with the Evangelistic Committee of New York city [*sic*], and as pastor's assistant at the Madison Avenue Reformed Church. Previous to his residence in New York he was for three years musical director of Bethany Presbyterian Church and Sunday-school in Philadelphia, of

which John Wanamaker is superintendent. Mr. Butts has recently removed his place of residence to Lebanon, Tenn.[54]

Yet, in 1912, "Prof. Benjamin Franklin Butts" is back again, as the *New York Times* reports. He directs a choir for a "Converts' Rally" at Carnegie Hall.[55] I imagine sweat standing on his face as his arms flail: his furrowed brow, his eager smiles.

After the early 1910s, there is a gap in ProQuest's intel on the Reverend.[56] I find him again only in 1921, using a smaller database, the California Digital Newspaper Collection, maintained by UC Riverside. In 1921, year of the Battle of Blair Mountain, the largest labor uprising in the history of the United States, the Reverend Butts has relocated to Northern California, where he is the minister of the First Presbyterian Church of Marysville, an institution still in existence. He continues to be married to my great-grandmother, although she does not appear in the papers. Butts's popularity is unflagging. He travels. In 1927, for example, he is in San Francisco, where he sings "one of his own compositions entitled, 'I Know He's Mine.'" He is a baritone.[57]

Butts is now the father of three more children, the youngest of whom, my maternal grandmother, Gloria Onna, was born in 1925. In 1930, the family will move again, this time to New Mexico.[58] This is in service of my great-grandfather's career.

The Reverend Butts drops dead in Las Cruces, New Mexico, in 1935, age sixty-nine, leaving my great-grandmother and grandmother to fend for themselves during the Great Depression. It's not clear from the newspapers where the other members of the family are.

Hymnary.org, where one may peruse the Reverend Butts's compositions, explains his life in the following terms,

> Born: September 7, 1867, Ohio. Died: May 25, 1935, Las Cruces, New Mexico. Buried: Home of Peace Cemetery, Porterville, California. Son of Samuel F. Butts & Hannah Colton, Benjamin studied music at a young age. He started

in business in Kansas City, but entered the evangelism field in 1888. He married three times: To Eva Grace Lambright (1867–1941), Mary Emma Rawlings (1869–1919), and Onna Barrett Mills (1896–1963). His works include: *Tears and Triumphs No. 4*, with Lycurgus Pickett & William Marks (Louisville, Kentucky: Pentecostal Publishing Company, 1910), *Good News Hymns* (Chicago, Illinois: The Biglow & Main Company, 1914).[59]

I don't know why I dislike this ancestor of mine so much. Maybe it's what I know about the lives of the children from his third marriage, my maternal ancestors. There's also something unsettling to me about his second union, how Mary Emma Rawlings dies at forty-nine and her widower immediately takes up with someone in her twenties. Or maybe it's the man's reputation for holiness and "pep."[60]

I, in fact, stalk many of my maternal ancestors online by means of genealogy sites and defunct newspapers. I have found this is the best way to obtain reliable information about them. My mother has told me almost nothing about her family. What I have learned from her hasn't always seemed true. Or perhaps a better way to put this is that the incompleteness of her accounts is stylized.

For example: As a child I often asked my mother about the members of her family, who it was she knew during her own childhood. These were bad questions for several reasons, first of all because my maternal grandmother was a reclusive alcoholic to whom we spoke by phone no more than once a year, secondarily because my mother had never met her own father, who may have been a teenager when she was born. Thus, little information was volunteered. My mother would, however, tell me about someone named "Uncle Ben," her mother's eldest brother. I asked my mother what had happened to Uncle Ben. "Oh," my mother said, wistfully, as if speaking of a casual acquaintance,

"I don't really know. We just stopped seeing him." Sometimes my mother said, "I think Uncle Ben was gay."

Uncle Ben, a.k.a. Benjamin Franklin Butts Jr., decommissioned his own head with a gun in Illinois, in 1994.

In 1994, I was fourteen. I'd heard nothing about this great-uncle, a living relative, except vague stories about a handful of times he had visited my mother when she was a girl. I assumed he was already deceased. No one ever said anything because there was no one to say anything, save my mother.

It's January 2023. I've just turned forty-three, the Reverend Butts's age at the time of his 1910 southern tour. I'm in a university library, working on this essay, and discover the following information on findagrave.com: "Benjamin Franklin Butts committed suicide by a gunshot to the head at 7:40 am, in his home. Ashes were released to stepson on 22 Feb 1994."[61] Is this taken, in part, from a police report? Perhaps these two sentences were published in a newspaper. The page is maintained by someone named Bettejean, who seems to be Benjamin Franklin Butts's grandchild and is therefore my cousin. Bettejean has added twenty-six memorials and currently manages twenty-nine memorials. They've added flowers to 146 e-graves, and their profile picture shows them squatting outside a wooden nineteenth-century building near what appears to be a garden. The caption of this photograph reads, "Myself on the grounds at The Banning Museum in Wilmington, CA where I did volunteer work for almost four years." They write in their profile, "I can hear the voicesOf those gone aheadI hear their ghostly whispersWhen no one is listening but meThey speak my name softlySharply, angrily and so sweetly."[62]

Benjamin Franklin Butts Jr. seems like a discomfiting spirit-guide choice to me ("angrily"), but what do I know? Benjamin Franklin Butts Jr. was survived by not only his stepson, but by a daughter and a spouse, my cousin's mother and grandmother, both of whom are now also dead. He additionally had a brother, a second sibling to my grandmother, my great-uncle Robert Colton Butts, who died three years after Uncle Ben, in 1997, when I was seventeen. Until today, this Saturday in mid-January when I've escaped downtown to do my research, I'd never heard of this Uncle Bob, a Paul Rudd lookalike who seemed extremely proud of his service in the Second World War and lived most of his adult life in Olympia, Washington.

I mean this quite seriously and in multiple senses: Who are all these people?

-:-

I float. I was born long after (the real) Benjamin Franklin's spooky prediction of the population boom of the 1850s, long after Thomas Jefferson's vision of yeoman-farmer-as-ideal-citizen was put to rest, long after the supposed efficiencies of the New Deal, long after the postwar boom and the perceived need to usher women back into the home, long after the G.I. Bill. There is no plan anymore. Isn't this part of the reason for the success of the internet? Google and Facebook farm us. They give a basic reason, a raison d'être, for humans, if not Americans: that some entrepreneur may track our movements and repackage this data for sale. We do call them "server farms."

I don't know what the Reverend Butts was looking for, as he traveled west, although I do know that he married serially and sang constantly about Jesus. I can't go back in time to understand the large Ohio household he was born into. That is what truly feels foreign to me, in my own ancestral past. I can vaguely comprehend the violence of the family as it moves into the mid-century, but what it was before 1900 is beyond my comprehension. In truth, disaggregating your face, skull, and brain with a bullet or, for that matter, descending into alcoholism make more sense to me than frenetic performative worship in Ohio, Pennsylvania, New York, Tennessee, California, or New Mexico.

Anyway, for years and years I've dreamed of catastrophe.

My earliest dreams were of genocide and enchanted corpses. As a teenager in the 1990s, I dreamed of monster weather events, storms with tornados beneath them like whips.

Last night I dreamed that the moon fell out of the sky. I was alone in my parents' house in Massachusetts holding my preverbal infant son (who in waking reality is a loquacious toddler). It was late. Three strange men who claimed their car had broken down along the driveway appeared. I opened the door to them holding my child.

"Look at the moon," I told them, pointing up.

The moon's face was changing rapidly. A hot-pink corona surrounded it or then a veil of orange lace crossed it. Stars appeared—five-pointed stars, as on the American flag—in a circle, and spun around the moon. Lines appeared in the sky. Perhaps these were stripes.

I didn't believe the three men, about their car trouble, that is. Their smiles were full of stress, and they kept showing me their teeth.

Suddenly it didn't matter. The moon's pyrotechnics were becoming outrageous. There seemed to be an animation of an astrolabe behind it, then pentacles in gold. The moon trembled, got bigger.

There was a terrible boom and an enlarging of this body as it became apparent the satellite was hurtling toward the surface of the planet we were standing on. There was a light like day.

I brought my son's face close to my face. I smelled him. I can't remember if there was time to say I love you.

I wake up after dreaming such a dream and have to go on living. That is the funny thing about dwelling here in the wreckage.

It is interesting to me, too, that only my son can accompany me in this dream. Neither his father nor anyone else I have ever loved is with me in that place. There are only the three mysterious men with car trouble, itinerant, like the Reverend Butts and his two offspring, yet people with power of a kind, people of force, people who want to convince me of something.

It used to be that I was alone in dreams of this kind and would simply die. Since the birth of my son, it doesn't happen that way anymore.

I don't die and I don't quite understand the ending of the dream. My heart thuds, and there are no more images.

The narrator of Toni Morrison's *The Bluest Eye* tells us that romantic love is one of "the most destructive ideas in the history of human thought."[63]

Suddenly I think, that is what the dream moon is.

The dream moon crashes to earth. It is a literalization of my earlier sentence, "The whole world falls away." The world falls since something strikes it. Something draws unbearably near.

When I examine my own life as a narrative item, as an ongoing attempt to make sense of the various, eccentrically interconnected presents in which I have lived, I see that romantic love is a form—perhaps even the only form, the singular form—that I have appropriated wholesale from the past. It is a sort of dream moon: real, massive, ancient. It is a cover for the wild fiats of my unconscious. Too bad it's world-ending.

I didn't criticize the dream moon much, at least, not until recently. I wrote hundreds of poems in praise of it, even. I lamented it, but I praised it. I perceived it as fundamentally better than other conceptual containers for my personality and hopes—things like meritocracy or heroism. The reason I seem to have thought that the apocalyptic dream moon (a.k.a. romantic love) was so good was that it was, allegedly, at once future-directed and transformative. It would allow me to get out of my current life and it would make me a more fully realized person. Most importantly, it would, I believed, emancipate me from my parents, something I urgently desired. It was, therefore, even more important than voting. The person who loved me, who engaged in romantic love with me, would recognize me. This person would understand me. They would know me entirely, and without effort. They would know how good I was. They would accept me and, by accepting me, save my life. They would make my individuality real. They would make me absolutely free.

I am sure that I held these beliefs about romantic love by the time I was fourteen, although, as I have noted, I could have indulged in similar premonitions as early as four, at which time I may have believed that a person in love was certain to receive gifts and be the main character in a story. Of course, a child has little use for romance, as such. It is, when you consider it, odd that I could have defined romantic love as a series of specific behaviors and outcomes even before I knew how to read and write.

I pondered this concept far in advance, is what I am saying. You probably did, too. This is to me one of the most unnerving aspects of romantic love: it is a visceral, all-consuming, private mode of thought and bodily arousal that is painstakingly explained to children. Prince Eric and Ariel kiss, mouths diagonally locked, cheeks perfectly still, eyes shut. Ariel, only recently driven for mysterious reasons to disinherit herself ("You want thingamabobs? I've got twenty! But who cares? No big deal. I want more!"), sacrifices her status as an elite merperson for a gamble at bliss among high-level humans. Foam. Merging. Paillettes of light on water, scales, pearlescent shell. Economic concerns obscure whatever is going on between Eric and Ariel (emotional obsession, telepathic sex), even as we are repeatedly assured that these two royals from different worlds are absolutely, positively not getting together with the express purpose of consolidating their respective dominions over soil and sea. In other words, while we need to know that there's a deal being struck here, that these two aren't "just fucking," we also require an erotic frisson to keep from sinking into despair over the fact that cash rules everything around us, even here in a children's animation. This is, by the way, what is known as a double bind.

It's 1989. Minstrelsy inflects various numbers sung by creatures of the sea. After seven decades of hard-won and unevenly distributed suffrage, we watch—enthralled, breathless—as this vivacious young gal is married at sixteen.

-:-

In a 1988 essay on the Grimm brothers' editorial interventions into the fairy tales they published in the mid-nineteenth century, the scholar Ruth B. Bottigheimer describes a systematic transformation of "lively tales of golden girls" into a series of stories in which "guilt inhered in the female persona." As the Grimms published new editions of their anthologies from 1810 to 1857, they "embedd[ed] ever more unpleasant outcomes for women."[64] With the accumulation of guilt, the girl-hero became (monetarily) impoverished, as well.

Although many believe that the Grimms' stories were taken directly from the toothless mouths of muttering crones lurking in the smokiest huts of the remotest and most authentic corners of the Austrian Empire, in fact, the narratives are palimpsestic regurgitations of other literary and popular texts. Many of the tales in the first editions are sourced from "young women of [the Grimms'] bourgeois circle in Kassel" and derived from those women's readings in French literature. In these narratives, "girls . . . could take the initiative: they could talk and even suggest that they have a chance to try on the tiny slipper."[65]

Later, themselves strapped for cash, the Grimms plundered cheap chapbooks, a bit along the lines of modern-day "airport novels," that were sold to travelers in the sixteenth and seventeenth centuries. The chapbook narrative or *Schwank* was often a bawdy, brutal affair, with a nagging wife and violent husband—Punch and Judy for grown-ups. Incorporation of these texts led to fairy tales in which the formerly talented or magical women disappear and are replaced by waifs who are slandered, exposed, imprisoned, isolated, generally tossed about like rag dolls, and enslaved. Absent fathers are exonerated for the debasement of their offspring. The girl at the center of the story is not permitted to speak. The tale of Rumpelstiltskin, which at first concerns a charmed girl who has the unusual ability to turn straw into gold, becomes a harrowing account of a hapless person who is falsely reputed to be able to turn straw into gold, thrown into a dungeon where she is instructed to accomplish this impossible task or else, and subsequently obliged to make a deal with a devil who seems resolved to traffic her firstborn child.

This trend toward materially deprived heroines—whose fault everything is—has something to do with a desire on the Grimms' part to establish a collection of supposed folktales that would appear concertedly German and not, for example, French in origin. The Grimms were nationalist participants in the Romantic movement, and they valued the German language and vernacular culture. Yet, they seem to have cut corners, emphasizing the harsh consequences of a pulpy mode of genre writing that itself imitated the supposed mores of rural society without having direct ties to such communities. And they did this in part to entertain. As Bottigheimer suggests, the *Schwank* doesn't so much originate in German-speaking rural areas as exist as an easy-to-read literary genre that addressed itself to less-educated audiences, along with anyone else looking to be diverted during a stomach-churning carriage ride. *Bump, bump, bumpity, bump, bump.*

The famous cruelty of the Grimms' fairy tale—noses cut off (a traditional punishment for those reputed to be sex workers or adulterers),[66] the need to beg the assistance of vermin, the resounding clank of the dungeon gate, tattered garments, the presence of knives and unfulfillable commands—is not, as I once believed, a matter derived from old wives' tales and the depths of freaky forests formerly inhabited by blue-eyed Goths. It is a function of a popular press. It is as commercially expedient as the bombast of contemporary podcasting.

For this reason, the transmutation of these tales into a, if not *the,* central source for what remains arguably the most influential form of children's entertainment in the United States, the so-called Disney princess narrative, is, even granting the simultaneous Danish and French influence, of great interest.

True that Disney tends to clean up the blood—no amputations, thank you—but the impoverishment, the helplessness, the orphanhood, the impossibility? Those have stayed in the picture. How else would she know she was in love? ("When you're in love, really in love," sings Jane Powell as Milly in *Seven Brides.*) It is only very recently, in such princess affairs as the *Frozen* franchise, that the heroine, here persistent Anna, is permitted to remain rich and politically influential. Meanwhile her sister, Elsa, also rich, retains her supernatural powers and commits to a self-imposed exile not unlike an artist's residency rather than descending to a dungeon where she must become the world's most prolific scullery maid in preparation for her marriage. ("Just whistle while you work!" trills the exiled Snow White. Nearby, a smiling fawn licks dishes clean. "Oh, sing sweet nightingale!" the disinherited Cinderella croons on her hands and knees, harmonizing with images of herself that rise in soap bubbles.)

-¦-

In either fall of 1995 or spring of 1996, when I was either fifteen or sixteen, I went to visit my best friend in the hospital. I'll call her Albertine, but this is not her real name.

I tell myself stories about Albertine all the time, but it isn't easy to write about her here. I feel shame when I think about Albertine. Simultaneously, I am entranced.

I remember what I wore the day I went to visit Albertine. I recall the outfit exactly. It consisted of a thrifted, electric-blue wool sweater, perhaps with some angora in it, a cheap, short, black wool-blend skirt with a hidden zipper in the back that was sometimes too small for me, black tights, and a pair of black brogues. The brogues were an addition I had purchased from a shoe store somewhere in the vicinity of NYU, and I was proud of them. They were the edgiest part of the ensemble, suggesting men's attire. They were a hinge in the look, a loophole.

I remember coming into the room. Albertine was in bed in a hospital gown. She was very pale, quite literally green, which I assumed was the result of blood loss.

She was also angry. I wondered if this was because she knew I was treating this as one of the closing scenes in a film about our relationship. Or perhaps she understood that I had been invited here by her parents, who wanted me to witness her folly. It was a sort of offering on their part to my parents, the least they could do.

This is why you shouldn't imitate Albertine. Don't idolize her. Don't say we didn't warn you.

I asked Albertine how she was doing.

She said something about better now, how they let her walk around a little.

Albertine's father appeared and said he was heading to the cafeteria. I accepted a theoretical cookie.

He told us he would leave so we could visit. He left.

I tried to sit on the edge of Albertine's bed, but she didn't like that. She made me stand. She was looking me up and down, assessing my clothing. "I can see why the boys like you," she said.

I still remember that line, hear her saying it from the janky-looking adjustable bed. Almost three decades have gone by.

This was a reference to my career at my new high school. At my new high school someone had asked me to date him. Albertine was aware of this. Although I continued to consume my lunch alone in a bathroom stall, Albertine apparently felt I had moved up in the world. Albertine's remark was not friendly.

I did not reply to the remark. Or maybe I said something about my clothes. Because I loved clothes now. Unencumbered by a school uniform, I could say something about who I was by getting dressed.

I had what I thought of as two "lines," speaking of speech: there was my "ultrafeminine" line—seventies-style high-heeled platform boots worn with flared vintage pants, polyester tops, and long, narrow skirts—and my "boy" line—often with the same pants and shrunken vintage knit tops, occasionally a short skirt, sometimes a skirt over pants. On a "boy" day, it was easier to walk, but I missed the power of the heel.

I reveled in these garments. I mostly bought them from the Goodwill and other thrift stores with my allowance. That was how far a pair of tens went in the mid-1990s.

This was New York and nobody gave a shit about "grunge," or dressed like that, except perhaps for the editors of *Vogue*. I listened to Sade, Mazzy Star, and the Cowboy Junkies. Albertine, meanwhile, didn't share my proto-emo stylings. She wore The North Face plus Stüssy plus a sterling Tiffany bean on a chain and listened to hip-hop.

Albertine was not about to be caught dead in someone's old clothing, and she was not a romantic.

I knew Albertine was not a romantic not because of her sartorial or musical tastes but because I had watched her fuck. I do not mean this metaphorically.

Albertine was obviously some sort of twisted substitute for my mother, but unlike my mother, a self-professed saint, Albertine was not very concerned about possible impropriety. She made a nominal effort to hide her two- or even three-figure body count from her parents, a pair of workaholics from Connecticut, but when she was fifteen, they found her diary.

As I write this, I worry that I still do not have the tools to explain this period in my life. You could say that Albertine and I are grooming each other to survive heterosexuality, but our obsession with each other is more complicated than this, given that it is indeed (and primarily) an obsession with each other—at least, it is from my side. Albertine, who at school is just a passable student, understands her sexual conquests as a form of education. She is far from stupid but sees little value in traditional subjects, Latin or Earth science. She does not want to derive status from anything except money. And sex is for her, already, a kind of work. It's a kind of real-life, adult work she has access to.

I have to be careful, because Albertine isn't exploited—not by people who aren't her parents, who are clearly using her as an outlet for insidious anxieties spawned by their codependent relationship. Albertine does what she can. She is destroying the leash that tethers her to this triad (she is an only child) the best way she knows how. Because we must reconstruct our families in the outside world at least one time if not many, before we can begin to leave them.

Of course, this is just how I explain this to myself.

In truth, I still consider Albertine's motivations a mystery.

In the past, I thought everything Albertine did was about power. Then I began to theorize her, speaking of theoretical cookies, in relation to commerce, commercial imagery, and misogyny. I will be honest: I hate that she is one of the first people I love. I hate that loving her means I love someone who treats every aspect of my person as something to be instrumentalized: my hands do this my eyes do this my brain does this.

Albertine steals liquid ketamine from her father's veterinary practice and cooks it to a dry mass in her family's oven. She somehow manually refines it and sells it to acquaintances. I'm not kidding. She even tries to scale her business.

She never gives me a taste. In fact, you might say she shelters me. I'm the innocent in our relationship.

She is in the hospital now because the human papillomavirus caused either warts or precancerous lesions to form on her cervix. When these were removed by a medical professional, Albertine, either at the time of the removal or after, had a lot of bleeding.

I don't really understand what has happened from a physiological point of view, and no one goes out of their way to enlighten me. I heard from Albertine that when her parents found her diary, her mother started screaming that Albertine's father never had to "fuck me in the ass to satisfy me." Even though I'm only fifteen or sixteen, it's not lost on me that this response is inappropriate. Maybe it's bizarre of me, but I admire Albertine's adventurousness. That's not the problem here. The problem is that the kind of men Albertine likes to sleep with are the kind of men who are nearly thirty years old, who have recently fled a civil war in Eastern Europe, and who do a kind of work that requires them to bring unregistered handguns to parties, some of which I, too, have attended.

The problem is that, although the membrane that separates the world of commerce—in which anything is interchangeable with anything else by means of the medium of cold hard cash—from the sensitive surfaces of our bodies is tissue thin and actually nonexistent, everyone goes around acting like it's this impenetrable barrier. Everyone associates money with violence, and they act like money doesn't really exist, or, failing that, like it's inaccessible to children.

Albertine has never acted this way. In a sense, she's the only one out of all of us who's really alive. Everything, to her, is an economic transaction. Sex is just another part of her business plan.

People are enraged by her, and her own mother calls her a whore (yes, this happened), but that's because you'll never be able to convince Albertine that romantic love is anything but a construct. She even knows, without being able to define the term *psychoanalysis*, that there's something sick about how her parents are together and how they want to enlist her in hiding this sickness.

Albertine can be very unkind, but the one thing Albertine is not is wrong.

Albertine is a cold genius, a perfect mind. It's why I fall in love with her, although I don't know this, at the time.

Anyway, soon enough it's over. We stop speaking once we

are in college. She's a corporate lawyer now. She works in debt restructuring.

-:-

The "classic" educational computer game *The Oregon Trail* taught fourth graders all about the fragility of human life, particularly in the context of settler migration. My classmates and I named our avatars Gonorrhea, Buttsy, Fartopher, Poopsmell, and Penis, and we set our rations to "bare bones," the ultimate austerity, racing along, whipping our pixelated oxen into a lather. We erupted in screams of laughter when Buttsy's life was claimed by dysentery or Poopsmell drowned while attempting to ford a river (we never stooped to pay a bridge or ferry toll). We treasured the tombstone vignette that appeared once everyone had succumbed. It was a morbid and hilariously twee detail that I imagine was programmed in by someone with an intuitive understanding of the lives of ten-year-olds trapped in an oppressive single-sex school for eight hours at a time.

We never, ever made it to the Willamette Valley.

R. Philip Bouchard, one of the game's authors, writes in his self-published history, *You Have Died of Dysentery: The Creation of "The Oregon Trail"—the Iconic Educational Game of the 1980s*, that such moments of transport were part of his life's work:

> I wanted to design highly engaging "micro-worlds" that would draw the user in. The user will be completely sucked into this entertaining environment, but to succeed in this world, the user will have to learn.[67]

It is a pleasant but rather unrealistic projection. Given that we were most interested in our own spectacular deaths, I doubt— although I could be wrong—that what we learned from *Oregon Trail* corresponded to the designers' intended lessons. Scarcity and sacrifice were built into the microworld of the *Trail*, but rather than accept the game's values as our own, we liked it for what it could, inadvertently, reflect back to us about language's status as an ambiguous substance porous to obscenity and absurdity. Our "family" was mostly identified with things you'd want to bury or hide, if, for example, you valued hygiene and propriety in close quarters. When its members died, we were pleased because it meant the game's interface was compelled to reiterate, in brutal sans serif font, the names we had, vibrating with giggles, originally entered.

Men in California had ordained that the beige plastic consoles we stared into during "Computer Lab" be created. They could supply our school with software and indirectly force us to interact with these glowing cubes, but they could not force us to name ourselves "Lucy, Ilene, Jennifer, Davina, Albertine." Our party was shit and the clap. It drove straight into a wall.

On the one hand, we knew nothing about that "biological weapon" of the 1850s, the "firehose of fecundity" that was transforming North American demographics. On the other, we knew all about it. We knew, intuitively, that *Oregon Trail* was about a perverted and risible idea of sex, perverted and risible since instrumental. We knew this because there was no option to turn back. There was no option to found a school or become an artist or live on a commune. There was no option to practice philosophy. There was nothing to do but be a family and head west.

And we continue to dwell in this country.

In 2015, as part of the rollout of a "Modern Love" essay by author Mandy Len Catron, "To Fall in Love with Anyone, Do This," the *New York Times* published a set of thirty-six questions formulated by a team of behavioral psychologists led by Arthur Aron. These questions serve as "a practical methodology for creating closeness in an experimental context," as Aron and his four coauthors wrote in a 1997 study published in the *Personality and Social Psychology Bulletin*.[68] These are questions about who you most want to be and whose death you most fear, and they are designed to promote vulnerability and self-revelation.[69] In other words (i.e., according to Catron and the newspaper itself), these three dozen queries might make you and your interlocutor fall in love.

Catron had the admirable goal of seeking "a way into a relationship that feels deliberate."[70] Out with an acquaintance who subsequently became her partner, she proposed they take Aron's formula for "accelerated intimacy" for a spin. At a bar, they traded questions from a document on her phone, then stepped outside to a convenient bridge to perform the scientists' final, boundary-dissolving task: stare silently into each other's eyes for a timed four minutes.[71] Here the essay slows dramatically. Catron notes, amusingly, that one of her date's no doubt soulful eyes is perceptible as "a clump of very useful cells," as sentiment falls away, replaced by a sort of materialist awe that includes the retrospective realization that romantic love might be an easily comprehensible action as well as—or, better yet, *instead of*—a mystical feeling.[72]

Whatever their opinion about the virality of Catron's essay, Aron and his colleagues were likely delighted by this etiological reorientation. As psychologists who focus on human behavior, they have reason to prefer an account of love that not only attests to the efficacy of their methods but holds out hope for the improvement of humanity through considered, elective, and possibly quantifiable action. As scientists who believe the laboratory is a good place to study people, they could hardly object to Catron's desire for control, either. So, while the 1997 paper does not make any claims about romantic love or falling in love or loving anyone, seeking rather to engineer "the development of a close relationship among peers" through "sustained, escalating, reciprocal, personalistic self-disclosure," no one from the team seems to have publicly criticized the "Modern Love" essay.[73]

In 2015, Aron's method probably reminded readers less of an MKUltra experiment than a Facebook quiz. Less paranoid Cold

War national-security-crisis vibes and more head-in-sand, cozy
self-improvement. What strikes me about its presentation in the
context of "Modern Love" is the suggestion (the hope/prayer?)
that one might be able to keep love in the present. Isn't that, after
all, the overdetermined dream? Keep love in the present by making it last and also: keep love in the present by choosing it con-
sciously. Don't let love be an old love, a repetitious love, a love
you got from a mediocre or dangerous parent, who got it from
an even worse parent, who got it from an even worse ancestor,
and so on. Don't let it be that infernally early thing, that thing
without origins no one can properly remember, and don't wait
for it to happen to you. Don't wake up on a roller coaster or at the
bottom of a mine shaft. Don't look up just as the moon is crashing
down on your head. Be intentional. Be rational—not desperate,
not an addict, not a codependent victim. Do all of these things
right now. Start today. Be here. And only here.

The problem with this style of thought is that it is precisely
those of us with the most work to do in relation to legacies of attachment who harbor the deepest and often most self-defeating,
labyrinthine, and delusional wishes regarding a nondestructive
form of love. We are the ones to whom the thirty-six questions
most appeal. We are also the ones who cannot simply "move on,"
as they say, who can't seem to wake up. We don't know how to
stop doing what we did before. We have already, as the authors
of the study write, made emotional closeness "an explicit task."
We've been doing this explicit task since we were children and,
for this reason, are also always loving as we did formerly, cruelly
optimistic that it will turn out differently this time.

We are the ones to whom the story of that girl—who is falsely
reputed to be able to turn straw into gold, thrown into a dungeon, obliged to make a deal with a devil—makes the most sense.
We watch as the tale unfolds: in the beginning, she is debased,
a bound girl, wrapped in a donkey skin, her skin marked with
mud and ashes. Lies have been told about her, in that many be-

lieve her worthless, despite her effervescence and authenticity. Perhaps animals or insects are her only friends. Perhaps she has nothing but a pair of old books and a sparkling personality. Perhaps she has even less than this: nothing but a body.

We aren't worried, though, because love is on the way. We're not going to spend overlong on the reasons for her debasement. Love comes and the bound girl is free.

This story is bizarre and illogical, but who among us has not, at the very least, found it entertaining?

Don't forget that the freed bound girl is so grateful for her rescue, for her transcendence to acknowledged personhood, that she is willing to spend the rest of her life providing that most necessary form of labor known to humanity, care. Care would be so expensive, unimaginably so, were it not for the debased princess in disguise, the bondswoman, that person with no one to cling to who has been brought back from the brink. Or so the stories tell us.

In an irony common to many American cultural products, *Seven Brides for Seven Brothers* additionally contains a curious array of contradictory messages about its veneration of heterosexual romance.

Michael Kidd, the film's choreographer, is famous for having refused to create any dance numbers "per se." He insisted that all the gestures and movements on screen resemble those that might plausibly be enacted by "real" backwoodsmen of the 1850s. While this obsession with authenticity can seem oddly borne out by the resulting movie, with its diorama-like painted landscape backgrounds and two-dimensional characters in form-fitting buckskin, Kidd's method nevertheless produced some very interesting dance. The film scholar Kathaleen Boche connects Kidd's ad hoc way of working to 1950s notions of white, male "improvisational ingenuity." "His kind of dancing is raw, close to the earth, and full of abandon," Boche writes of the hypermasculine "cowboy/ frontiersman."[74] If contra dances seem to break out spontaneously throughout *Seven Brides*, this may be a way of figuring American postwar identity as well: The citizen of the United States is a self-starter and a product of a dynamic folk culture distinct from that of Europe. He's also a better dancer—wilder, more original—particularly if he's a man.

But Boche's reading, while convincing to someone who hasn't seen the film, doesn't capture what takes place in Kidd's numbers, which are less raw displays than exhibitions of well-honed collaborative skills. All the dancing in the film is outclassed by a single performance filmed in three days, the celebrated barn-raising sequence. Kidd apparently summoned it to life in a sort of reversal of the sorcerer's apprentice scenario, asking a prop man to "go down to the prop shop, find anything that you can that would be lying around when they build a barn: bring planks of lumber, bring sawhorses, bring an axe, bring anything you can find there that would apply."[75] Subsequently, the dancers were enchanted by these things into acrobatics on a pair of planks set on sawhorses, fancy footwork on the wooden winch of a small well, jumping repeatedly over an axe. But far from being individualistic in nature, this choreography is about social ties, mimicry, and mutual support. Five of the seven brothers (two of the actors did not dance) express cheeky antagonism toward the townsmen, even as everyone collaborates and shows off for one another, frequently joining hands. Although the scene ends with a mild tussle (heads thumped and thumbs hammered), it's hard to feel that we've just witnessed anything other than a pretty sexy series of come-ons recoded as faux-vernacular moves from various choreographic schools. It's not clear if it's the girls of the town, the boys of the town, or both and preferably at once, that are the objects of the brothers' intense affection. As the ever-amazing Julie Newmar, who portrayed my favorite abductee, unshy Dorcas, said in a documentary about the making of *Seven*

Brides, "The word *lust* is the thing that seems to come across about this film."[76]

Among the brothers are Tommy Rall, one of the greatest gymnasts and ballet and tap dancers of 1950s musical film, and Jacques D'Amboise, a dancer with the New York City Ballet from 1953 to 1984. Their dancing is explosive, clever, and highly trained. It establishes a sensual language that differs greatly from Milly's pious troths and Adam's priapic winks and dull bluster. We note not just the ingenuity of these moves but also their familiarity. This dancing seems to arise from the affect and tensions of the social world of the film's actors, which in these moments seems believably of a piece with our own world; dancing is a means of expressing irritating and exciting tensions, of making that which is personal into a series of shared and often meditative gestures. Even the solos accomplish this. As he sings about his loneliness on the remote ranch, Matt Mattox (brother Caleb) swings a long axe around his body as he crosses his legs in a modified plié in artificial snow. It's a slow, deliberate dance that accompanies a sad song that was at one point flagged by censors for lingering a little too long over the possibility of intimate relations with farm animals.[77] "A man can't sleep when he sleeps with sheep," the brothers moan.

Like most of the dancing in *Seven Brides,* the "Lonesome Polecat" number doesn't really have to do with romantic love. It's about moods and bodies. It's about luxuriating in states of nonsatiety, relishing liminal feelings, dreaming of sex. The purported remoteness of the homestead and the emotional distances this geographic distance analogizes are quite useful for art: the brothers are always having to pantomime something or other they don't quite have the words to express. It's visually arresting and surprising in that these straight men seem to have quite a lot to say, physically speaking, about their psychology and the contents of their hearts. They are eloquent, even. Meanwhile, unscripted glances travel. The dancers trade tools and coy looks of appreciation. We all know they aren't actually related. We all know this was an unusually gregarious and warm set.

The bound girl isn't really a girl. The bound girl is feminized, of course, but this is just a disguise used to make her figuration more palatable to the squeamish. Because the bound girl isn't a person. She is a figure for infancy. Although in the stories her hyperbolically gendered activities—the constant cleaning and wooing of tiny baby substitutes like mice and elves—scream, "YES, THIS PERSON IS VERY MUCH FEMALE," the bound girl isn't female and is not a person. It's the screaming that should tip us off. The screaming is there to distract you as the unconscious flashes by. However, if you can get past the screaming, you will see that the image the unconscious is lazily stroking here is one of an infant that cannot lift its head. The infant cannot speak. The infant must survive a period of non-agency, a kind of imprisonment in its own body. After this, it will be "married" to the world.

The gowns, tiaras, and lacquer-like makeup, which look so much like so-called baby clothes and counterfeit the smooth faces of young children, are there to repulse and attract. In either case, you are invited to look away—to look elsewhere. You are invited to get obsessed with gender and cash and fabulous realms (or to go back and play with your trucks and guns) and forget about the thematization of agency and attachment that is fundamentally at play. It's too awful to recognize that the beginnings of our lives, of all our lives without exception, were times when we could be strangled or beaten or raped or abandoned or shut into a drawer or otherwise abused by people who not only would face few repercussions for such activities but whom we would later be compelled to love.

This is not to say that all infants are abused. But child abuse is very common. You have friends who were abused even if you yourself were not. There are people in your community who were abused as children. It seems strange to even bother to type these sentences given we at once take the reality of what they describe for granted and refrain almost absolutely from speaking of it.[78]

This is an essay about romance. It is an essay that defines romance by means of an eccentric series of artworks, histories, intellectual typographies, and personal anecdotes. Its goal, however, isn't to show you how real romance is or how you can better negotiate this ambivalent thing. Its goal, my goal, is to convince you that it could be worth considering the notion that your idea of what is romantic, of what is sexy, compelling, might originate in emotional survival techniques you no longer recall acquiring, because you acquired them before you had full access to language. It is my suggestion that, if we are willing to entertain this story about romance—call it a sort of fairy tale, since it is very much a narrative about rescue and what can be survived—then we might want to simultaneously entertain the notion that romance is not all there is and not the best thing possible. We might want to ask if we are capable, as adults, of something other than infantile mind games, to use a metaphor literally.

Thus, being intentional in relation to romantic love wouldn't simply mean deciding when and with whom to do it. It might mean deciding not to do it at all.

In this case, one would need to learn to love differently. You would have to teach yourself how.

On this last point ("how"), I don't have prescriptive advice. This is not for want of looking. Years ago, I began compiling a bibliography related to romantic love. This bibliography included such rarities as the *Hypnerotomachia Poliphili* of 1499, a bizarre architectural fantasy about a quest on the part of one Poliphilo for his beloved Polia. The "love bib," as I call it, is also stocked with slightly more predictable psychoanalytic titles and sociologies, as well as Renaissance guides to elegance and courting. I put contemporary self-help books (e.g., *The Rules: Time-Tested Secrets for Capturing the Heart of Mr. Right*, which I first read when it was published in 1995) alongside classical texts on mysticism and other unclear approaches to the problem of fate. I reluctantly added poetry, along with the Old Testament. I have removed items. I continue to update my list.

"And Jacob was left alone; and there wrestled a man with him until the breaking of the day."[79]

I'm not the bound girl, not Donkeyskin[80] or another disguised princess, and I am definitely not an infant, but if we are choosing roles with eyes open, I think I can live with the baffled agonism of that traveler left alone on a riverbank—who lingers, wrestling and maybe dancing, with a stranger who arrives from somewhere seemingly beyond the world.

The stranger isn't my love or my lover. The stranger is someone I seem to have forgotten, whose story I must nevertheless tell.

Again, today, if I must choose between love and memory, I choose memory.

A Love Bib[81]

Arendt, Hannah. *The Human Condition.*

Aristotle. *Nicomachean Ethics.*

Baldwin, James. *Just Above My Head.*

Bagley, Benjamin. "Loving Someone in Particular." *Ethics,* 125, no. 2 (2015): 477–507.

——. "(The Varieties of) Love in Contemporary Anglophone Philosophy." In *The Routledge Handbook of Love in Philosophy.* Edited by Adrienne M. Martin. Pages 453–64. New York, NY: Routledge, 2019.

Baier, A. C. "Unsafe Loves." In Solomon & Higgins (1991). 433–50.

Barthes, R. (1978). *A Lover's Discourse.*

Benjamin, Jessica. *Like Subjects, Love Objects: Essays on Recognition and Sexual Difference.* New Haven: Yale University Press, 1995.

Everything by Lauren Berlant

Teresa Brennan, *The Interpretation of the Flesh: Freud and Femininity.* New York: Routledge, 1992.

Delany, Samuel. *The Motion of Light in Water.*

Dufourmantelle, Anne. *In Praise of Risk.*

Charles Fourier

Erich Fromm, *The Art of Loving*

Garber, Marjorie. *Bisexuality and the Eroticism of Everyday Life.* Hoboken, NJ: Taylor and Francis, 2012.

Jean Guitton, *Essay on Human Love*

Glück, Robert. *Margery Kempe.*

Habermas, Jürgen. *Knowledge and Human Interests*

Hegel, G. W. F. "A Fragment on Love."

Helm, Bennett. *Love, Friendship, and the Self: Intimacy, Identification, and the Social Nature of Persons.* Oxford, UK: Oxford University Press, 2010,

hooks, bell

The Way of Love by Luce Irigaray

Melanie Klein and Joan Riviere. *Love, Hate, and Reparation* (New York: Norton, 1964).

Eva Illouz, *Consuming the Romantic Utopia: Love and the Cultural Contradictions of Capitalism* (Berkeley:
   University of California Press, 1997).
Claude Lévi-Strauss, *The Elementary Structures of Kinship*
Teresa de Lauretis, *The Practice of Love*
Jean Laplanche and Jean-Bertrand Pontalis, "Fantasy and the Origins of Sexuality," in *Formations of Fantasy*, eds.
   Victor Burgin, James Donald, and Cora Kaplan, 5–34.
Lin, Tan, "The Patio and the Index"
Lorde, Audre, *The Uses of the Erotic*
Morrison, Toni. *The Bluest Eye.*
Nussbaum, Martha C., 1990, "Love and the Individual: Romantic Rightness and Platonic Aspiration," in *Love's*
   Knowledge: Essays on Philosophy and Literature, Oxford: Oxford University Press, 314–34.
Plato, *Symposium*
Rémond, dit le Grec Agathon, *Dialogue sur la volupté. Receuil des divers écrits*. Publ. par Saint-Hyacinthe (pseud.
   Voltaire, Paris 1736: (33-4) "La volupté c'est la plaisir pénétré de l'intelligence: la sensation pure est brutalité, mais la conscience de la sensation est délicatesse."*
Jacqueline Rose, *Sexuality in the Field of Vision* (London: Verso, 1986).
The Marquis de Sade
Eve Kosofsky Sedgwick, *Epistemology of the Closet*
Lady Sei *The Pillow Book*
Singer, Irving, 1984a, *The Nature of Love, Volume 1: Plato to Luther*, Chicago: University of Chicago Press, 2nd edition.
———, 1984b, *The Nature of Love, Volume 2: Courtly and Romantic*, Chicago: University of Chicago Press.
———, 1989, *The Nature of Love, Volume 3: The Modern World*, Chicago: University of Chicago Press, 2nd edn.
Solomon, Robert C., Kathleen Marie Higgins, and Arthur C Danto. *The Philosophy of (Erotic) Love*. Lawrence, KS:
   University Press of Kansas, 1991.

---

* "Voluptuousness is pleasure penetrated by intelligence; sensation on its own is brutality, but consciousness of sensation is refinement."

D.W. Winnicott, *Collected Papers: Through Paediatrics to Psycho-analysis* (London: Hogarth, 1958); D.W.
Winnicott, *Playing and Reality* (London: Routledge, 1971); and D.W. Winnicott, *Home is Where We Start From: Essays by a Psychoanalyist* (New York: Norton, 1986).
Slavoj Žižek, "The Spectre of Ideology," in *Mapping Ideology*, ed. Slavoj Žižek (London: Verso, 1994), 21 [1–33]
——, *The Sublime Object of Ideology* (London: Verso, 1989).

The End

> ... indeed, it is precisely the way theory
> misses its target that produces incalculable
> and interesting effects elsewhere.
>
> —*Barbara Johnson*[1]

A is for apocalypse and for apple. A is the reddest letter in the alphabet, laterally symmetrical, widely preferred. A is for experience. A is— blushing—for innocence.

In 1995, when I was a person with a lot of hope about, even a longing for, the future, I began to dream about the end of the world. I was fifteen. The world always ended the same way, sky filled with tornadoes that consumed everything in sight. I was always standing in front of a very large rectangular window. It framed a rural view. I watched the tornadoes and felt terror at being a witness to a cataclysm that would soon bring an end to me, along with everyone else on the planet.

The dream recurred with variations, some of them witty, if I may compliment my unconscious on its cinematography. In one dream, earth and sky were reversed, and spiraling cones of soil silently perturbed a blue void. In another, the tornadoes were fashioned from wire, wool, and cellophane, as in the crafty style of stop-motion animation that might have been used for a Björk video. There were additional permutations. In all cases, fear was a paralytic beverage. I was planted in place, eyes open. Not much use in running.

B is for the sister I do not have, for Barbara and blue. B is for "plan B." It's for when a system, method, or theory still seems functional, but

you know this isn't going to last. B is for binary, for be and belief. For
beauty. Fold her in half.

My tornado dreams had to do with a real storm that killed three
people—two students and a member of their school's staff—in
late spring of 1995 in western Massachusetts near the border with
New York State. (The car they were in was flung "about 600 feet"
from the road into a wooded area.)[2] Tornadoes, while uncommon
in the Northeast, are not unheard of. There have been some big
ones. A Northeasterner myself, I wasn't aware of the possibility
of such weather events until 1995, at which point, learning of
the May 29 storm, I began gathering anecdotes and information
about North American twisters, a hobby I ultimately turned into
a science project for my high school chemistry class. I became
obsessed with stats and models, along with the rating scale devised by Dr. Ted Fujita of the University of Chicago.

I sent away for documentary footage of large storms that had
been compiled, for fans like myself, on VHS. I watched the tornadoes others—now, vicariously, I—had ecstatically collected over
and over. They looked like objects, these vortices, although, in
fact, they were debris- and water-filled channels of wind. At the
center of their cones was stillness. The storms were nothing but
atmospheric transformation, products of unevenly heated air,
yet they behaved like a sentient species. Meanwhile, inside them,
strange miracles took place: a corn stalk impales a car radiator.
Everyday hierarchies of matter do not inhere.[3] Within a tornado,
as in the children's gambling game, paper will slay rock, a tissue
penetrating granite.

C is for clarity. Clear and distinct. C for scissors, for cutting off, for
immutable, blinding distinction. Crisp. Paler than the pale edge of a
white seed. The bright light of shipwreck.[4]

Four years have passed. It's 1999. I am a sophomore in college. I
no longer study the weather and have breezily (*groan*) exited the

realms of STEM by passing a short standardized test and taking a pair of general education courses, one on apes, the other on bombs.

I'm in a lecture. The following diagram is projected on the wall:

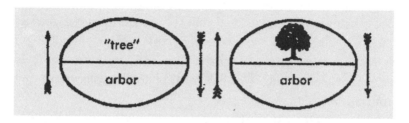

Or perhaps the professor does not project it on the wall or on a screen at the front of the lecture hall but merely refers to it on a xeroxed handout. Or she only describes it in words, without recourse to supplementary materials.

It would hardly have been unusual to share this diagram, taken from Ferdinand de Saussure's *Course in General Linguistics* (1916),[5] with undergraduates who were majoring in comparative literature (almost everyone seemed to do so at the time), yet to me this map of the dynamics of language was an ultrastrong taste, a confounding revelation. Saussure's bilateral sign is a pair of sliced eggs flanked by feathered arrows. We find the signifier, represented by the Latin word for "tree," *arbor*, below the concept it relays. This concept, the signified, is the notion "tree" in the left egg and, in the right, a deciduous silhouette.

Saussure's sign is generated by psychological association; you experience the signifier's "sound-image" and intuit the signified, an idea. As I sit on my hard little flip-down seat in dingy Emerson Hall, this schematic renders electrifyingly clear—is a lightning bolt, a sudden surreal shift—a suspicion I have held all my life, namely, that words are mushy tokens, that there is a part of them, not an insignificant part, that has little to do with meaning. This part is an arbitrary image. This part is an illogical sound. It is recalcitrant, expedient, yet a magnet for our weirdest fantasies, ironically the liveliest element of expression. The diagram also confirms what I've always suspected about dreams (to some extent what Freud teaches), that the pictures in them have been sheared off from life by some mercurial force and stitched back together in a riddle.

Whatever we take to be a real tree could fly away from its mooring in a word. Then, alarmingly, this mooring might begin to cling to other things. Words can become meaningless, obsolete, confused. (*Wads.* Words.) Yet this doesn't mean we won't continue to use them.

Language's most basic operation is, I realize, to cause us to believe that something invented is a given.

D is for distraction and disenchantment. It's for difference. D is for god, spelled backward. Deleterious effects. Barking. It's for the delights of decreation, doubt, and death. It's for laughing open mouths.

Dr. Barbara Johnson, who is teaching this course in late 1999, is the author of ingeniously constructed, brief, dense essays, among the finest I have read. She is a former wunderkind, a student of Yale's Paul de Man as well as a translator of the work of Jacques Derrida. An extremely neat person—in blazer, turtleneck, and ankle-grazing skirt, her fine and very straight graying hair gleaming in a long bob—she appears not to have updated her wardrobe since the early 1980s but is eternally the best-dressed individual in any room. She, like Mary Poppins, carries a genuine carpet bag, does not smile frequently, always seems to be smiling. She is the most intelligent human I have ever met.[6]

Welcome to "Deconstruction and Psychoanalysis." This course is graduate level and we, the undergrads cowering in the third row, have been duly informed. You should probably take something else, they've warned us. All the same, the Department of Literature is ISO naive geniuses who can light fires using their eyes, forecast twenty-fifth-century fashions, or (relevant for the syllabus at hand) cold read Jacques Lacan with perfect comprehension. After the department has let us know that we'll probably do badly and there will be no compensatory curve, they make no further ban.

"Deconstruction and Psychoanalysis" is ostensibly about a disagreement. It concerns two interpretations of Edgar Allan Poe's short story regarding knowledge and theft, "The Purloined Letter": the first by psychoanalyst Lacan, the second a response from Derrida. Professor Johnson, an expert in both Derridean deconstructive criticism and Lacan's style of psychoanalysis, has written a rejoinder, demonstrating how both Lacan and Derrida are mistaken.

But in practice the class turns out to be about other things.

E is for everyman. It's for the end. Hello. We're here.

I'm nineteen and write all the time. I use ninety-nine-cent notebooks purchased at drugstores, THE ORIGINAL MARBLE COVER— 150 SHEETS, wide ruled, by Roaring Spring Paper Products of Roaring Spring, PA 16673. The front cover reads USE YOUR IMAGINATION, and I try to live up to this command. I'm not just interested in something called "literature"; I'm obsessed.

I've realized that language makes a visual image. Language is effective. It's a good screen. But I'm not thinking, on the page. I'm thinking: in your head. By way of the eyes, words go inside, hover, remain. (*Words are spinning eggs. Arrows shoot from them. They dissolve into myriad images, and the images inhere within the reader. Images enter the bloodstream, traveling, nesting at the cellular level.*) I envision this, and then, as if there were never anything else to think, it overtakes my world. This is my sole goal in life, generating images with language. Nothing else matters. I'll sacrifice everything for just one perfectly bright, indelible verbal picture.

F, meanwhile, is for Francis Fukuyama. It's for France and friends. F is
an axe or a comb. A false flag.

Professor Johnson brings examples of language she has found in
the world into the lecture hall and shares them with us before
she begins her presentations. One day she mentions a poster she
has seen while walking to the course meeting, emblazoned with
the question, "How do I know if I'm eating enough?"

This was an advertisement, I believe, for a student organization that provided peer-to-peer counseling related to eating disorders and body image. I recall this poster as part of a series that
addressed the undergraduate population by means of mentalist
questions, the idea being that if you recognized your own inner
dialogue in the sample interrogative, you might need help.

I had, of course, passed these posters many times. Rather
than reassuring me, they inspired an alarming thought: *Why am*
I in no way worried about how much I am eating? And: *Does the fact*
that I have never had a thought such as this—that I know with cer-
tainty that I am eating more than enough, that there is way too much
food on every plate I clean—a sign that I should be eating a whole
lot less? If I have never had to wonder if I might be starving myself
and liking it a lot, does that mean I lack all self-control? If I were a
thoughtful person (which I see now I am not), would I often experience
the joy of noting that I have starved myself for days on end?

Johnson repeats the question. "'How do I know if I'm eating
enough?'" She switches to the second person. "'How do you know
if you're eating enough?'" She pauses. "You're not dead!" She then
summarily begins her lecture.

Johnson is irritated. She is a thin woman, and so it seems
as if some of the mental noise that falls to me as a reader might
miss her. Or maybe she hears this noise and steps a step further.
For it is gendered, the question, not even implicitly a question
only a female student asks herself, and thus it has an in-group
as well as an out-group. I am part of the in-group. Meanwhile,

those in the out-group are likely to pass the poster by and laugh. I can imagine the question in the mind of a member of the football team who lives in the same residential house I do and who, one recent weekend night, ripped an allegedly firesafe and riotproof door off its hinges with his bare hands when he could not open it by other means, causing a report heard throughout the building. Maybe that person passes the poster and thinks, *"Q: How do I know if I'm eating enough? A: I am conscious and upright and can rip a door off its hinges."* Or perhaps it serves as a wholesome reminder that food is important. Or of this person's weight-related struggles as a wrestler, before he switched to football. Or of something else altogether. I'm just guessing.

Johnson indicates that the question is unstable. It seemed natural enough when I'd passed it on previous speed walks to class but give it a moment to reverberate in the lecture hall and it starts to seem hollow and uncanny. By converting it to the tautology "The way that we know we have not starved ourselves to death is that we have not starved ourselves to death," Johnson shows how the question fails to pose a question. It claims to offer help by means of a disclosed state of mind (vulnerability and uncertainty) but in effect serves to make the reader more vulnerable to and uncertain about the very misapprehension it purports to ward against. "Why haven't we starved ourselves to death? Because we haven't yet eaten little enough to starve ourselves to death. Who are we? We are the ones interested in the possibility of starving ourselves to death. We are the ones who distinguish themselves by exploring this possibility."

One way to exorcise or disarm this false question, Johnson shows, is to take it as literally as possible, to render it stupid, since it is stupid, stupid and cruel and sticky, loaded with all the norms and categories it claims to want to help you survive.

There is also a quiet note about the extremely local abode of death in the question, for the question "How do I know if I am eating enough?" is another way of asking, "Is there a chance I am killing myself?" Further, "Is there a chance society wants me to kill myself (less work for it than actively murdering me), and I—late to the game, as ever—have not yet adopted this imperative as my own?"

G, at least, is all good. Very good. A bright sphere. Great expectations.

It was the fall of 1999. It was still vaguely the time of theory. Of high theory. The French invasion. Post-structuralist hijinks. Whatever you want to call it, mocking it lightly. It was coming to be the end of the time of theory, and I was barely Barbara Johnson's student and hadn't been alive in the 1970s, theory's US heyday, so I missed the moment when human culture was laid bare by a group of philosopher-critics who borrowed from anthropology and linguistics, among other disciplines, to devise reading strategies that allowed them interpret any form of discourse, knowledge, or information as a constructed narrative.[7]

I took a single class with Johnson but never considered myself her student, although no other teacher has made so lasting an impression on me. I have never wanted to be like another person so much nor been so convinced that such a feat would be impossible. I was an unremarkable, silent participant in a course led by a famous scholar of French literature. Someone who spoke with an eloquence I can barely recreate. Even if, by means of some form of magic, I were to return to her lectures today, if I could sit in them as my forty-year-old self, I doubt there is much I could contribute. It's not that I did not understand what Professor Johnson was saying. Her speech was larded with double meanings, chickens and eggs, inversions and striking impossibilities: ironies, which is to say language that pondered the fact that a single word can mean more than one thing, including its own apparent opposite. What I am saying is, what she said meant too much. She seemed already to be saying anything I could want to say.

H is for the here and now. Ha. Haha. Ha! Human, humility, aspiration. Who and how.

Before I met Barbara Johnson, what I knew of language games came to me from my teenhood in the 1990s.

The reader will recall a certain scene in the film *Reality Bites* (1994). Asked to define irony at the close of an unsuccessful job interview, Lelaina Pierce (Winona Ryder) blurts, as an elevator door closes over her face, "I can't really define irony, but I know when I see it!" Subsequently, the downtrodden Pierce asks Ethan Hawke's character, Troy Dyer, if he can define irony. Dyer quips, "It's when the actual meaning is the complete opposite from the literal meaning." At this moment, we see that Dyer, who is seated at an appropriately unfussy diner counter, is reading a copy of *Being and Time* (1927), by Martin Heidegger. Presumably, this prop helps us understand why Dyer is more fluent in the rhetorical structure of irony than Pierce. Dyer reads existential philosophy associated with the global shift in consciousness following World War II.[8] He may not see himself as a postmodern rhetorician, but for sure he is an innately resistant, thoroughly traumatized, disaffected, cool dude who defines himself in distinction to what he perceives as simplistic consensus. He coldly contemplates tropes that for Pierce blend into the larger mass of culture.

Pierce, for her part, only intuitively senses the presence of irony; she is a documentarian, not an interpreter. Or, she is someone who hasn't yet learned to defend herself from language's seductive ambiguities. Irony is for her an amorphous quality that circulates in the landscape. She's at its whim. It is part of words and might be a god. She films it while sucking down a cigarette, squinting. In her Super 8 scenes, irony is a swampy mood, texture, or affect. It is weather. It is nature. It is very human. If irony is a way in which the world responds to—and therefore reads and interprets—her, Pierce will, ironically, need someone else to explain that.

I is for the obvious. It is for eye and I. It is invention and interest. Intervention and intellect. I is for idea. Ironically, a line. It looks a little like me. Inscription infinitely inspired. Idols. Idiocy. I can't find my head.

As eager readers of Alanis Morissette's 1996 song "Ironic" have pointed out,[9] its examples of irony are really examples of co-incidence and frustrated hopes: a traffic jam in the commute of a worker who is already late; a sign telling the same worker that they are not permitted to smoke during what they perceive as their "cigarette break"; a multitude of spoons in a drawer opened by someone possibly looking for a knife to cut a cake (for an of-fice birthday party?); and so on. These are not examples that teach us much about polysemous speech or hidden meanings.[10]

If we are generous enough to understand Morissette's lyrics as not incorrect but rather redefining irony, she seems to con-ceive of it as a quirky cosmic force, a "funny way of helping you out" on the part of a personified entity she calls "life," or perhaps "Life." We are invited to understand the dashing of our hopes as redemptive, instructive. Perhaps we shouldn't rush, shouldn't smoke, should just use one of the spoons as a makeshift knife. We should cope, try to see the good—rather than engaging in a paranoid reading that diagnoses the traffic jam as somehow en-gineered by nefarious elites to slow us down precisely when we least need to be slowed down, thereby converting us into unfor-tunate subjects of Foucauldian bio-power.[11]

The miasmic irony of *Reality Bites* is, meanwhile, an irony of frustrated hopes, yes, but it is more unpleasant even than the adjective *frustrated* (from Latin *frustratus,* past participle of *frustrare,* "to deceive, disappoint, make vain," from *frustra,* "in vain, in error," which is related to *fraus,* "injury, harm," a word of uncertain origin [see *fraud*]) lets on. If we were to rewrite the Morissette song as a synopsis of *Reality Bites,* it might go some-thing like,

It's a desire to have a passionate, honest relationship with the mate of one's soul **when** you're living in a society in which most people suffer from attachment disorders that prevent them from bonding with people in general and specifically with those with whom they might, in theory, experience deep love.

It's a wish to contemplate one's role in contemporary socioeconomic inequalities and broader histories before choosing a path in life **when** you're living in a society in which there are no paths that do not contribute to the increase of inequalities and in which such attempts at historical reflection are thoroughly mocked (even by the very film in which they are occurring) and possibly punished, with far-reaching consequences for one's (economic and social) future. See Pierce's loss of her job, blackballing within the industry where she is desperate to have a career, and unfortunate sale of her documentary to a network that edits it beyond recognition.

And isn't it ironic, don't ya think? Despite what Troy Dyer/ Ethan Hawke says, despite how satisfyingly impressive his definition is, it may be more accurate to see irony as something most of us know only vaguely and intuitively. Here irony is a zeitgeist, a cloud, a whack-a-mole double that pops up when you least expected it (but when you always expected it, let's be real). In *Reality Bites* there is no time to meditate on the scarcity of love and lack of time for contemplation. There is so little time for discussing how things may mean in a world swayed by the exigencies of capitalism (a problem the film admits) and the destructive demands of romantic love (which are generally approved of by the film, given they make for a shapely plot), that it is unsurprising that this snippet of dialogue regarding the definition, which is to say the *meaning*, of irony is the most memorable part of the whole production. Nobody remembers what happens to the various characters or why they are at odds; the film makes only a cursory attempt to parse their conditions, anyway. No one remembers that *Reality Bites* is about the germination of a proto-reality television show; this plot gets buried by various kinds of handwringing about sex. What's crisp and clear here—*clear and distinct*, as some philosophers like to say—is the sight (image) of the elevator closing over Winona Ryder's face as she tries to parse the linguistic substance known as irony. Someone fumbles in the face of language's dominion. She is unable to speak, rendered (ironically) silent by a word.

J is for Jacques and jacks, a game. Jesus. JK, just joshing. For jokes and gestures. Hi there, Juicy Lucy.

But the academy knew all about the importance of irony, even before *Reality Bites*. In 1989, kicking off the tongue-in-cheek, slouching 1990s of US imperialism and economic boom, the American philosopher Richard Rorty published *Contingency, Irony, and Solidarity*, a book version of a series of lectures he had delivered in the UK. Synthesizing developments in late nineteenth- and twentieth-century philosophy with post-structuralist theory (Derrida, in particular), as well as readings of novels, Rorty presents irony as an important personal and cultural good, a device that supports liberal democracy by making it possible for there to at once be no truth, as such, and for people to understand themselves and one another.

As Rorty puts it, the ironist realizes that "anything can be made to look bad or good by being redescribed" and therefore renounces the temptation of any absolute set of criteria to be employed by all people, ending up "in the position which Sartre called 'meta-stable': never quite able to take themselves seriously."[12] The ironist rescues contemporary social and political life from the evil twins of "Enlightenment rationalism"[13] (vivisection and cotton plantations) and postmodern nihilism (terrorism and culture wars) by inventing a style of speaking by means of which "she" at once debates the possibility that she has completely misunderstood the nature of her position as a human, having been equipped with a mistaken vocabulary about her own condition, and acknowledges the impossibility of discovering a perfectly fitting vocabulary. The ironist dwells between two fantasies: one in which there is a truth, and another in which everything is a lie (and, therefore, why bother with words at all?). Or, she acknowledges these fantasies as fantasies, engaging in public discourse in a world that has no "intrinsic nature."[14] But nowhere in Rorty's rather unfunny publications do we find anything but the haziest of descriptions of this apparently delightfully zesty linguistic demilitarized zone.

K is for repetition. It's for a kick in the pants, disorder, Franz Kafka, a partly squished X. K is anarchic, the strangest of letters. Special K. Antinomian K. Kool-Aid, and other crimes against C. K is an expression, somehow, of the deepest and most intractable alienation. K is an asymmetry.

I remember speaking freely. I was friendly, I was funny; I was shy but reasonably loquacious. In 1999, things changed for me. I never really knew why.

I recall walking around the university thinking, *I have to put an end to this terrible feeling.* I felt defined by this feeling yet never spoke about it with anyone. Social media, in the contemporary sense of the term, did not exist. Moreover, the notion of mental health as a form of temporary and shifting grace, seldom achieved without struggle, was decades off. As I conceived of things then, in 1999, one was either sane or one was crazy. If one was not sane, then one was not sane. The only thing I knew was that I could not be crazy. If I was not sane, then I was crazy, and crazy was something I could not be.

The pain I felt in these days was the pain of having lost someone with whom I was close. Perhaps it was even myself I had lost. Because I could no longer find this person, I wasn't sure who they were. The term *panic attack* had not yet entered the popular lexicon; therefore, I could not name the symptoms that took that form. There were other symptoms, as well: recriminations, despair, crippling self-loathing, paranoia, insomnia, auditory hallucinations, the belief that I might in fact be dead. I dragged around. I was determined to stop the feeling. It was the most important thing I could do. Sadly, I was failing.

When I write about the experience of meeting the critic Barbara Johnson, I am also and at the same time the person who has the terrible feeling. I am the person who is experiencing the terrible feeling for the first time. I sit in the lecture hall and plead with myself. *Please,* I think, *become intelligent again, Lucy. Please use words and use them simply, easily, thoughtlessly to think.* The terrible feeling is so powerful that it can make it very hard to think, and I am desperate to think. Meanwhile, language is an ungovernable substance. It has exploded and gone everywhere, staining my clothes and parts of the inside of my brain. I must, before all else, begin thinking again. I'm desperate just to be *interested* in something, other than my own unaccountable suffering, in which I am not at all interested but which commands my attention—like an annoying bell, chilling breeze, or edge of a very steep and attractive cliff no one else can hear, feel, or, more generally, perceive. "Everywhere he looks, his own thoughts look back":[15] it's a sentence meditating on a poem by Charles Baudelaire in one of Johnson's best essays. Unfortunately, it also describes me.

For a long time, I have been using writing in my battle with the terrible feeling. Once or twice a day I find a location outside, weather permitting, and I put language into one of my Roaring Spring Paper Products notebooks with a pen. I don't try to write in sentences and often I write down combinations of words I don't fully understand, words that enter my consciousness seem-

ingly of their own accord. After I've done this for a while, I'll attempt to focus my attention on the physical world and will write
down only things I can see. I try not to include any feelings.
Subsequently, I'll try to write about my feelings, but strangely,
despite the staggering vigor of the terrible feeling, I often can't
discover if I have any. I'm very compelled by the notion of romantic love (a topic of poems I consider good), yet I love nobody.
Occasionally, I become obsessed with someone and write about
our supposed bond. I write about my failure within it.

The only thing I seem to be good at, in fact, is writing. In
creative writing classes, I'm praised and even idolized by the instructors, who usually attempt to cultivate some sort of friendship with me until they discover how unhinged I am.

In summary: I've stopped believing I exist. I have no idea why.

I'm therefore practicing a form of ascesis,[16] or self-discipline;
it's the one solution I've been able to devise. I'm nineteen and
the only thing that matters to me is becoming a great writer.
Paradoxically, perhaps, I don't care about publishing or fame,
both of which I consider the opiates of fools. I'm harsh and domi-
neering, studying diction and syntax. I believe in technical mastery, and I seek this with the zeal of a patriarch. I do not believe
in god, but I do believe in irrevocable error and have come to
the conclusion that the world will end during my lifetime due to
catastrophic nuclear war, environmental degradation, or some
combination of the two.

In some ways, I ignore my own life. I'm incoherent: I have difficulty buying shampoo or razors, since I believe that these are
not just unnecessary but heinous pollutants, yet I smoke ciga-
rettes. I drink Diet Coke. I consider the purchase of new clothing politically unconscionable and wear only items I have rooted
out of thrift stores or found on the street or on floors at parties.
I don't read the news.

A graduate student, with whom I have a brief and mostly chaste
liaison, tells me that I remind him of Euphrosyne of Alexandria,

a medieval saint who in the fifth century disguised herself as a man to avoid marriage and enter a monastery. Euphrosyne took the name Smaragdus during his life as a monk and was obliged to seclude himself in the desert in order to devote himself to prayer, given the distracting interest on the part of other monks in his beauty.[17]

The graduate student makes no attempt to liberate me from my isolation. I'm not really that into him, anyway.

What I am into is language.

Wads. Words.

I've concluded that the most literal uses of words are the best, miraculous. Common nouns and simple verbs astound me. They point. They are earnest, mute other than in pointing. They are brilliant in their pointing, cutting. They don't need me, or any of us, for that matter, in my fantasy. In my fantasy, these words will survive the end of the world.

Figurative language, on the other hand, revolts and disturbs me. It seems like vomit or a weapon. It's not just that I find it unethical, a lie; it makes me more aware of the presence of the terrible feeling. It's part of my sickness. Literalism seems to protect me. Calling a green thing green keeps the terrible feeling at bay.

A leaf is green.

One to one.

I am safe. I am sane.

But the paucity of literal language in everyday speech sets me at a disadvantage. To compensate, I try to speak as little as possible. I'm certainly doing a good job of this in Professor Johnson's class. I still have friends, but I'm not able to write a college-level paper. It's only sophomore year, and the road ahead does not look promising. I consider most sentences falsehoods. I intend to somehow overcome the untrue nature of language. My project has become so important to me that the threat of bad grades or even expulsion doesn't move me. I continue, a secret fanatic. I tell no one about the words. I tell no one about the terrible feeling. I no longer believe in the existence of knowledge. I wonder about the existence of history, too; I consider it real but largely inaccessible—and am awed by its inaccessibility. I believe all but exclusively in language, in the qualities and potencies of letters, of marks I can draw, of these visual-conceptual-musical chimeras. Nothing exists except language, a mark of fundamental absence. I don't believe that I can share, which is to say, communicate, anything with anyone but am determined to leave behind me a trail of the linguistic objects I, a stranger, have touched, the little blue or black indentations I have carved into white with a ballpoint pen. For years, years that begin in 1999, I hold my breath.

Lovely. Ludicrous. Luxurious. Loose. Light. Literal. Liminal. Lucky. These are but some of the troubling adjectives that begin with L. I said, "Elle." A loop. C'est moi. L: here is a shelf to save her.

Something never mentioned in any class I took in college is that the United States is a creation of apocalyptic—which is to say, millenarian, eschatological—thinkers. Descriptions of the Pilgrim Fathers who landed at Plymouth Rock in the early seventeenth century elide or euphemize this sect's anti-historical predilections. They believed themselves to have escaped a Satanic Europe in order to build an exceptional "Zion" of refuge in the "New World." As John R. Hall writes, the Puritans, "sometimes invoking the ancient Jews, pursued a redemptive quest in time by moving through geographic space, from perceived persecution in England to the promised land."[18] John Winthrop, a second-wave Puritan settler, enthused about New England's exemplarity (recall his "city on a hill") and its distinctness from the sinful cataclysm of Europe, proclaiming that "the church hath no place to fly into but the wilderness."[19] The Puritans' metaphor for migration, invoking the psychedelic landscapes of Revelation, has analogues in the thought of German Pietists, Mennonites, the Amish, Huguenots, and schismatic Lutherans. John Edwards, the influential eighteenth-century revivalist preacher-celebrity, maintained that the end times were near. For some revolutionaries, Britain was literally the Beast of Revelation 13:14.[20]

The Shakers, otherwise known as the United Society of Believers in Christ's Second Appearing, emigrated from England in 1774 and subsequently settled in Watervliet, New York. They lived in intentional communities in which sexual intercourse was forbidden and all aspects of daily life were spiritualized. Following the teachings of their founder, Mother Ann Lee, the group averred that the end of the world had begun. There could be no point in living a life cluttered with objects and babies, as these would encumber one's relationship with Christ.[21] Shakerism's streamlined and apparently apocalyptic decor provides an interesting gloss on contemporary waves of revival of minimalism,[22] showing how easily we skip over the widespread obsession with eschatology in early colonial America. One can buy a "Shaker peg rail" at Home Depot or any number of online retailers but in no description of this product are you likely to read that its stunningly chary design is due to its inventors' belief that secular time was short and a new age beyond history was dawning.[23]

The American nineteenth century's best-known monger of end times is William Miller, who predicted that Christ would return to earth in 1844. Miller served in the US Army during the War of 1812 and was left unscathed by a shelling that injured or killed others around him. After this lucky miss, Miller became convinced of the presence of an interventionist god who determines human events.[24] Challenged to justify his beliefs, Miller began a period of intense Bible study that culminated in his calculating a termination date for the world as we know it based on a creative interpretation of Daniel 8:14.[25] Miller's prophecy circulated by means of a Vermont newspaper in the early 1830s, and by the time of the so-called Great Disappointment of October 22, 1844, his followers, the Millerites, numbered at least fifty thousand.[26] When Jesus did not descend from the clouds, concluding secular time, many left the faith and a handful of believers joined the Shakers. Others founded new churches: the Advent Christian Church, the Jehovah's Witnesses, and the Seventh-day Adventists. The latter two organizations report tens of millions of adherents today.[27]

One schismatic offshoot of Seventh-day Adventism, the Branch Davidians, became a subject of public fascination in 1993, after a botched raid by the Federal Bureau of Investigation at their Waco, Texas, compound resulted in a conflagration and gun fight that left eighty Branch Davidians dead, twenty-five of whom were children.[28] David Koresh, the sect's self-proclaimed messiah, had been involved in violent conflicts with other Branch Davidians in the late 1980s and was known for his pursuit of polygamy and weapons. Despite the twisted nature of Koresh's separatism, military veteran Timothy McVeigh took inspiration from him, attending the 1993 standoff in person and distributing literature regarding gun rights there.[29] In 1995, McVeigh and Terry Nichols undertook the deadly bombing of the Alfred P. Murrah Federal Building in Oklahoma City, in order to obtain revenge for what had taken place two years earlier in Waco and the Ruby Ridge, Idaho, siege of 1992. McVeigh was particularly distressed that women and children were killed in these police actions[30] and that military-grade weapons, with which he was personally familiar as a result of his service in Iraq, were used.[31]

In a twenty-three-page letter to his childhood friend Steve Hodge before the bombing, McVeigh wrote,

> I know in my heart that I am right in my struggle, Steve. I have come to peace with myself, my God and my cause. Blood will flow in the streets, Steve. Good vs. Evil. Free Men vs. Socialist Wannabe Slaves. Pray it is not your blood, my friend.[32]

A hideous irony: The Alfred P. Murrah Federal Building contained a daycare center. McVeigh claimed after the fact that he and Nichols did not know this.[33]

But recall that *apocalypse* does not mean "end." Apocalypse means "uncovering." It means "revelation," that sacred mysteries are elucidated. Farewell to the veil. Angels speak to the hero and explain what was and what is and what shall be. They offer visions of history, take him on a tour of the heavens, show him God's gorgeous four-wheeled throne. In the literature and cinema of the world, there are many such fantastical apocalypses (see *The Divine Comedy*, see *It's a Wonderful Life*).

Martha Himmelfarb writes, "The association with eschatology derives not from the meaning of [*apocalypse*] but from the content of the Book of Revelation and other related works."[34] In other words, *apokalypsis*, a Koine term for a mystical ascent to the realm of the gods by a hero, is used today, all but exclusively, to refer to revelation of the preordained (and often very violent) end of the world, particularly in a Christian millenarian context. It is taken by many of us, incorrectly, to mean "end of all things." For there is no knowledge, apparently, without an end. No truth without cataclysmic violence. Send the horses of various colors, the earthquakes, a moon the color of blood, skies without light, innumerable falling rocks, hail, thunder, lightning, fire and fire and fire, angels with destructive music, poison for all the rivers, dangerous meteorites, a woman pregnant with god, assorted vicious hybrid beasts, some of whom use language to confound what remains of the devastated human world. Smash the light out. Consume the light within a brighter light. Immolate the planet with all its ironies to at last produce something incontrovertible.

My blood, my friend, my mystery. Mastery. Mister. M is for mothers, for mine. M is for memory. M, the valley and the mountains. The body in bed. Peaks. M is the sound of another's heart. The voice in the mind. Hum. Um. The voice is always that of someone else.

Funded by the Ford Foundation and hosted by Johns Hopkins University, the consequential academic conference that brought

French theory to North America had the rather clunky and indirect title "The Languages of Criticism and the Sciences of Man." It was at first imagined as an exploration of the influence of anthropologist Claude Lévi-Strauss and linguist Roman Jakobson on contemporary literary criticism. It was meant to be about the hottest trend in the humanities: structuralism, which is to say, methods of research and argument that take as their starting point the notion that all human understanding is ultimately beholden to language. In practice, however, the talks concerned the passé-ness of structuralism—inaugurating a critical movement called "post-structuralism" that attempted to criticize structuralism's lingering rigidity. The conference was the first simultaneous public airing of the thought of critic Roland Barthes, philosopher Derrida, and psychoanalyst Lacan in the United States. It was drunken and at times rancorous.

In a biography of René Girard, today the best known of the conference's organizers, author Cynthia L. Haven lingers over some of the seamier details of the four-day event, October 18–21, 1966. Lacan demanded that his silk undergarments be laundered by hand and ran up a nine-hundred-dollar long-distance phone bill after his presentation, complaining to friends back in Paris about how poorly he had been treated.[35] Meanwhile, rich wines and liquors flowed. Angus Fletcher, the respondent for Lacan's talk, was blitzed on gin-based French 75s when he ramblingly compared the analyst to "a spider" who makes "a very delicate web without any human reality in it."[36] This was just one among many rather personal exchanges at the "standing-room-only" talks that were broadcast via closed-circuit television into a library lounge to accommodate the crowds.[37] Derrida and Lacan spatted at a certain dinner party.[38] Paul de Man informed Barthes that he was "somewhat disappointed by the specific analyses that you give."[39] Another participant walked away with the sense that he had "just heard a paper that destroyed everything that I stand for, but," as the scholar noted, "it was a very important paper."[40]

Carefully edited versions of the presentations and discussions at "The Languages of Criticism and the Sciences of Man" were published as a paperback edition titled *The Structuralist Controversy* in 1972 (an earlier 1970 edition retained the original conference title). *The Structuralist Controversy* went through two printings during the 1970s, an unusual feat for a conference transcript, as American literature and humanities departments were seized with a hunger for stylish interdisciplinary explanations of language and human nature. Never mind that the two key speakers the conference's organizers had originally wanted to invite—Lévi-Strauss himself and Michel Foucault—had been unavailable, or that the symposium's emergent star, thirty-six-year-old Derrida, was considered a marginal figure at best back in France. Never mind the total exclusion of women and near-total exclusion of nonwhite participants. (Edward Said was among the colloquists.) "Miss Susan Sontag," who in 1963 had noted anthropology's colonialist underpinnings in the *New York Review of Books*, was, for example, dinged for "faintly hysteric ignorance."[41] Who cared about intrinsic identities or linear histories? This gathering announced the death of rational man and the birth of something called "the subject," a being whose psychological, social, and political nature could not be separated from either the prison house of grammar or the fundamental instability of meaning—and who would grasp, mostly vainly, to find its way in a postwar society of unreal spectacle and all too real control.[42]

N isn't for anything. Nope. Never. N doesn't. No. N is knots, denial. A crack-up. The persistence of a strange whining. Hissing that crackles. N's sharpness and unpredictability. Strangely the letter of fire and shadows. Naughty not nice. Not as much nonsense as necessary.

I studied the following languages in college: French, German, ancient Greek, Latin, Mandarin, Russian, Arabic, Spanish, Sanskrit.

I dropped or failed multiple courses. I had no interest in mastery or even rudimentary communication. I wanted only to see the event of expression unfold. Meanwhile, I was forever in the library. I could not "think." I could not write a topic sentence. I comforted myself, attempting to believe my impulsivity and dilettantism were somehow modernist. I was in danger of being expelled. Someone said something to someone who called someone who made a note, and I was advised to take time off.

A year had gone by. It was late 2000 and I was ushered into a dean's office. I lied, saying that my parents were undergoing a messy divorce.

The administrators chewed this over. You could tell it didn't taste as good as what they usually got.

I used money from a summer job to purchase a plane ticket to Los Angeles, where I rented a car from a dry-cleaning business that advertised on the back of a pamphlet available near the Hertz counter. It was a red two-door with rims and a decal in the back window of a pissing Calvin (no Hobbes). I told the man at the dry cleaners that I would use the vehicle within the city limits exclusively but then drove up the Californian coast over a period of five days. I took Route 1 so that I could see the ocean.

There are hundreds of miles of fat green hillside into which this road has been blasted.

I remember getting out of the car to climb over a fence and walk in a field that had two horses in it.

I wandered around small towns and my heart would race whenever someone in a supermarket or convenience store looked me in the eye. I would have gone to live with anyone.

I drove into areas of cultivation off the coast. On an empty road I did 120 and was picked up by aerial radar. Later a police car pulled me over.

I practiced writing landscape. Over and over I stopped and attempted to write what I could see. I believed I could drive into an image. All I wanted was to be able to stop the terrible feeling—

which I believed was located in the swirling, uncertain, figurative dimension of words.

I arrived in San Francisco where the red car was towed one afternoon after I got lost in the Tenderloin. I retrieved it at great expense from a dusty lot. Seeing it for a second time I had a vision of myself standing beside myself. I was almost out of money.

When I returned to LA I stayed in a youth hostel. I kept to myself. In the central courtyard I met a man who said he was driving to Las Vegas and wanted company. We talked about the sitcom *Friends* and he gave me a white rose. It becomes stranger in that he was selling an early technology that allowed one to convert internet into international phone service, or so he told me, opening the trunk to reveal boxes printed with a photo of a manicured hand caressing a receiver.

He had a rented Chrysler like a yacht. I remember the largest thermometer in the world and the light from the Luxor.

Letter O: oblique oblivion. O is a bald vessel. For me, O is pale blue, a mass made to appear translucent with respect to the sky by distance. O is out there, gaping, a faceless face.

There are approximately thirty Roaring Spring marble-cover notebooks currently in my possession, which I believe I kept during the years 1998, 1999, 2000, 2001, 2002, and some parts of 2003. There may have been more notebooks. If so, I no longer have them.

I find these notebooks frightening and a little sad.

I find them frightening because the person writing in them seems to have been hit by a wave or something else very big that continued its forward motion long after it plowed through her.

I find them sad because the wave left the scene, but she did not.

Yet, I also find them comforting. This person, the writer of the notebooks, did something, even though there was nothing she could do. She toiled away, therefore, at a form of irony.

By late 2002 or so, I've figured out how to navigate, in the wake of whatever it is that has passed through me. I still have panic attacks (these have no name; they're just a feature of my existence), I hold extremely pessimistic views about the future of human civilization and the United States in particular, and I find it impossible to connect with other people emotionally, possibly because I am, one, sure that we are living in End Times and, two, possessed of a nagging suspicion that I may actually be dead. When the United States invades Iraq in 2003, I spiral for a few months, but I know how to bob, how to drift. I've taught myself a technique for managing the obliteration of my self. I'm surviving in the absence of a world.

The notebooks 1998–2003 contain few notes about material conveyed by professors or graduate students at the college where I am enrolled. They contain almost no notes on texts assigned for courses. There are, instead, pages and pages of quotations from my extracurricular reading, which is extensive and eccentric. I'm searching for something. I feel a kind of rage that nothing has been written down that will explain my own experience to me, yet I find glimpses of insight in the writing of others.

An example of a list of books I instruct myself to read:

1. *Cane* Jean Toomer
2. *The Information Man* Edward Ruscha[43]
3. *History of Sexuality* M. F.
4. *The Ice-Shirt* William T. Vollman

And there are magpie quotations. Pages of them.[44]

From an obscure text by Gilles Deleuze: "This manner of reading intensely, in relation to an exterior, flux against flux. . . . It's a manner of loving."

From *Forms in Japan*, by Yuichiro Kojiro: "When a form complies with the downward pull not only of gravity but also of the pushing power of water down an incline, it changes the forms of 'weeping' to the forms which 'flow.'"

From one of Tocqueville's astonishing descriptions in *Democracy in America*: "You might call it a fertile meadow covered with the debris of a vast edifice."

From James Baldwin's book-length essay on American media, *The Devil Finds Work*: "Revenge is not among the human possibilities."

Perhaps it's rage that's keeping me alive; I'm not sure. I've lost myself and all I have now are these *wads*, words.

I write:

> that hell is a world/scape with no horizon

I write, in a series of notes toward a brief, now-lost play:

Rules for the Ghost
1. She has been dead for 20 yrs (in their time)
2. She is still in the instant of her death, i.e., the consciousness she experiences is in opposition to time. Her appearance in their world is a forced one?
3. Or simply, she is alone. They are not.

I write:

> Look there is a tree shaped like
> a dog, there is one with a nose
> in its branches, all those
> leaves are a head that shakes

I write.

There is one notebook that is different from the others. It is handmade, bound in brown leather with covers of blue hand-dipped marbled paper. I call it Blue Notebook. It is the notebook I took with me to California in early 2001, a special purchase for my travels.

Its contents vary. Mostly, I write in the sort of poem-language I've devised at college. I use this language to describe what is around me. And some of my thoughts. Which is to say, I treat my thoughts as a type of furniture that is connected to, sometimes confused with, the material world.

The notebook opens with the following three lines, written in blue ink, probably in February,

> an airplane on
> fire; a practice-
> burn they always do

I'm not sure what I'm referring to here. Maybe fuel is being ignited or perhaps an airplane has been experimentally or prophylactically set aflame ("a practice-burn"). It's certainly a weird thing to be writing about on a flight, since that's where I think I must have been when I wrote this, although I can't be sure.

When I read this today, I can't help wondering if I'm having some sort of vision of the future.

In this writing, as in much of my writing from this time, I'm extremely suspicious of the systems I participate in from day to day. I refer frequently to the "decadence" of American society. I describe interior spaces in brief visual spurts such as: "light entering through plastic curtains and / playing in white O's on the far wall." I compose cryptic little aphorisms: "even a church can be on television." I write about my own writing process in semi-desperate terms: "a lite / line one can choke, truss, and / teach one's self with, the only / hope there is."

I write: "I admit I'm resisting the landscape." I exhort myself: "try again."

I'm spooked by the ubiquitous image culture of America and simultaneously in awe. Everywhere I go, I take note of advertisements. I refer to these as "the backdrop / of every action, grief, even." Again, most of my accounts take the form of short poems. This is a rehearsal for something. It's an exercise.

It's mystifying to me now, looking back into these pages, the conviction with which I put myself through these paces. I'm alone and don't speak frequently to others. I'm twenty-one and travel with two pairs of pants, a pair of shorts, three shirts, and a leather jacket. I have sneakers and the vintage boots I wear most days. I wash everything in sinks. I wear sunblock, no makeup. There's something tragically serious about all this. If I were a man, people would be afraid of me.

P is for perfume and it is for person. P is for paces and perfection. Pores. P is for Poe. Purloined. Peace! Police! Purple prose. It's for poetry, a hook or spoon or spade. It's for coincidence. P is polite. It stands or dangles. It does its deed.

Edgar Allan Poe had a strange death. On October third of 1849, in Baltimore, Maryland, the poet and inventor of the detective story, aged forty, was discovered by strangers, semiconscious and dressed in rags that did not fit him. Four days later, he passed away.[45]

Only an acquaintance was on hand in the hospital. An enemy who wrote Poe's obituary and, in an odd twist, became his literary executor, put abroad the notion that Poe died of excessive inebriation. This story lingers, even in the present. Others think Poe was a victim of political violence. Given that he was discovered on an election day, he may have been abducted by a gang and compelled to vote multiple times for the political candidate who employed them. By means of a then-common practice known as cooping, enforcers would pen unfortunate individuals, intoxicating them against their wills and beating them into submission. The detainees would sometimes be given new garments between rounds at the ballot box. Thus, Poe's strange clothes and delirium.[46] In some interpretations, Poe suffers from rabies contracted from rats also present with him in the "coop."[47]

A decade before his death, in 1839, Poe published an apocalyptic short story in *Burton's Gentleman's Magazine*, titled "The Conversation of Eiros and Charmion." (Poe was familiar with William Miller and the Millerites. Everyone was.) The story is a chat between a pair of spirits in the afterlife. Eiros has died during the course of the cataclysm and explains what happened to

Charmion, who died a decade earlier and therefore missed out.[48] That "The Conversation of Eiros and Charmion" attributes the end of the world to the arrival of a comet that alters the composition of the earth's atmosphere, adumbrating in detail the environmental effects, pushes it into the realm of science fiction. Poe combines popular fascination with comets (Halley's had returned in 1835) with Millerite evangelical celebrity culture and with other oddities derived from his wildly synthetic sensibility; although he's far better known for creating the genre of the detective story, this futurist-gothic, crypto-Christian, eco-horror mash-up is none too shabby.

About that detective story: "The Purloined Letter," which I mentioned earlier, was the final installment in a trio of detective fictions concerning Poe's infallible sleuth, C. Auguste Dupin, a gallic Holmes before Holmes. It was first published in late 1844, year of the Great Disappointment, in *The Gift for 1845*, a journal intended to be gifted during winter holidays. The story has almost nothing to do with the apocalypse or apocalypticism, in the contemporary sense, although death, or the threat thereof, certainly has a role to play. Unveiling is, however, key. Thus, "The Purloined Letter" *is* an apocalyptic story, if we hew closely to etymology.

The story concerns a certain personal letter whose contents, if known by the king of France, have far-reaching consequences for the recipient, a woman who may or may not be the queen (Poe's narrator does not specify). In a palace boudoir, this woman is compelled to hide a piece of correspondence suddenly when the king walks in. A sly minister, perceiving the woman's anxious dissimulation, takes advantage of the situation to steal the letter, replacing it with a similar-looking missive of his own. The minister plans to blackmail the woman.

When the story opens, these events have already taken place. We are in Dupin's smoky quarters where he, an impoverished aristocrat, hangs out with the story's comparatively bland narrator.

A prefect who has been engaged by the woman robbed of the letter enters. This policeman wants Dupin's help. When, in time, the prefect returns to Dupin's abode, Dupin is in possession of the letter and demands a share of the reward. It's a high fee that will restore him to his former wealth or something like it.

Dupin acquires the letter by fascinatingly simple means. He imitates. He knows the canny minister well, having in the past been deceived by him. All he must do is to put himself, imaginatively speaking, in the minister's place. Visiting the minister's home on an anodyne pretext, Dupin catches sight of a shabby-looking piece of mail hanging in a cheap card rack suspended from a mantelpiece. The letter was addressed by a woman, judging from the calligraphy, and bears the minister's seal. This nonsensical combination of feminine handwriting and male imprimatur tips Dupin off: this is the stolen letter, turned inside out and lightly disguised. Dupin makes plans to return, creates a distraction, robs the minister of his prize. Of course, Dupin can't resist leaving a calling card; the look-alike he substitutes for the purloined letter contains a vengeful little scrawl to the effect of "This is your own damn fault."

What is this story about? On its surface, it appears to be a romp concerning the triumph of one form of cunning over another. But look again: there is something so eerie, nearly haunted about that letter (speaking of gothic mash-ups)—for the tale of Dupin's triumph is long since concluded, yet we still have no idea what the letter *says*.

In fact, we will never know.

It seems, even, not to matter.

For the letter is a site where the desire to see and, thereby, police desire mixes with other sorts of desire. We have to presume that these "other" sorts of desire are carnal or affective in nature (the woman's desire for sex with somebody), but, again, we don't really know.

When Jacques Lacan reads this story, he says that it is another way of talking about what takes place in psychoanalysis—an "*allegory for psychoanalysis*," as Shoshana Felman summarizes. In Felman's words, in his "Seminar on 'The Purloined Letter,'" Lacan interprets "the intervention of Dupin, who restores the letter to the Queen," as similar in nature to "the intervention of the analyst, who rids the patient of the symptom."[49] The "Queen" is healed when the letter is returned to her. She can stop worrying. Her mind is set at ease. If a symptom is a sort of loss, then, sure, the symptom/loss ceases when the letter goes back in its rightful place. Pursuing this allegory: it doesn't matter what the letter says, doesn't matter if the psychoanalyst knows the full contents or history of the case, just so long as what is out of place is identified, then restored.[50]

My own reading of Lacan's "Seminar on 'The Purloined Letter'" tends to humanize it a bit, and it's a reading I've come to only over time. What struck me first, when I read the essay in Professor Johnson's course in 1999, was the letter's otherworldly power. I took Lacan literally (having no personal experience with psychoanalysis and unable to read between the lines.) I thought: *What is this thing, this thing that controls everyone's movements and thoughts, that isn't even alive? This thing is writing,* I thought. *This thing is marks on a page.* I skipped over the bits about healing. The bits that pointed to a certain collaborative release devised in therapy. I read only the parts in which a "letter"—think of it metonymically and it can be a single written character, a letter of the alphabet, little more than an abstract squiggle—is more successful at being human than human beings are, is the entity with most perfect agency, the agency that comes from being perfectly free and sought by everyone, the agency we all desire.

I thought about this so much, in fact, that I had very little time for Derrida's critique, which we also read in Johnson's class. I buzzed through it, mostly uncomprehending. Derrida is annoyed that Lacan has ignored the role of the narrator in the transmission of this letter, obviously preferring the glamorous

Dupin, along with all his sparkling hiding and seeking, to the dynamics of the literary text itself and the narrator who makes the whole story unfold. The homely and supportive narrator is, despite his simple role, necessary to the possibility of revelatory "truth."

Barbara Johnson, meanwhile, points out that the "symbolic structure" Lacan discovers in the story is much the same as Derrida's favorite unit of literary analysis, *différance*, in that both are, like Poe's letter, "known only in [their] effects."[51] We can't really know what this "letter" everyone is after is, Johnson tells us, except insofar as it is something that is fundamental to literature and "not constative but performative."[52] In other words, the text exists not to tell the reader a singular, quantifiable, preordained content, a truth separate from the act of writing, but to teach the reader how to read it on its own terms, thereby putting the reader's own sense of "literal" truth into question, bringing the reader into an uncertain and interpretive space. The text reaches out to you—is, in fact, reading you. Johnson muses, "The true otherness of the purloined letter of literature has perhaps still in no way been accounted for."[53]

There is, Johnson maintains, something infernal in literature, something inhuman that is yet constitutive of our sense of humanity, as such. Just because poems and stories are full of characters, it doesn't mean there are any people in them. Literature reminds us just how tricky it is to describe a human. It reminds us of this not merely by showing us that humans are "complex," as we like to say, but by revealing that acts of description often occur in advance of what they purport to describe (*chicken and egg*). For this reason, it can be difficult to discern where the line between describing a human and creating a human begins or ends, in literature, in law, or in life in general. Has anyone, Johnson asks elsewhere, ever met a "natural person,"[54] which is to say, someone entirely unaffected by letters?

Q is for question. It's for quackery and for quietude. Q is for the outlandish, but it is also for the soft, the minor, the gentle, the floating, the sweet.

Among Miguel de Cervantes's short stories is the tale of a young law student, abandoned as a child and raised by kindly strangers, who comes to believe, after consuming a noxious and apparently ineffective love potion, that his body is composed entirely of glass.[55] The glass lawyer insists that he must be transported in a bed of straw lest he abruptly "break." The glass lawyer, nicknamed Vidriera, becomes famous for his delusion and ability to make witty remarks. However, revolted by the effects of his own celebrity, he enters the military and dies in a war.

Although Vidriera's tale may seem fantastical, it is a fictionalization of a very real delusion of the late fourteenth through seventeenth centuries in Western Europe. At this time, glass became a valuable and widely used material. "Glass delusion" seems mainly to have affected the upper classes, who would have come into frequent contact with this novel substance.[56] King Charles VI of France is history's first recorded sufferer and, according to an observant member of a fourteenth-century religious order, "clad himself with iron splints" so that no one in his vicinity might inadvertently shatter him.[57] Charles's initial experience of the delusion supposedly coincided with an episode of August 1395, when he was unable to recognize members of his own family, exclaiming and running to and fro. Charles was sometimes known as "the Beloved," more frequently as "the Mad." Several centuries later, the polymathic Tommaso Garzoni, author of a history of all the women in the Bible as well as an encyclopedic treatment of mental illnesses, describes a man traveling to Murano who "plans to fling himself into a kiln and be transformed into a goblet."[58] By the time of Richard Burton's *The Anatomy of Melancholy* (1621), the ailment was relatively well known. Burton tells of people who claim that they are "all glass, and therefore will suffer no man to come near them";[59] for Burton, glass delusion is next door to melancholy, what we might today term depression. Certainly, to believe that you are untouchable is to engage in despair.

As is obvious from the preceding anecdotes, a key symptom of delusion makes its home in the fraught space between bodies and language, in stories we tell ourselves about our status as persons, stories about the bodies we are or imagine ourselves to be, stories about the bodies that surround us. Delusions, as the American Psychiatric Association's *Diagnostic and Statistical Manual of Mental Disorders* (DSM-V) maintains, are "fixed beliefs that are not amenable to change in light of conflicting evidence."[60] Capgras syndrome, for example, is the delusion that a person close to the sufferer has been replaced by an imposter; this ailment plays a key role in Rivka Galchen's novel *Atmospheric Disturbances* (2008).[61] Delusion is commonly associated with schizophrenia, among other disorders affecting perception and self-experience. Of course, delusion is frequently observed in so-called normal people. To repurpose a phrase from the philosopher William Hirstein, delusion "involves absence of doubt about something one should doubt."[62]

Delusion may additionally be present in depersonalization disorder (now termed "depersonalization-derealization disorder," as per the DSM-V); here delusion takes the form of various species of perception of "unreality"[63]—in this context, a medical rather than an aesthetic term. Reading the Wikipedia entry for this condition of mind is an uncanny experience for me.[64] It is the feeling of perceiving something click into a slot, the words bizarrely written only to refer to my life, although I know, rationally, that this is not the case: "Individuals may report feeling as if they are an outside observer of their own thoughts or body, and often report feeling a loss of control over their thoughts or actions." (The phrase "feeling a loss of control over their thoughts or actions" is particularly moving to me.) "People who are diagnosed with depersonalization also often experience an urge to question and think critically about the nature of reality and existence. . . . In rare cases, symptoms . . . can last for years. . . . First experiences with depersonalization may be frightening, with patients fearing loss of control, dissociation from the rest of society and functional impairment. . . . Onset is typically during the teenage years or early 20s, although some report being depersonalized as long as they can remember. . . . The onset can be acute or insidious. With acute onset, some individuals remember the exact time and place of their first experience of depersonalization."[65]

An additional symptom: some individuals who suffer from depersonalization disorder do not recognize their own reflection in the mirror.[66] This "special effect" is quite familiar to me, even now, after years of treatment. In a strange rhyme with what I believe is largely an internal difficulty on my part, to this day I am sometimes told by acquaintances that I look so different from week to week that they have difficulty recognizing me. What can I take this to mean except that some aspect of the quality of my mind affects my body? "You could be a spy," people have said to me at parties. Or a terrorist, they do not say.

But to return to myself as I was in 1999—and subsequently in 2000, in 2001, in 2002, in 2003, nineteen years old, three years and counting older than the mean age for onset,[67] yet hardly impossibly remote from this time of life, either—I was experiencing what I believe was the acute onset of depersonalization-derealization disorder, a condition that was to be chronic and would expand to fill two decades of my early adulthood. But I want to add something here.

A rarer condition, Cotard's syndrome, does not appear in the DSM-V and may now be considered apocryphal, yet it, too, is vividly evocative of this time in my life. Identified in the late nineteenth century by Jules Cotard, a French neurologist and psychiatrist, the syndrome is the delusion that one is dead or does not exist. Cotard termed it "the delirium of negation."[68] Curiously, it is the only delusion that is self-certifiable in the Cartesian sense, since to claim that one is dead while engaging in the (lively) act of making this claim is obviously a contradiction. Indeed, as if spurred on by the perversity of the contradiction in question, the sufferer may begin to deny everything, including the world.

A person diagnosed with Cotard's may proclaim that the world has already ended or is about to end. They may no longer recognize themself as the owner of their own experience; therefore "the resultant existential predicament may well be best conveyed in terms of being dead, disembodied, nonexistent."[69] Given that such a description of what is being experienced internally (an impossibility) will be quite hard won, the sufferer may well attempt to avoid any situations or information that would tend to contradict their explanation of their own sensorial and mental situation. As with schizophrenia, self-isolation is common. Researchers have, meanwhile, linked the symptoms of Cotard's to a multistage onset process, by way of which a discrepancy emerges "between one's body-image—which has a certain spatial and linguistic structure—and one's awareness of one's inner bodily sensations."[70] It seems important to me that one's body image might be partly linguistic in nature—and that this language-based image could come to seem *empty*.

To return to the fall of 1999, I can't speak, can't perform, can't—above all—adopt the knowledge that is being imparted to me.

If I can put the world inside me (pictures like a phantasmagoria), then I can show it to other people. I want to be a medium of a kind.

Everything is about striving for greater impersonality, along with greater clarity.

If I am empty, at least I will be clear. If I am clear, perhaps I can be useful.

R is for reading. R is, above all, for letter. For seeing in reverse.

Here is how to write an image:

1. Isolate yourself—you must do this in order to hear what passes through your own brain, which will take the form of language.
2. Isolate yourself completely.
3. Be truly alone.
4. Have no ties to anyone.
5. Having isolated yourself, preferably outdoors (a window will do, in a pinch), make use of your eyes. Allow your eyes to fill with what surrounds you.
6. Forget yourself. Forget the story you know about yourself. Stop trying to think.
7. Stop thinking.
8. Now, allow your gaze to soften. Permit your eyes to choose a thing.
9. Describe it.
10. Don't think about what this means. Think about what this is. Think about: blue shadows, the red profile of a piece of grass, the green line of the horizon. The infinitely small fire that seems to be inside the light. Give names to the landscape. Forms. Allow yourself to begin—possibly with color.
11. Stop trying to think about what this means!
12. Stay in the realm of the visual.
13. Stay in the realm of the visual.
14. Stay in the realm of the visual until you can't take it anymore.
15. At this point, you may record a few remarks about what you are thinking.
16. Stop yourself before it goes too far.
17. Now stand up.

You feel somewhat bleary. Your feet and one of your calves are numb. You stomp in place, try to get the blood moving.

The dread is with you still. You swallow. You don't understand. Something is amiss, but you don't know what. Or, you know "what," in the sense that you are not functional and have not been so for a year and counting. Your mind seems capable of anything, save comprehending your own inability to stop feeling this way or the reasons for these feelings. You are only able to feel this way. You are only able to feel this way and *not* know what causes it. It is a rock. You live under it now. It is the only world.

Part of what you do, then, when you write in this way is to mourn the person you used to be. That person seems so distant now. That person was alive. You aren't. What's imperative is that you generate a reality of a kind through exercises with language. Everything else is wrecked. There is no chance for you. You're already dead. You can't have a life. But if you can manage to write in a good way, what may be a sort of a true way, a simple, clear way, then that articulation may survive. You can give it the life you no longer have, and it may, in turn, pull some remnant of your self through. I repeat, you are dead. No one can reach you. And here is what is terrifying: you know you are dead, that this is fact, but you appear to be living still. Meanwhile, you don't know how to correct this error. Sometimes you have the impression that, because you are already dead, you may not be able to die. You experience this as your own fault, a nonsensical and exceedingly shameful crime.

When I first arrived in Los Angeles, I stayed with friends of my parents. Probably these were friends of my mother, given that most of my parents' friends were, in fact, my mother's professional acquaintances. I can't remember where they lived, although it was suburban and the house was a rectangle on the side of a hill, packed in with other rectangles. I recall their laundry room—it was adjacent to the space where I slept. It impressed me, because in New York we did our laundry in the basement.

I do remember this couple's bafflement when I told them that my plan was to drive. There could be no reason to do that. Or, perhaps they understood this as a poorly conceived literary adventure.

There was something to this time, the early post-millennium, the dawning of the popular internet, in that it nominally resembled a series of times (the nineteenth and early twentieth centuries) in which young men went out into the landscape to find themselves and test their minds and bodies against nature. Perhaps we had officially passed this point in history—the couple weren't sure; I wasn't either. At any rate, I was not a young man. I was clearly some sort of feminist, but my commitments did not really compute.

I left the couple and drove up Routes 1 and 101 as far as Crescent City. I visited the ocean repeatedly and the redwoods, eventually. I was in San Francisco. I had walked to a park in search of green and was drifting downhill through the Tenderloin, lost. I remember a pair of kindly older men, a couple, stopping me. It's not the best idea to just wander around, around here, they said. For a moment my heart leapt. I imagined them adopting me. But they only gave me directions. They told me: stay safe.

What do you do when *you* has left you? She left me without warning. Surely, something must have happened to bring about these events. But nothing had happened. There was nothing.

And worse than this, my present life was consumed by oblivion. I was losing the ability to exist in the moment at all.

In the redwoods, there is at least one mystery spot, a place where the laws of nature do not apply. Here a ball will roll uphill.[71] I never paid a fee to go behind a fence, to see physics undone. Instead, I wondered about Cold War newlyweds, stopping in search of novelty.

I go alone into a forest where giant trees are. It's a weekday in an odd part of early spring and there are no other visitors. It is like an alien planet, probably an impression produced by *Star*

Wars. I want this place to tell me something. It is too cold in the shade, and I am beginning to run a fever. I find pieces of sun.

I stop in Morro Bay, so named for the volcanic plug that sits in the ocean just beyond the beach and estuarial bay. I walk in a large parking lot.

There is nowhere for me to be. Nowhere I am due or awaited. I've never lived like this. Time is a recalcitrant shard.

When it gets dark, I have to find a place to sleep. I can afford a motel, so it is not as if I will have to sleep in the car. Yet, I might prefer that. I wish I had to drive all night to be somewhere.

I make strange lists:

> topiary
> rooftops
> oven lights
> dashboards

I twitch with the need to become part of the world. I know that I cannot.

I can't concentrate. Can't stay still.

It's possible I drive back south inland, on larger highways. Many parts of this trip are impossible to remember.

It's the voice that says, I am trying something out. I'm praying. The realization that one is human and, meanwhile, that this means all bets are off. It's staggering: anything can happen—but is this what petrifies me?

My maternal grandmother is living as a recluse in San Diego. It never occurs to me that I might visit her.

I am in awe and in terror. I'm no one.

I want to replace everything that is inside me with something else.

I write:

> the thick horses and white wheels are a
> bank sign

I write:

> I saw the fields beside the road
> trees died
> slowly there
> I saw identical cars

I write.

I wake up in the morning and panic. I remember that I am still here, trapped in this situation, this situation in which nothing makes sense.

There is no one watching me, but it is as if everyone is watching. Translucent devils dance around me all day long. I panic but maintain myself in a state of calm. I must be still in these odorless, heatless, colorless flames. I cannot protect myself from the delusion that surges into my consciousness, but I can choose which form it takes, and so I attempt to make my delusion counterfeit reason. I wrestle it into a form.

Here is how to write an image:

Begin with the intention to write an image.

S is for symbol and suspicion. It is for situation. It is for the spirit of the law. S is a sinuous letter, scintillating, switching. A snake worn as a belt. A spirit is a law.

Eventually, I come back to the East Coast. On my way, I stop in with some friends who are squatting in dilapidated buildings in Austin, Texas. I stay with them for late spring and part of the summer of 2001. We don't need much money. We cook communally and go to shows. I am very high one afternoon and jump off what seems like an enormous quarry cliff into beautiful water. There are people drinking beers in a pontoon boat below and they clap for me as I come up, nose burning, crying, relieved not to have broken my neck, wishing I lived my life in a social world that would allow me to do things like this every day.

I don't know how tall that "cliff" was.

But soon it is September. College will begin.

I now reside in Somerville, Massachusetts, in a witchy three-story house with a single mossy bathroom and five roommates, plus a caged rabbit and mildly neglected midsize dog whose greatest delight is the clandestine consumption of cigarette butts.

Hardly anything has happened; it is a Tuesday I am too preoccupied to think of as anything other than the day before classes start. I am supposed to be a senior but am in the second half of my junior year.

It is morning and my roommate R. has his door open, his television on. He is the only one of us who has a set. He is probably the most serious student, too, writing on Indian nationalism, and he watches CNN as part of his work. Now he is smoking, barefoot, in shorts.

"Lucy," he says, poking his head out. "You should come in here."

We are the only ones up.

I pad over. I don't remember if I accept a cigarette.

I hear the voice of a female anchor. On the screen is a tower with a plume of smoke rising from it.

"What is this?" I say.

"It's New York," R. informs me. "Now."

CNN cuts to ABC. A male anchor is interviewing an eyewitness. An airplane enters the image. The plane is fast and silent and smooth. The words do not narrate what is happening. This plane races into the vicinity of the smoke plume and tower, which is, in fact, another tower.

"Wait," I say. "What? Should I wake everyone up?"

R. isn't saying no. One of his legs is shaking. He's shaking his head. "This is it," he tells me.

T is for trees and teeth. It is for enunciation. For adulthood. T is for knowledge. T is success. T is for the T-Zone and perfectly clear skin and the and therefore. T, T, what begins with T? Textual tribulations in technocracy!

One of the curiouser chestnuts in *Irony, Solidarity, and Contingency* is Rorty's contention that "the only important political distinction is . . . that between the use of force and the use of persuasion."[72] Rorty would have us believe that force and persuasion are by nature—and semantic necessity—distinct; that neither term can be defined without the other. Persuasion has meaning precisely because it is *not* force; force has meaning, because of the absence of the attempt to persuade in its exercise. I strike you down because I can't be bothered to persuade you. I strike you down because your life has apparently become such an impediment to mine that I view your flourishing as a form of violence and am more committed to striking you down than I am to your safety; I can't be made to listen to (your) reason.

However, as anyone who has experienced assault knows, force and persuasion are not so easily cleaved asunder; they are, as Rorty's contention also inadvertently suggests, two sides of the same coin—of the same letter. We plead with our attackers and with bystanders, attempting to match choking, kicks, hair-pulling with sympathetic language (or, failing that, alarming screams). We don't do this because we are better people than our attackers. We do this because we seek advantage. Any advantage. We do this because our voices are all we have. Anyway, persuasion may be a prelude to the use of force, a tool associated with enabling force, as when we are convinced to isolate ourselves in someone's company, or when a demagogue speaks to a crowd to incite action. In other instances, someone may respond to language with violence, striking us for wearing a message-bearing T-shirt or holding a sign. I understand that Rorty probably has in mind the last example, wanting to remind us that the violent person responding to the apparently offensive message must, in democratic society, be forbidden from exercising force. And that, for this reason, force may be used to restrain the individual exercising force. In Rorty's understanding of liberal democracy, the police must choose between persuasion and force, decide which is which, because otherwise you can't protect speech—or, for that matter, irony. And irony is a nice thing.

Rorty's confidence in the fundamental decidability of the difference between force and persuasion (and the universal recognizability of this difference, once decided) is odd. One could easily have spent a whole book discussing the practical and semantic complexities of drawing such a distinction, but *Irony, Solidarity, and Contingency* sees this as a done deal. When Lelaina Pierce fails to define irony, she not only fails to be an ironist on Rorty's model but fails to properly venerate persuasion. She cannot enter Rorty's "liberal utopia."[73] Simultaneously, Pierce fails to be a private person, which is to say, a useful person, as *Contingency, Irony, and Solidarity* would understand this category. She does not see herself as participating in a language game. She had not realized that the word *irony* might run the world and therefore didn't gird herself against its dominion. She isn't zesty. She's not quick or free. She's sweaty, hectic, flattened. She's frantic just to be a part of something. She'll say anything you want her to.

As my reading here suggests, *Reality Bites* is most interesting to me in its minor resemblance to a John Cassavetes film: its recessed images of addiction and emotional scapegoating nestled among scenarios familiar from teen drama and romantic comedy. It also reflects well on the uncomfortable intermingling of the private and the public spheres in the early 1990s. "Sometimes I get that not-so-fresh feeling," Vickie Miner, portrayed by Janeane Garofalo, says into a camera held by Pierce in a brief performance of a douche advertisement voiceover elicited during a postgraduation celebration. This hangout takes place not in a backyard, living room, or bar, but rather on the roof of a large office building, probably part of the Houston campus of the University of Texas but nevertheless a location that places the recent graduates in a corporate environment even in their leisure.

This overdetermined setting rhymes with the most effective critique of Rorty's depiction of (neo)liberal democracy in that it shows that Rorty's assumption that the private realm of self-creation may remain apolitical is false.[74] Irony, a tool Pierce and her friends dally with in a space in the air, does not protect them. Irony is an antic substance that, ironically, suffuses their supposedly rebellious, private drunken chatter and vintage clothes with the vicissitudes of commerce, seemingly compelling them to speak and act in ways that are beyond their control, that are entertaining, commodified, and ripe for purchase once they have been filmed by the extremely game Pierce, who, we should note, is working in her downtime. These aren't her friends; they're actors. This isn't reality; it's, in too many senses to name, a moving picture. The viewer is concerned that one or all of these young people may jump from the unfenced side of the roof, pushed, as it were, to self-sacrifice by the incomprehensibility of the capitalist workforce they are entering, by the mystifying "end of history"[75] in 1992, by the many-layered persuasiveness of unreality.

U is for undergraduates and understatement and unguarded. It's a near-perfect yet flawed reflection of its neighbor.

Barbara Johnson, whom I encountered in 1999, was a product of theory's highest heights, and she was also, interestingly, someone who changed with the times. While her first publication was a book-length study in French on nineteenth-century prose poetry and her first English-language work, *The Critical Difference* (1980), a series of essays performing deconstructive readings mostly in French literature, she soon became preoccupied with transferring her powers of perception and "differential reading strategy" to spots treated as exterior to the Western canon, locales she somewhat facetiously, responding to detractors, termed "the 'real world.'"[76]

In her discussion of the poster about eating disorders, Johnson proposed we dig for beliefs undergirding the supposedly altruistic question "How do I know if I'm eating enough?" We were to excavate its ironies, its self-contradicting meanings. But Johnson wasn't interested in these ironies in a vacuum, as a series of patterns that affected the objective interplay of various words. She was interested in the ways in which the contradictions of literal and figurative meaning had entered the world to produce something called a person, which was an entity each of us was meant to be.

A world in which some people are eating enough and others are not was, of course, a foundation of the poster's question, but there were many other tributaries creating its notion of difference: for example, the presupposition that "eating enough" is not and cannot be tied to scarcity of food or physiological restrictions but is rather always an aesthetic choice, that the question is asked in a world without scarcity. A related line of thought: that there might be a "safe" way of eating as little as possible, and that those who are deemed women should band together to find out what that is, so that they may continue to eat as little as possible (safely, of course, and with supervision). Like many critics of a poststructuralist persuasion, Johnson showed how what is apparently open and clear may be attached to something hidden, something already determined by other sanctioned metaphors, and that this hidden aspect of a given statement more powerfully determines its meaning than what sits, glibly and showily, on the surface. The critic works to draw our attention to such underpinnings, Johnson maintained. For these underpinnings are reality. These shadowy, figurative underpinnings *are* the "real world."

What was different about Johnson's critical method was how intimate, how divorced from despair, despite its vertiginous rigor, and how devoted to the present it was. She showed that what we'd believed to be our most private and personal selves were, in fact, composed of linguistic items that we might take to be fixed and objective but were better described as public or historical. We were all engaged in collectively constructing "the subject" in language—we were all participating in this, all the time.

I was so transformed by these ideas that today I can't reconstruct an intellectual self that precedes them. Through Johnson's criticism I came to see how every thing I encountered was composed of my attempt to differentiate it from myself—and thereby control it. I was walking through the world, complicit in the strangest of effacements: of an echoing, shimmering cacophony of multiplying, discontinuous, metamorphic meanings, images, affects, vibrations. I was effacing the interdependent nature of being in language, in favor of a painstakingly policed condition called personhood. What was I going to do about this?

Johnson was alive for the early popularization of the internet and the appearance of the Republican Tea Party, but she missed the advent of smartphones and the rise, after Barack Obama's first presidential win, of the online right (about whose methods she would have had much to say). She passed away in 2009 after an eight-year battle with cerebellar ataxia, a rare neurological condition. Her memorial service, which she apparently planned herself, may be seen on YouTube.[77] Within this two-hour video, there is brief footage of her lecturing. It's a video of a video, a lecture from 1997, given at Yale Law School, titled, "Anthropomorphism in Lyric and Law," a version of an article later published under the same title. In the excerpt we view, Johnson responds to the question "What is a person?" She tells us that her paper is an attempt to describe the rhetorical figure of anthropomorphism ("a rhetorical figure that confers human characteristics upon a non-human entity"), but that there is a "lack of articulation" of the link between anthropomorphism in the law and in the context of literature, specifically the lyric. We're supposed, she says, to listen for this lack. Her speech moves with her thoughts, carefully measuring each word as she says it. She tells us she will explore a Supreme Court decision alongside an essay by Paul de Man that takes poetry as its subject. She is going to explore what a "juridical person" is, according to the highest court of the land, and she going to explore de Man's "outrageous" (her term) claims. The clip ends abruptly. As of late 2023, I have not been able to find additional recordings of Barbara Johnson on the platform or elsewhere online.

"Anthropomorphism in Lyric and Law" may be my favorite of Johnson's essays. It is simultaneously challenging and learned and very plain. The gist: contemporary definitions of who or what is a natural person, entitled to protection by the law, are underwritten by selective attention to a ubiquitous lack of finality where the line between human individuality and something merely metaphorically similar is concerned. To speak a bit more plainly myself: it seems wrong to say that the US Congress has a "'natural' intentionality"[78] and should be treated as a nonmetaphorically anthropomorphic, legally person-like entity, while a prisoners' association must be understood as artificial (i.e., only weakly and metaphorically anthropomorphic), and any similarity between this association and a person, as such, is impossible to recognize in court. Judges, Johnson suggests, may have self-interested reasons for making so flimsy a distinction—such as that they've been seeing lots of cases from prisoners' associations and want to reduce their workload. Still, such bald asymmetries—unfortunately for judges hoping to go on vacation—only make it easier for Johnson to know where to look. Reading legal language together with de Man's remarks on the rhetoric of Baudelaire's lyric poetry, she wants to know: is the lack of a satisfactory definition of who or what a human person is the fault of language (i.e., a structural problem), or is this lack the definition we've been searching for all along? If it is the latter (Johnson leans in this direction), we might need to rethink our laws, along with the social role we accord poetry.

Thus Johnson produces a reading the implications of which are at once philosophical, literary, and meaningfully directed to unequivocally pragmatic political questions unfolding in the present.[79] Johnson shows, contra Rorty, that you do not have to choose between public and private life—because you *can't.* For it is precisely when and where language ceases to make sense (except to a select group), when and where it ceases to be something we can describe as universal, when and where it becomes undecidable and thus a matter of life and death, that it is, simultaneously, a matter for urgent public discussion.[80]

V is for varieties of experience and waves and valleys and vistas. V is for victory and viciousness. It is the taste of snow, it's knives. V is for victim. V is for the vile days in a butterfly's life, veering. V is antennae. It is virulent. It is intuition.

I find a paragraph—typed up, printed out; page folded, taped in— at the back of Blue Notebook. It seems like notes toward a fiction I never completed:

> They meet in L.A. in the late morning while she is still not eating, at the place where they are both staying. They speak and do not disagree, and so he invites her to lunch. She notices his short hair. Later she is late to meet him. But they eat, and he offers to take her away. She assents on condition of several hours. He takes her to a mall. He fails to kiss her. They decide to make peace in Las Vegas. At sunset they drive out in an upgrade to his original rented car. They get nachos from a drive-thru. They put the top down. They see the largest thermometer in the world. They stop to watch the stars from the desert floor, and on the desert floor he cries. He wants to kiss her. I am ugly, he says. He asks her to drive so that he can pray. She accepts, but only until the outskirts of Las Vegas. When they enter the first curtain of light, she pulls over. He drives, she stares. The pyramid

with a lamp at its peak, a ray stuck in heaven, a white high-
way full of birds hunting insects. The pirate ship. The palaces. Venice and Paris, and sirens, and laughter. They find
their hotel, where they fight and put down $35. He begins
weeping, and even though she is tired, they must go to a ca-
sino. She gets quiet, plotting her escape. He despairs. And
later, she lies to him and does a drama for the concierge.
Thinking of a spy she sneaks from their room while he is
sleeping. She does not return. Hard to imagine his anger in
the morning.

W is for world.

That famous diagram I first saw in 1999, Saussure's sign, could
also remind one of a bubble wrapped around a tiny, hermetic
world in which there are no people. It's a glass bead on a string.
A single Edenic tree sprouts there.

The critic Edward Said was present in Baltimore at the Johns
Hopkins conference in 1966, when capital "T" theory arrived.
Said's early and somewhat obscure essay, "Abecedarium Culturae:
Structuralism, Absence, Writing," first published in *TriQuarterly*
in 1971, elaborates a series of misgivings concerning Saussure's
description of language as a model for broader structures of
knowledge, particularly those promoted by Lévi-Strauss. In the
structuralist paradigm, Said maintains,

> Order is a limit beyond which it is impossible to go, in which
> moreover it is impossible to think. Order is the mind's choice
> of syntax over semantics, the choice for the existence of mo-
> mentary, discursive sense over the certainty of rigid and de-
> tached meaning. The structuralists, in short, do not believe
> in the immediacy of anything; they are content to under-
> stand and to contemplate the alphabetical order of sense
> as a mediating function rather than as a direct meaning.

Order, they claim, is just on our human side of nothingness;
it preserves us from the blankness of undressed duration.[81]

According to Said, the problem with this "alphabetical order of sense" is that it is merely another "limit," another veil beyond which, barring the intervention of angels, we cannot see. As Saussure's diagram contends, linguistic difference isn't a singular, material thing like a pencil sitting on a table; rather, it is a contingent, comparative quality. However, as Said notes, relying on difference won't keep us from becoming myopic or even biased. In critical philosophies dependent on difference, "our minds remain rooted in a doctrine of signs, fastened upon the paradox of absence, committed to difference rather than value."[82] Such thought is radical, according to Said, yet nihilistic. It takes us to a fascinating place, then doesn't offer much once we are there. In a jab at Derrida, Said compares him to Fyodor Dostoyevsky, fretting excessively over "debilitating paradoxes."[83]

Said will develop these remarks in *The World, the Text, and the Critic* (1983), where he identifies some postmodern thought as a form of "religious criticism," which is to say, "critical ideas whose essence is some version of theory liberated from the human and the circumstantial."[84] This "basically uncritical religiosity" has its antecedent in the thought of theorist Marshall McLuhan, whom Said singles out as granting a questionable, nearly animist agency to media and inscription, which in turn, paves the way for the success of deconstruction and semiotics in the United States.[85]

Said is wary of religious criticism because it "serves an agent of closure, shutting off human investigation, criticism, and effort in deference to the authority of the more-than-human, the supernatural, the other-worldly." Said supports "a sense of history and human production"; he rejects "what cannot be thought through and explained, except by consensus and appeals to authority." The basic function, according to Said, of religion is "either to compel subservience or to gain adherents."[86] By analogy, religious criticism is not criticism at all. It's evangelism or a species of gnosticism.

Writing on Said, John Guillory takes a mildly ironic position—that literary culture "occupies a realm of social fantasy, which yet testifies to a certain reality."[87] At the end of the day, the poststructuralist critic is a literary writer and participates in collective, imaginative activity. It may be an unreasonable bar to set, to require the critic to be a scientist. After all, the critic deals with unreal things—images, dreams, songs.

Intellectual historian Amy Hungerford, meanwhile, is broader than Said in her concern about deconstruction:

> Derrida, and de Man as well, are informed by religious thinking in a subtle and profound way. . . . In the effort to demonstrate the utter absence of presence in the written word, these writers posit the text as radically autonomous, then return language to an intensified version of presence by personifying the text so conceived. Language in their hands becomes immanent in much the same way that the names of God are imagined to contain God's presence in Hindu and in Jewish tradition and in the way Christ is said, in the Gospel of John, to incarnate the divine Word.[88]

"In the effort to demonstrate the utter absence of presence in the written word, these writers . . . personif[y] the text." But do they personify it or anthropomorphize it? In other words, do they use the written word to make claims about what a person is or to investigate the very possibility of successfully defining this term? What I think Hungerford and Said miss, and that Johnson brilliantly centered in her criticism, is that by experimentally anthropomorphizing, and *not* personifying, the text, one may call into question facile certainties regarding what a person is. And not only what: when and where.

X marks the spot. And dot, dot, dot. X is for xenos, a stranger, and X, too, is for world.

We turn to etymologies for comfort, where language is concerned. They reassure us as to the storied-ness of words—that meaning is shifting and not infrequently determined by handling, by the existence of human speakers. *World* is an old word, its first use preceding the twelfth century, according to Merriam-Webster.[89] It is derived from Old English *woruld*, "human existence, this world, age," and is a portmanteau of two shorter and more concrete Old English words, *wer*, man, and *eald*, old. Whereas in contemporary English we tend to think of "the world" as a spatial extent, in previous usage it was a temporal quantity or quality, defined by the ephemeral existence of humans. The world is man's age, an anthropomorphic span.

Of the fourteen definitions of the noun *world* offered by Merriam-Webster.com in 2023, the first, "the earthly state of human existence," is probably closest in spirit to *woruld*, even as it diverges from this ancestor. Definitions number 8, "human society," and 12, "the whole body of living persons," seem relevant, too. Given that we so frequently use *world* to mean "the place where I live," it is of interest that most present-day definitions do not privilege place or, if place is part of the equation, then place is created by a multitude of persons. *The world* is less a planet or country than society. It is a bundle of shared and contested perceptions and beliefs. It is a conversation, a public, a crowd.

This would suggest that the end of the world, if we hew closely to language itself, is the end of a collective form of time, the end of collaboration. It might also be the end of understanding. The end of the world is less infrastructural devastation, conflagration, and inundation, although it may be and is these things, than the curtailment of knowledge and lifeways. The end of a world, of *the* world, is an end of expectations, certainties, security, comprehensibility, artworks, inheritance, banter. It is an end of things that pertain fundamentally to humans as social, mortal, interdependent beings. (An end of words, too.) In this sense, the world has already ended. It has ended in forced migration and the destruction of cities and the impossibility of agriculture and is ending. It is about to end, is complete, nearly shut, even if, for you, the end remains up ahead, in coming decades, somewhere out there, in a realm of anxious speculation. For you, too, the world is ending.

This is not to propose that anyone relax into the devastations of the contemporary global order. Rather, it is to point out the temporal and social dimensions of recent manifestations of climate apocalypse—as when, just a week and a half ago, New York City's Air Quality Index climbed above 400,[90] the air turned yellow-gray-brown in an ill all-day dusk, and an eerie campfire smell clung to everything. I sat in a room in Manhattan hyperventilating and performing pointless internet searches as the sky got more obscure and olfactory conditions got worse, which is to say: invisible wood on invisible fire, everywhere. The government, meanwhile, said as little as possible, and the paper of record published a raft of air-purifier recommendations.[91]

My son was in daycare, and I was meant to be writing this essay. I was already behind to the tune of several weeks, nearly a month, on a promised revision, and the irony, in the Alanis Morissette sense, of the world seeming to end just as I was meant to be completing a long essay thematizing the end of the world, was only slightly lost on me. I was seated in front of a rectangular window as devastating weather rolled in. To rewrite an earlier sentence: *I* ~~was always standing~~ *am sitting in front of a* ~~very large~~ *rectangular window. It* ~~framed a rural~~ *frames an urban view. I watch*~~ed~~ *the* ~~tornados~~ *smoke rich in particulate matter approach and* ~~felt~~ *feel terror at being a witness to a cataclysm* ~~that would soon bring an end to me, along with everything else that lived on the surface of the planet~~ [I don't know how to end this sentence].

At some point, I forced myself to text people. I texted people

I knew in the city and people on the West Coast. I sent out a few emails. I began to get replies. I'm telling you, this made absolutely no difference to the environmental hell out of doors that was exactly what it appeared to be. But to me, it made a difference.

Y is for yes, and for yet, and for you. Y is for why. You are asking me. Y is a slingshot and a perch. It is a surprising view. It is among the sunniest of letters, a relative of vowels yet its own creature.

I've tried to leave out what happened on that trip from Los Angeles to Las Vegas.

Speaking about myself to a friend, decades later, I say (we are eating lunch on a dais of grass in a park near Chelsea Piers and behind us a photo shoot for what looks like a small athleisure brand goes on; GoPros are involved), "I used to put myself in danger."

My friend seems to understand this. My friend is a philosopher who uses literature to allegorize partly invisible things like emotions and social games. She has powerful vision.

I switch subjects. I'm thinking about this essay, which is in progress at this point. I mention my tenuous acquaintance with Barbara Johnson.

My friend is mildly astonished. "Oh," she says, "you know someone was just trying to get me to write about her?"

It is not clear to me if my friend intends to write about Barbara Johnson, and I don't press her for details. I also don't explain anything further about danger—although later, after we have parted, my friend texts me the phrase "delirium of negation," which I must google to see is a synonym for Cotard's, something I seem to have forgotten, despite all my research. "Oh my Lucy," my friend writes.

Part of what my friend is pointing to is Barbara Johnson's affiliation with the so-called Yale School, Paul de Man, and criticism that supposedly sees language as a site of vertiginous absence (see

Said, Hungerford). The delirium of negation could be a method of critical reading. It might be a way of reading that discovers "nothing" undergirding that which we had originally taken to be great or deep or invaluable meaning. So there's no "there" there, as they say; chicken and egg.[92]

I think my friend is saying, Hey, I'm sorry you got mixed up with complicated critics at such a young age. I think we can both laugh about this a little. As I write elsewhere in this essay, there's something tragically serious about all this, by which I mean, tragically comic.

But I think my friend is also saying, I'm sorry. Depersonalization-derealization disorder is generally understood to be strongly correlated not with post-structuralist theories of language, but with emotional abuse.[93] The disorder appears, as I understand it, when the sufferer attempts to live in broader society using maladaptive emotional strategies acquired at an earlier time, usually to cope with a verbally manipulative or habitually degrading caregiver. The sufferer, no longer a child, has on their hands a self of an exceedingly odd shape, a misshapen self, a little like a fingernail peeling or a translucent scrap one should definitely not attempt to use as a blanket. It takes some time, a certain span, an age or a world, to realize this and—if one is lucky, a luck I wish for everyone—to transform.

"Zed," the British say. Z is for zipper, zebra, and zoo. Z, like X, feels like an outlier, feels rare. Z is green to me. A deep green, at times indistinguishable from black. A letter with wisdom to impart but nothing to spare. A kind of perfection. Zero. A crook. I would say that Z is for the end, but I don't think so, no. Z is a trace and a clue. Z is an echo.

In the end, it is not theory but language itself that is my great philosophical love, a version of myself, a temporary and artificial self I adopted when I lost the self I previously took to be my own.

Perhaps there's nothing more to say, yet I feel ambivalent, because on the one hand, my love of language is what allowed me to survive several decades of mental instability and illness, and, on the other, my love of language seems to have delayed my recognition that I needed help—but perhaps it's wrong to blame language for this. I think it is wrong—or, at the very least, ineffective—to blame language.

This isn't much of a political point, but I want to tell you that part of what makes living in our time bearable for me is that I no longer experience the mental anguish that was my reality throughout my early twenties (and which continued into my thirties). I have my difficulties and my view of things is distorted in its own way, but I would not describe myself as pathologically deluded. Mainly, I do not wake up into a field of disordered, painful ideations that continue until I manage to sleep again.

I sometimes think, if I was able to do this for myself, what else is possible?

Letters miraculously allowed me to keep hold of a self, even as myself became unreal.

On the question of language and the fate of meaning: The funny thing (the irony?) was that in order to carry out my project of description I became dependent on conjunctions, in particular the conjunction *and*.

The more I used it, the better things got, even if only incrementally so.

And is a word that unites gesture and meaning. It's like a particle, a faint flavor, a blink, a comma, close to nothing. There is no depth to *and*, and yet. *And* is everywhere in the world. It may be the only word with undeniable ontology.

Above all: this is not the logic of either/or. Not that logic. This is the logic of or/and, which is actually the logic of *and*. *And* is a rock that wins every round of Rock Paper Scissors. The logic of *and* is the logic of magic, yes, and it is the logic of complexity, the logic of paradox, of impossibility. Is *and* authentic? Is *and* true?

    And is stubborn, short, and stubby. *And* is dear. A human holds this wor(l)d close.

    So, this is the end. The *and*.

    She stayed alive and

The Three-Body Problem

> My usage of the word "generation"
> implies less a chronology than a
> *signifying space*, a both corporeal
> and desiring mental space.
>
> —*Julia Kristeva*[1]

If all memoir can be said to be in some sense literary—and I think it can—then by far the most common, the most widely shared and numerous subgenre of this wide, wide literary genre is seldom written down and even less frequently published. What is this enigmatic, often unwritten yet ubiquitous narrative? It is the birth story, of course. Because every person on Earth knows someone who has one such story, if not more.

For a long time, the only birth story I believed I knew involved hay raked out in a little nest and effigies of donkeys and sheep. I'm joking but I'm also deadly serious: that passage about how they could not find room at the inn (Mary droops in the saddle) becomes far more affecting once one has attempted to exit a car while nine centimeters dilated. "And she brought forth her first-born son, and wrapped him in swaddling clothes, and laid him in a manger; because there was no room for them in the inn."[2] It is only today, as I type this, that the obvious becomes, well, pristinely obvious: Mary labored. Had labored. Was in labor. I have not seen many Christmas pageants, but the few I have witnessed did not involve a youthful Mary in her bright blue sack groaning to cause her chest and forehead to vibrate and thus disperse the overwhelming sensations produced by the oncoming deity.

There is material here for a musical, I just know it. A silent Mary is such a missed opportunity!

Indeed, it might really be helpful, were there such a musical, with clever songs one could memorize and sing (causing one's chest and forehead to vibrate), were one to be in one's own nonfictional labor. It might also be helpful because of the relative absence of usable images of pregnancy and birth in our society, even given recent changes to Facebook and Instagram's policies regarding "graphic" content and birth.[3] I write "usable" because, on the one hand, there are plenty of images of pregnancy and birth, and, on the other, so many are unhelpful.[4] I indicate the 1980s Hollywood suburban caper trope: water breaks, *whoosh*, and a screaming woman chews the air in a station wagon, cursing her husband's genitals all the way to the hospital, where a wailing infant is instantly produced, along with predictably sweaty male overwhelm. (Chevy Chase [or similar unimpeachable blockhead] faints dead away.) Forty years later, a gravid celebrity in a bandage dress picks her way across a red carpet. Her elective cesarean, scheduled years in advance, receives little scrutiny; pictures of her infant, published to social media, accumulate nine digits of likes. Meanwhile, if tomorrow you seek the advice of an American who has never given birth, they may tell you that if someone is in labor you should first become very afraid, then rush them to the emergency room.

When I became pregnant in late March of 2020, Year of Dread,™ I packed my fear away. I felt it. I knew that it was there, but I tried to keep it at bay, a finger's width between us. Now I could say that this fear reminded me of certain nightmares from childhood when I would be compelled to climb a staircase that led nowhere, that led directly up into a ceiling. But then, back then, I did not know how to speak about it. There was the anticipatory fear of the labor to come and there was the stress—of ignoring the fear. For new fear, like a wraith or phoenix, rises from those feelings we do our best to overlook.

I got the basic books. I was diligent. I sought out copies of *Active Birth: The New Approach to Giving Birth Naturally*, by Janet Balaskas;

Childbirth without Fear: The Principles and Practice of Natural Childbirth, by Grantly Dick-Read; *Ina May's Guide to Childbirth* and *Spiritual Midwifery*, by Ina May Gaskin; *The Birth Partner: A Complete Guide to Childbirth for Dads, Doulas, and Other Labor Companions*, by Penny Simkin; as well as *Real Food for Pregnancy: The Science and Wisdom of Optimal Prenatal Nutrition*, by Lily Nichols. Oddly, although maybe not oddly, this writing left me cold. I did not know what the question I was trying to formulate was, but these texts, intended to soften (what was for me) the raw unfamiliarity of pregnancy and labor, along with the enormity of the appearance of offspring, a second body from one's body, could not coax it out. I did have a question. It was always just retreating, a rogue hair basking in my mouth.

During pregnancy I read. It was something I unexpectedly became extremely good at. A hundred pages in a sitting? Not a problem. Two hundred? Give me more, friends. On a Saturday afternoon I'd polish off a contemporary novel. I made progress on works of philosophy, collections of critical essays, lists of esoterica I had been meaning to investigate. I remembered how, several years earlier, someone at an artists' residency had told me that in his opinion the perfect novel to read at this moment in this nation was the very novel he was currently reading. Of this perfect novel, he said: It distracts you from *everything*.

The title of this novel was *The Three-Body Problem*. I had long kept it in mind and thought it was, meanwhile, a very good title and I will tell you why: this title makes you wonder, Why are the three bodies such an enigma? Simple words, fascinating concept. And once you learn that the phrase refers to a problem in astrophysics, that of the instability with respect to pattern of movement (i.e., chaos) of three massive entities orbiting around one another, you are entirely sold. Not to mention, the plot concerns alien encounter and existential threat. All this feels big and important. And there is not just one book; it is a satisfyingly expansive three-part series.

The curious thing about this series of so-called hard science fictions, Liu Cixin's Remembrance of Earth's Past trilogy, is, as I found, its aesthetic and ethical contrasts. The books are simultaneously in possession of sparkling narrative hooks aplenty and some pretty alarming notions about the nature of humanity. After I had read all three novels, I went looking for further biographical information in the way one does: knowing that it's not supposed to matter (it's "fiction," after all) and convinced that only the command of such personal data could crack the project open. What I found impressed me. First, because it turned out that I was researching Liu during a period when it had come to the attention of Western media that his views on the ongoing persecution of the Uighur people were, distressingly, in favor of. Second, because no one, not even those writing about his views on ethnic cleansing, seemed to have pointed out the similar themes around treatment of one's supposed enemies already present in his best-selling trilogy.[5]

I additionally felt some perplexity regarding former President Obama's citation of *The Three-Body Problem*—obvious to anyone with some acquaintance with the history of the twentieth century as a love letter to the ambition on the part of architects of the Cold War to militarize everything—as "one of his favorite books."[6]

What follows is riddled with spoilers, yet I doubt that knowing the fate of humanity in a fictional intergalactic conflict can entirely extinguish the interest inherent in prose dealing with these themes.

In summary: Ye Wenjie, a brilliant and, importantly, *female* physicist, daughter of an academic cruelly murdered during the Cultural Revolution, decides, during her exile at a remote defense research facility named Radar Peak, to broadcast a message into space advertising the habitability of Earth. (Ye is personally and politically isolated. She may be insane with grief.)

Her message is received by a functionary at a similar station on a planet known as Trisolaris. Trisolaris is, tragically for its inhabitants, at the mercy of its three suns, around which the planet orbits erratically, leading to unpredictable ice ages and ages of fire, as well as periods during which its surface is tolerable to sentient, rational life. The Trisolarans, a far more technologically advanced civilization than humanity, have survived their chaotic climate(s) through a singular physiological adaption: like the real Earth-dwelling micro-phylum tardigrades ("slow steppers"), a.k.a. little water bears or moss piglets, Trisolarans can desiccate their bodies at will and become dormant during extreme ages. (Tardigrades have survived mass extinctions caused by astrophysical events and have tolerated temperatures as low as −460°F, as hot as 300°F, pressures greater than those of undersea trenches, hundreds of times more radiation than is instantly lethal to humans, as well as the vacuum of outer space.)[7] Despite their handy anatomy, the Trisolarans are bound to leave their home. The chaotic movements of the three-body solar system must inevitably lead to the death of their planet; Trisolaris will either be shot out into space or consumed by one of the suns. The Trisolarans are, therefore, colonizers. They just haven't found the right planet to colonize.

The functionary who receives Ye's message is unconfused. If Trisolaris's autocratic government discovers its source, everyone on that planet will soon be dead. Even more significant for the functionary, he will be out of a job. The functionary therefore messages back: Whatever you do, don't reply to this message. Ye replies. So begins a process by which the Trisolarans travel toward Earth—a journey of roughly four hundred years—even as they take steps to establish remote contact with humans and sow a kind of phenomenological disinformation that will ensure that during the four centuries to come, humans cannot make scientific and technological progress such that they might present as worthy foes once the aggressors arrive.[8]

One of Liu's great gifts as a storyteller is to devise scenarios that dramatize the fate of individual human intelligence amid difficulties of epic consequence. Although Liu seems neutral-tending-to-negative regarding people in general, he is amused by those who don't know their own strength, and his appreciation for the underdog is what makes his work so likable. Without this grudging admiration, the Earth's Past trilogy would be bleak indeed. Of course, the underdog qualities that entertain Liu and solicit his empathy seem present only in men—and in the trilogy, there are only men and women on Earth, just two genders, eternally differentiated, distinct and opposed, a fact that is of primary consequence to what transpires and functions like an unspoken curse.

I read the novels and quietly noted this curse.

Soon, it started to be that each time I spoke to a person about the books it turned out that that person had been reading them, too. I spoke to a doula about the books, and they reported that everyone at the farm where they were employed part-time was reading them. I spoke to a visual artist over the phone, and he had been reading the first book. "But I had to stop," he told me. "It was too sad."

Fear. There should be a whole manual on fear related to pregnancy and birth. Having typed this sentence, I laugh to myself, for there is! In 1942, British obstetrician Grantly Dick-Read published *Revelation of Childbirth*, subsequently brought forth in the United States as *Childbirth without Fear*, a "worldwide bestseller" from my original autodidact's list. The drolly named Dick-Read stipulated that women experience pain while giving birth because they become frightened and therefore tense. (Essentially, your uterus screws itself shut when you get freaked out—a refined etiology, to be sure.)[9] If, according to Dick-Read, women could simply not become frightened, then they would not become tense while giving birth and would, therefore, deliver painlessly. To do so would be for a given patient "to fulfill her biological purposes," much like "primitive" women who—according to Dick-Read, alas a racist and no feminist at all—allegedly felt no remorse regarding their own hemorrhaging and demise in childbirth because they saw that it was better that they *die* attempting the highest task available to them.[10]

At least one current edition of Dick-Read's classic of so-called natural childbirth has the most remarkable cover image I have ever seen: a white woman with small symmetrical features wearing a soft bra shrieks in agony—or, is it ecstasy?—as the head of an infant emerges, grapefruit-like, from her vulva.[11] The photograph has been taken in such a way that we see the baby but no part of the model's genitals. A man, presumably husband to the birthing person, brings his happy face down to examine his spawn's exit. As I contemplate typing the next sentence, I think: can this really be? For this cover feels like something my brain would invent in a nightmare. And yet it is: the shrieking beauty is an aspirational image. Be this individual pressing a baby out in a yoga top, diamond ring, and hoop earrings, hair scooped into a perfectly disheveled bun. Do not even appear pregnant at the time of your child's birth. Astound everyone. Or, perhaps, be this glad man. Oversee her birth and praise her for her gameness. Claim your neatly born child.

A friend with a two-year-old who saw the image had a different reaction: "*That's* supposed to make you unafraid?" she snorted, returning the book facedown to its shelf.

An infrequently cited statistic: In the contemporary United States, you are about *thirty times* more likely to die from childbirth than you are from an abortion.[12]

If I could go back in time, I would amend my autodidact's bibliography, which I abandoned so quickly in favor of speculative fiction. I would amend it to focus on the history of American birth practices. I would amend it to include such titles as *Reproducing*

Race: An Ethnography of Pregnancy as a Site of Racialization, by Khiara M. Bridges; *Coming Home: How Midwives Changed Birth,* by Wendy Kline; and *Cut It Out: The C-Section Epidemic in America,* by Theresa Morris. I would read these books and reflect: for what was terrifying me in those days, I might have realized, was not—or was not simply—my own body.

One afternoon when I was about a month and a half from my due date I was standing in line to buy lunch from a window. A stranger approached and asked if I was pregnant. She was older. She said, "I know you're not supposed to ask, but here we are." It was fall of 2020 and Covid was making folks friendly.

Yes, I told her. I am.

"You look great!" She smiled, obviously relieved. And proceeded to relate the story of how her husband, an obstetrician, had twice "made" her get cesareans because he "did not trust" her to give birth vaginally.

"But that won't happen to you," she quickly reassured me. "You're going to do well!"

Because I am not married to my partner, who is not an obstetrician, there were various truths hovering, dodging in and out of dreck, but I only thanked her and stepped up to collect my takeout.

"Goodbye, goodbye! Good luck, good luck!" She waved, as if we were passengers aboard a ship that had traveled far, and I was rashly disembarking at the first stop.

Mechanical and surgical interventions into vaginal birth, also known as instrumental birth or operative vaginal delivery, date back as far as ancient Rome for live births (see one bas-relief in which a male figure brandishes a forceps-like implement as a newborn is collected from the floor),[13] with stillbirths extracted

instrumentally in earlier Sanskrit texts.[14] Forceps as we understand them today were invented in the early seventeenth century
by the Chamberlen family, Huguenots who had fled France for
England. The Chamberlens jealously guarded the secret of their
device across generations, growing wealthy in the process. They
arrived at the homes of their clientele bearing an enormous gilt-
encrusted box, which I imagine as a pseudo ark of the covenant.
Lugging this thing indoors, they shut themselves into the birthing chamber, where they further disguised their activities by
means of a blindfold and carefully arranged sheets. Terrified
family members would apparently have heard bells and other
strange noises, as if an enormous clocklike machine had been
set in motion.[15]

The Chamberlens' secret got out near the end of the seventeenth century, and for several hundred years "men-midwives,"
who professionalized under the title *accoucheurs*,[16] made use
of forceps, sometimes greased with lard or covered in leather
to ease entry.[17] In cases in which a child was believed dead or
the life of the birthing person in danger, forceps could be employed to "perforate" (i.e., crush) the infant's skull[18] and a sharp
hook known as a crochet, sometimes attached to one handle of
the forceps, used to dismember the body.[19] Episiotomy, or "surgical enlargement of the birth canal . . . performed with a pair
of scissors or scalpel," was thought unnecessary except in extraordinary circumstances.[20] Episiotomy was not, as today, a
handmaiden of instrumental extraction, a process now more
frequently undertaken with a vacuum, or *ventouse*.[21] Cesarean
section, meanwhile, was not performed on the living with any
frequency until the late nineteenth century, given the likelihood
of executing the patient.[22]

Contemporary American obstetrics—which we might nick-
name the Episiotomy-to-Cesarean Era—seems to officially begin in
1920, with the publication of Joseph Bolivar DeLee's article "The
Prophylactic Forceps Operation," in both the *American Journal*

of Obstetrics and Gynecology and *Transactions of the American Gynecological Society.*[23] This was a transcription of an impassioned and controversial speech DeLee delivered to the American Gynecological Society in Chicago the same year. DeLee had developed a technique for managing birth from onset of labor through delivery by chemical and surgical means, such that the birthing person was incapacitated throughout the process and underwent a major incision. Labor was met with sedatives and, once the fetus began to descend, diethyl ether (a.k.a. sweet oil of vitriol), a highly flammable organic compound, was administered. The patient was meant to be unconscious when the time came for the removal of the baby, for DeLee recommended aggressive episiotomy. A deep, diagonal cut was made through the skin and muscles of the perineum. Into this intimate wound, a gaping combination of bloody severed tissue and vaginal canal, metal forceps were inserted to seize the baby's head and drag the neonate forth. Removal of the placenta was obstetrically managed, as well. The surgeon reached his left hand into the vagina while pressing on the stomach and pulled. Next, ergot, the fungus now famous as a psychedelic, was administered to cause the uterus to clamp down, preventing possibly fatal bleeding due to manual extraction of the placenta, an organ a conscious birthing person is perfectly capable of expelling on their own. The parent was sewn up and, after several hours (DeLee recommended that additional sedatives be administered post procedure), regained consciousness, perhaps to be permitted to see their child, who would of course need time to recover from the heavy sedation conveyed into its small body during the operation.[24]

DeLee reasoned that it was better to be proactive. Better to make an aperture yourself than to permit tears to occur in the vaginal canal and labia in unpredictable ways. Better to excavate the infant than risk brain damage ("epilepsy, idiocy, imbecility, cerebral palsies")[25] from the excessive force of contractions, long labors, or poor positioning. Better to be in charge of the pesky placenta. Birth was "so pathogenic";[26] DeLee compared it, vividly, to being impaled by a pitchfork. Risk was ineluctably present. Only a man of science could meet this risk. DeLee claimed that his procedure prevented prolapse, that it restored "virginal conditions,"[27] once the patient healed, and—most remarkably—that no long-term damage could result from his surgery.[28] No one, he proudly announced, had ever died from the prophylactic forceps operation. At the same time, he admitted he had no empirical proof for his assertions. "Experience alone can decide whether it accomplishes its purpose," he said.[29]

There were dissenters at the time of the speech. I mention this in part because the horrors are bad horrors, and it is encouraging to know that as they were being successfully institutionalized some people did stand up and say, "Hey, this is insane." Two obstetricians, John Whitridge Williams and Thomas Watts Eden, expressed doubts, with Williams asserting that it was safer for women to work with a midwife. Eden, meanwhile, was concerned, correctly, that the operation would do nothing to prevent prolapse.[30]

In his commandeering of the birth process, DeLee was addressing a field that, since the late 1800s, had staged a takeover of white, middle-class birth in the United States and was now expanding its purview. In the first and second decades of the twentieth century, births in the Northeast attended by midwives dropped significantly, without improvements in outcome for parent or child. In Washington, DC, for example, as scholar Barbara Katz Rothman writes, "the percentage of births reported to be attended by midwifes shrank from 50% in 1903 to 15% in 1912," even as "infant mortality in the first day, first week, and first month of life all increased."[31] Midwifery was entirely banned in Boston by the 1910s; it dwindled in New York City. Black lay midwifery or granny midwifery, a profession that had functioned through spiritual calling and long apprenticeship, faced regulation via the Sheppard-Towner Maternity and Infancy Protection

Act of 1921,[32] surveillance, and racist disinformation campaigns that reduced the number of deliveries attended by granny mid-wives from thousands in the first decades of the twentieth century to a handful in the twenty-first century.[33] DeLee and his colleagues had scads of patients on their hands and were only going to see more. They had triumphed in an ideological and economic war between the obstetrician and the wise woman that had been rag-ing since the Enlightenment and now had to avoid becoming vic-tims of their own ambition. Obstetricians had to show that they really could deliver babies more safely and with less ado than midwives could—since for several centuries they had been mak-ing claims to this effect. By 1930 in the United States, childbirth was widely viewed as pathological.[34]

Here an important note for the informed reader who raises a questioning hand: historians of birth believe that it is not obstetrical intervention itself that has reduced maternal mor-tality since the nineteenth century but rather family plan-ning and birth control (see feminism's first wave, 1880–1920, and pursuant declining birthrates), antiseptic methods, anti-hemorrhagics, availability of blood transfusions, and cesareans in true emergencies—all interventions that *postdate* the appear-ance of the man-midwife or accoucheur, that trend of the eigh-teenth century, but which coincide with improved outcomes in birth.[35] Meanwhile, in the decades that followed DeLee's speech—and in the present—aspects of his prophylactic forceps operation have been emphasized, while other aspects deemphasized, al-though the ghost of this procedure has yet to fall away from the profession of obstetrics.

Then there is the question of pain. For pain isn't, or so we are told, modern. Upper-class women had demanded pain man-agement during labor and birth since the middle of the nine-teenth century, when Emma Darwin, wife of Charles, and Queen Victoria received chloroform.[36] The requests of the well-to-do were met with various affordances, the most faddish and briefly successful among which was "twilight sleep," a translation of *Dämmerschlaf*.[37] The twilight sleep anesthetic cocktail of scopolamine and morphine was imported to New York from German clinics, where the combination had been painstakingly administered to mostly wealthy people beginning in 1902, resulting in amnesiac and supposedly painless delivery. Twilight sleep patients were sometimes restrained, blindfolded, and had their ears plugged; they labored in the dark, surrounded by attendants who wore garments specially designed to minimize sound. Tragically, the implementation of the procedure beginning in 1914 in the United States was shoddily managed with sometimes horrific results, and the term was largely abandoned after 1916, although scopolamine remained in use through the 1960s.[38]

Nevertheless, twilight sleep popularized the notion that unconsciousness or semiconsciousness during labor was medically feasible and appropriate, something DeLee's method also exploits; it, like the prophylactic forceps operation, further normalized hospital birth.[39]

Sedation during labor continued to be a regular practice through the 1950s and '60s,[40] along with the use of restraints and episiotomy—a procedure whose effects were not studied until the mid-1970s, more than fifty years after DeLee's influential recommendation.[41] The appearance of Fernand Lamaze's Soviet-influenced method in the 1950s in France offered some autonomy for parents but did not exactly mean liberation from medicalization. Imported into the United States and popularized as a breathing technique to aid in drug-free delivery, it became a way to manage the hospital situation, site of knives and restraints, with a male partner serving as supervisor and women told to "politely" request that they be allowed to have their hands unbound during labor.[42] Lamaze, Virginia Apgar's ground-breaking research into fetal drug effects, and the so-called natural birth movement notwithstanding, when Nancy Stoller Shaw observed hospital births in the 1970s she wrote, "These patients are totally alienated from their birth experience. They are treated like lumps of flesh from which a baby is pulled."[43] Until 2006, when the American College of Obstetricians and Gynecologists made a recommendation against its routine use,[44] the most common obstetric surgery performed in America was episiotomy. Today this form of surgery has been overtaken by cesarean.

Doubtless many factors have contributed to the excessive medicalization of childbirth in the United States. The motive of profit cannot, of course, be ignored. Labors and deliveries are shortened and often converted into "emergency" cesareans in the course of the use of Pitocin, a synthetic form of estrogen that intensifies contractions.[45] C-sections, in turn, "are associated with a higher risk of injury and death to women and babies than vaginal birth."[46] Despite this widely recognized medical fact, a person scheduling an elective cesarean is unlikely to view themself as endangering their own life or that of anyone else.[47] The rise of fetal personhood, changes to tort law since the 1980s and 1990s, and an institutionalized fear of malpractice liability have meant that pregnant people are encouraged to see themselves as incompetent to vaginally manage the exit of the "person" stuck inside them, even as medical professionals continue to privilege chemical and surgical interventions as miracles of safety.[48] Consent in a hospital is, meanwhile, a murky thing.[49]

In a 2019 book on nationalism and birth, *Homeland Maternity: US Security Culture and the New Reproductive Regime*, Natalie Fixmer-Oraiz draws unsettling and convincing connections between illiberal notions regarding risk, national identity, and security—and institutional control of individual Americans' reproductive power. The drugged children cut out of white women's bodies in the 1920s were citizens born under the sign of a sanitized but nevertheless storied patriarchal knife. As Fixmer-Oraiz writes, "The use of reproductive and sexual violence as weapons of racial domination characterizes a broad pattern of reproductive injustice in the United States."[50] Citing accounts of grisly

rape and dismemberment of Native women by war-making settlers, along with later genocidal policies toward Native, Black,
and immigrant communities, including forced sterilization programs and deportation of pregnant women, Fixmer-Oraiz argues that the use of violence to control birth is foundational to
American society. Today, the maternal mortality rate is far higher
for people of color, who are simultaneously more likely to be subject to draconian punishments around fetal personhood, with
this latter trend only showing signs of becoming more prevalent
with the Supreme Court's decision in *Dobbs v. Jackson's Women's
Health Organization* in June 2022.[51]

For some it may be overwhelming to contemplate these re-
alities of birth in our time—perhaps a reason for the promotion
of cuteness and the ongoing commercialization of the entire
endeavor, the advent of the ickily named "push present." It is
disheartening to me how little I knew about the history of how
all of us got here until I began bringing someone here myself.
Indeed, the only fact I have ever learned from my mother regarding my own birth was that she was mildly surprised to have
been "shaved" at Mount Sinai Hospital in January of 1980.[52] I have
always puzzled over this detail. Until recently I believed it had
something to do with pubic hair being considered unsanitary,
and I assumed this might happen to me, as well, should I give
birth, although I was planning never, ever to give birth. *It's just
part of a medical thing I can't really understand because I am not a
doctor,* I told myself, hearing the story. I now understand that my
mother's perineum was shaved because it would have been standard procedure to cut it open, extract me with tools if necessary,
then stitch it up again. I do not know if this occurred. I do know
that my mother, whether subject to an episiotomy, and instrumental birth, or not, was, when she entered the hospital, ignorant of the prevalence of these procedures.

─┼─

There is a prenatal imaginary. Things move into it.

For what had previously seemed unimaginable becomes merely actual. If you live through the prenatal into the postnatal, you live through a violation of the bounds of rational thought. You double, triple, quadruple, and so on. You become part of the impossible. You join up with it. As Rachel Cusk has a character say in her novel *Kudos*, one of the "fun reads" I selected for myself for the oncoming hours and months and years of breast-feeding, and I paraphrase: Even during a "normal" birth, you basically experience your own death, and then what is there to do afterward but talk about it?[53]

But that is only later, long after, months gone by, years. This is when you figure out how to start talking—when you keep figuring out, over and over, how to start talking. To say anything at all. Here I am, then, in the endless after, talking to you. If you are like me, me as I used to be, a person who had not had a child, who thought that probably they would not have children, that it wasn't for them, perhaps you wonder: Did I? Did she basically die or experience her own death?

Because I have lived these things, lived through them, under them, with them, inside them, I answer *yes*. But that's not precise. English betrays me. Yes, but I experienced only *the proximity* of death, death in its strange, plain availability. It was like drawing near an unknown planet.

Gender is a major problem with respect to planetary survival. As Liu would have it, a woman turns out to be the proximate cause of the destruction of Earth and humanity. In Liu's narrative, the fate of all extant life in the universe containing our solar system, as well as all other universes, is in a state of cold war. It is a dark forest; kill or be killed.

Eternal deterrence is ultimately impossible—or becomes impossible—because of humanity's innate distaste for war, a distaste most strongly experienced and perhaps embodied, in Liu's account, by the female element of the species. In order that humanity live, it, or at the least its elite leaders, must be willing to destroy. When a supposedly feminized society comes about in a time of peace, humanity elects a woman to serve as its chief agent of deterrence. As an anonymous "young mother" in a crowd beholding Cheng Xin, the female soon-to-be planetary defender (a.k.a. "Wallfacer") exclaims, somewhat woodenly, "'Oh, beautiful, kind Madonna, protect this world! Do not let those bloodthirsty and savage men destroy all the beauty here.'"[54] Not long after, Cheng will fail, causing the destruction of "all the beauty" through her softheartedness.

Liu's own position on matters of gender, sex, and their possible linked characteristics is ambiguous. Still, it is difficult not to read his decision to cast a woman as the last, failed hope of humanity as an indictment of a kind. While there is a conciliatory and fatalist interpretation near to hand—namely, that any attempt to deter ultimate destruction must eventually fail, given the infinite possibilities for alien technological progress—this interpretation falters in the face of the fact that humanity *could always have been* preserved for just a moment longer, for in such a moment lies an infinity of possible worlds. In truth, I don't think Liu means to suggest that the destruction of Earth is, in the fictional futures he has created, inevitable or even morally acceptable.

In this account, only aggression and refusal of empathy can provide us that moment longer. Only the hero's wiles. Or, as the extraterrestrial underling who crushes Earth and its surrounds thinks to himself as he perfunctorily executes this task, "When survival was threatened, all low-entropy entities could only pick the lesser of two evils."[55]

Of course, we can read Liu's speculative narrative as an exploration not just of an imaginary future but of the origins of misogyny. That the tendency to love, care, value life must, in some views, lead to loss—must be a kind of denial of biological and physical reality. *If one is not willing to use any means possible to survive* . . . Here "woman" would seem to be the one to admit this refusal. "She" is the one who, through "her" caring, paradoxically ensures humanity's ultimate nonviability, although we must bear in mind that without "her" (or someone's, anyone's) caring, human life would not have been possible in the first place, given that humans are born, as we all know, previous to full maturation. No newborn can survive on its own and requires months of feeding, holding, warmth. As someone said to me, "Without the mother, there is no baby." Important to note that I read this statement as in some sense metaphorical, for there can be various kinds of mothers—mothers who are multifariously "female," multifariously "human."

In *The Three-Body Problem*, meanwhile, woman/mother is the one who opens us/humanity to the vagaries of space and all that is foreign within it. She, distinct in her biological and philosophical perversity, is the one who does not defend us.

But I didn't come here to complain about people not liking *women*, that limiting term—which is to say (what amounts to the same thing), not liking themselves. Not liking birthing people. Not liking birth. Babies. Children. Adults. Bodies. Thresholds. Asymmetrical holes. Anatomy that hides itself. The vulva with its brown-red-purple-black folds. Blood. Shit. Slime. The sweaty work associated with all the above. The endurance. Straining. Bearing up under what cannot be borne. Vomiting. Weeping. Begging to be allowed to sleep. Rolling on the floor. Knowing, even as I might wonder if I exist at all, that I exist. For I do. I. Do. This.

Ughhhhhhhhhhng. Vibrating with the voiding body. Getting through it. Breathing.

I came here, to this page, to talk about a vast and, I would now say, holy nothingness.

-:-

On May 29, 2020, I wrote in my journal:

Ultrasound yesterday. It is painless and the baby swims and dives inside me, rolls, touches its face, does headstand. The baby is larger than makes sense for the current due date; they move me from 11 weeks, six days, to 12 weeks, six days,[56] meaning that in either case, as of today, I am out of the miscarriage zone. At this stage of development, it is apparently the case that the baby's size does not vary with respect to the size of parents, etc., and so there really is a definite indication that I was pregnant sooner than I believed. Exhausting conversation afterward with _____, a Certified Nurse Midwife, which Peter joins. I am warned to thin my blood with aspirin and that labor may need to be induced because of issues with the placenta in older mothers. I intimate that I am not about to be induced. I try to hold on to the first piece of information: "The ultrasound looks really good." And it did: even the technician could not resist exclaiming at the fetus, so fully and finely formed (its fingers and toes visible), "Look at those hands!" Its face in profile and then its repeated decision to "look" right at us. I am told that the scientific opinion is that the fetus cannot see the light of the ultrasound probe, but the technician does not seem so sure. I receive a massive book. The nurse tells me not to look at the images at the end. There are also many intake questionnaires, the detailed queries indicating an epidemic of poverty, opioid addiction, and domestic violence. There are several questions about whether I have access to food.

I can barely speak during the drive home. Feel obsessed with work and questions around writing, unable to think about the fetus, who was simply there—luxuriating, dancing in its fluid, flexing. Feeling as of having ventured onto an alternate planet, in the ultrasound room—which now drifts away from me. Will I return there? What is that place, with its small alien ruler?

It is embarrassing to me to read this writing now. In the dark room, cool since air-conditioned, I could not believe—I want, for some reason, to write, "I could not swallow"—this dancing, swimming entity. He posed. He stood on his head. He seemed to turn to look right at us. "Are they attracted to the light?" I asked, as if we were gazing upon a cave-dwelling fish or aquatic insect (or a tardigrade). It felt as if the question should be posed as for a nonhuman species, *Ooh, look at that thing there!* But perhaps more is known about nonhuman species that move about in the world than is known about this intrauterine, anthropomorphic, proto-human arrangement of cells, the metamorphosing matter that may one day become a person and whose putative personhood (I felt this so viscerally yet inarticulately, even then) the state has seized on as a site of advantage.

"The word is, no," the technician said, in response to my question about light. Then: "That's the official word." It was not clear if she agreed.

"In your experience?"

"Oh, I don't know," she replied, cheerfully cultivating inscrutability. "In my experience it's very mysterious what they do."

Allow me to amend my bibliography further. I would like to add two essays: "Fetal Images: The Power of Visual Culture in the Politics of Reproduction," by Rosalind Pollack Petchesky, and "Exterminating Fetuses: Abortion, Disarmament, and the Sexo-Semiotics of Extraterrestrialism," by Zoë Sofia.

For it occurs to me now that the problem is not with the classification of fetal becoming, but rather with the category of *person* itself. For everyone knows that we must protect *persons*. The ultrasound technician, a friendly young woman, instructed me: the baby was there, somewhere, alone, intelligent, free, possessed of inalienable qualities. He amused himself in *his* space. He was possessed of a personality and gregariously shared it. One day he would vote and own money, soon enough that we might as well conclude that he already did. A wand entered my vagina, but the image extracted seemed to come from some-where outside my body and perhaps somewhere beyond space it-self, even if (impossibly) what it showed was within. In any case, *I* wasn't in that picture.

What is that place? I ask in a journal entry.

That place—I answer, looking back, frank, unamused—is your uterus, Lucy. You were looking at the interior of your uterus by means of a technology first used to detect submarines in the time of the First World War and which today has commercial applica-tions in motion detectors and nondestructive product testing, as well as "nonlethal" sonic weapons used by police against protest-ers and migrants.[57]

In the ultrasonic image, I saw what Petchesky identifies as "abstract individualism."[58] This magic picture at once effaces the pregnant person and, significantly, "the fetus's dependence."[59] Like an astronaut floating in the vacuum of space, the fetus re-vealed by ultrasound is a technologically generated subject: it is free of the bounds of Earth and of mother; it has independent will, wishes, life, goals, preferences, interests, and, possibly, hobbies. It is not fundamentally characterized by need. It is, in a sense, a "lone survivor," as Petchesky writes.[60] Shipwrecked even before life, it must be rescued from an alleged void. Ponder the implications of such an inhospitable and empty scene of gestation—for we can surely put no trust in the radiation-rich desert of outer space. Amazing to find death lurking within the womb! The hostile-space metaphor is far-reaching; as Sofia has it, "The pro-life fetus may be a 'special effect' of a cultural dream-work which displaces attention from the tools of extermination and onto the fetal signifier of extinction itself."[61] Here is what I think Sofia means by this fascinating and disturbing sentence: The "extraterrestrial" quality of ultrasound images contributes to a reading of intrauterine containment as presaging human colonization of space after the death of Earth. We shouldn't worry about the development of weapons of mass destruction, because, according to this "dreamwork," we can just move on to another planet.[62] At the same time, we find ourselves obsessed with the fetus's perceived isolation.

But my fetus was not alone. My fetus wasn't alone in outer space and didn't need to be defended, any more than my liver needed to be defended, as far as I knew, on that particular day. But the image made me feel otherwise. This feeling went beyond questions related to anyone's health.

After this first ultrasound at the university hospital, I was told that the images looked "really good" by a member of the midwifery team there. (We could not be assigned a single midwife but would need to work with the entire team.) This midwife told us, "It doesn't get any better than this," regarding what could be assessed. She also warned me, as you read above, that "the recommendation" for my delivery "would be" that I be induced at thirty-nine weeks.

This was phrased in a strange way, because the midwife did not say that *she* would recommend or, *in fact*, recommended that I be induced at thirty-nine weeks. Rather, someone else recommended it. Somebody. Although the recommendation was not yet in full effect—it was merely being mentioned, teased—it seemed likely that in the future it might metamorphose from recommendation into requirement. When I tried to pin the midwife down on this modal matter, she seemed to float away. Her body remained in the room, but she became extremely distant. It was unnerving, as if I were breaking a well-known law. Clods of blame began to stick to my body, even as the cocreator of the fetus inside me sat next to me, his hand in my hand, his ears open to these ambiguous statements and, meanwhile, his body apparently innocent and upright: legally preserved from harm.

The next day I called a friend who had a one-year-old. I told my friend about what I had been told at the hospital. Yeah, said the friend, that's the thing, you think: great, hospital, it's the best, they'll keep me safe, they've got all the technology and the research and the experts, but you haven't factored in obstetric violence, that they'll do whatever is easiest for them for getting that baby out of you, your consent and body be damned. You think, great, they have midwives, it's cool and progressive, but I'm telling you right now, it is not at all cool and progressive and I'm being very vulnerable right now because plenty of people would say I'm a death-dealing wacko[63] for telling you this in no uncertain terms: do not have your baby there. Have a homebirth.

Each experience associated with pregnancy was one thing and then it was another, its near opposite. Each thing was terrifying, and it was new and brilliant, and anything could happen, as I imagined, anything at all.

This is why I have to narrate certain events in this essay once and then again, and perhaps a third time.

It seems there is always an extra body. Was always and ever. A pregnant person doubles and doubles. Chimeras swarm.

You
Non-Urgent Medical Question

Hi _____,

I hope you are doing well today.

I was writing because I have been continuing to think about my birth and labor and wanted to get more details about the birthing process at _____. I have some questions about how longer labors may be handled and what the team's general philosophy is regarding any interventions that are not merely physical or involving heat, water, etc.

If my pregnancy goes longer than 40 weeks, for example, would I be able to have access to the Birthing Pavilion and a midwife; also, what are the requirements for admission during labor (must I be dilated to a certain measurement, etc.)? What are the circumstances that might cause me to be denied a non-medical birth, and to what extent are midwives able to use their discretion to determine what might constitute a truly dangerous condition as opposed to a variation still within normal bounds?

I am interested in avoiding an epidural as well as episiotomy and the use of forceps or suction. (These fall into the same category as induction for me, procedures I would not consent to.) I also want to avoid being made to lie on my back, being strapped down or sedated (totally unacceptable), or having a bright light shined on me while I am laboring.

Do midwives at _____ generally remain present for all or most of a given birth? Is there any possibility of consultation about a plan leading up to the due date? And, lastly, is it possible to tour the facilities beforehand?

Apologies for the number of questions here! I did want to put this in writing so as to leave a "paper" trail that can be referred back to.

Warm wishes,
Lucy

_____, CNM
your note

Hi Lucy,
I saw the message you sent today, that the our [sic] nurse intercepted and wrote back to you about. These are things we do talk about with women/couples as the pregnancy

progresses. I'll give you a little bit of information now—as
our nurse said, these are things better talked about than
written about so I'll only say a bit now and you can talk
further at an upcoming prenatal visit.

—Yes you would definitely have access to the Birthing
Pavilion and midwifery care if you go longer than 40 weeks.
—We generally recommend women stay home for their
early labor and be admitted to the hospital in what we
call "active labor" which is usually but not always around
4 cms. Every woman is evaluated individually though, in
terms of what she needs and when she needs to be in the
hospital so this is not at all a rule.
—Your second question cannot be answered in a simple
sentence. There are many things that are variations of
normal and sometimes these required [sic] physician
involvement. We work with closely [sic] with the doctors
in our department, and consult as needed, and because
we've been part of the department for so long, they trust
our judgment. In labor, if a physician is needed we stay
involved in the woman's care. There are some conditions
in pregnancy for which we will generally transfer women
to the doctors—twins for example or high blood pressure
requiring medication.
—Unless there is a reason otherwise, women are able to be
in any position they prefer. The practices of lying on one's
back, being sedated or strapped down are outdated for
good reasons, not done by us and I don't think by anyone
anymore. A bright light is generally only used after the
birth to do any stitches that are needed.
—The midwives are present for as much of the labor as
possible given that they may also be taking care of other
women in labor. I'm not sure what you mean by consultation about a plan—it can be talked about. Right now tours

are not possible because of covid 19. Hopefully that will change.

Again—these are quick answers to questions that require much more conversation at a visit but I hope it's helpful.

RE: your note

Hi ⸻,

Thank you so much for taking the time to reply to my message which I know was quite long. I worry it was a bit overwhelming, as well! I'm very grateful for all the additional information you provide.

I am planning to make a decision about how I would like to envision (and plan, to the extent that I can!) my son's birth in the coming month or so. My foremost concern is to find a way to feel as relaxed and as positive as I can about the experience, which I hope will be joyful. When I say "plan," I think I mean that I want to decide where I would imagine having the birth, as well as who might be present, and so I am hoping to have more information about how things work at ⸻. If it's not possible to see a birthing room in person, are there any pictures?

Of course, I know you have much to do and you have already been extremely generous with your time! If it's easier to speak by phone, I will be happy to call the office and make an appointment with you or someone else. A final question (and apologies again!): does ⸻ publish birth statistics with information on rates of various interventions, including episiotomies and c-sections?

Hope you are well today & warm wishes,
Lucy

_____, CNM
RE: your note

Hi Lucy,

I appreciate your thoughts and concerns. From what you write, it sounds like you may be considering other options for where to have your baby, and it is definitely important for you to be in a place where you can feel positive and relaxed.

In terms of continuing this conversation and giving you the information you need, I think it would be best for you to have a conversation with one of the other midwives who are more directly involved with labor and birth here than I am (I attended births for 20 years here, but am now just working in the office). You have an appointment with _____ in July and could talk with her at that visit, but if you'd like to schedule something sooner, let me know and I'll have a scheduler contact you and set something up.

Also there are some videos about the Birthing Pavilion—
https://www._____.html

And about the midwifery service (midway down the page)—
https://www._____/obgyn.html

Hopefully these will get you to the right webpage.

Let me know what you'd like to do.
Best, _____

RE: Appointment

Thank you for your message.

For now, I will be working with a homebirth midwife for my care and birth and will not require further care at _____.
If anything changes in the pregnancy etc. I will get back in touch.

Warm wishes,
Lucy

-:-

The drug used to induce labor and intensify contractions is a synthetic form of oxytocin, the so-called love hormone. It is sold under the brand name Pitocin, among others. Oxytocin was identified in 1906 as playing a fundamental role in labor; its name, derived from Greek, means "rapid birth."[64] Pitocin, whose name is, meanwhile, a portmanteau of *peptide* and *oxytocin*, can, administered via IV, save some birthing people from cesarean section, but it, like so many common interventions into physiological birth, is likely overused in the United States—the most dangerous industrialized nation in which to give birth[65]—and has been linked to increased risk of uterine rupture, particularly in vaginal birth after cesarean (VBAC), elevated bilirubin in neonates, postpartum hemorrhage, as well as postpartum anxiety and depression.[66]

The contractions produced by Pitocin are stronger and sometimes more painful than unmedicated contractions, particularly if the birthing person is not already partly dilated before receiving Pitocin. Induction is a gamble: the pain experienced during induced labor is said to be more intense, increasing the likelihood that a birthing person will request an epidural, which simultaneously increases the likelihood of other interventions and unwanted outcomes. Induced labor can also be riskier for the fetus, given the force of Pitocin-powered contractions. Induction is, therefore, linked to increased risk of cesarean section.[67] Cesarean section is major surgery. Major surgery is major surgery.

The obstetrician Marsden Wagner, writing in 2006, describes the American, although not exclusively American, desire to "override normal uterine function."[68] Wagner diagnoses this desire as partly irrational in nature, a symptom of fear of the uncanny birthing body. Yet Wagner also sees the wish for institutional control of birth and bodies as pragmatic and venal: "Vaginal birth takes twelve hours on average and happens whenever—twenty-four hours a day, seven days a week. C-section takes twenty minutes, and most of the time it can be conveniently scheduled."[69] Interventions nudge birthing people toward cesarean, a site of management of risk through surgical expertise, as well as increased medical costs and damage to the birthing body. A commonly cited statistic: In 2021, the rate of cesarean section in the United States was 32.1 percent.[70] The WHO recommends a maximum rate of 15 percent, with 10 percent the threshold beyond which outcomes do not improve (from 10 to 15 percent there is a plateauing of improved outcomes; after 15 percent, negative effects appear). A less frequently cited statistic: in 1963, the cesarean rate in the United States was 5.1 percent, although presumably other interventions were rife.[71] In 1985, in an article in the *New England Journal of Medicine*, authors G. Feldman and J. Freiman suggested that anyone giving birth should be required to sign a "consent form" if they wished to attempt a vaginal birth. Recalling Joseph Bolivar DeLee's writing of sixty-five years earlier, this piece was titled "Prophylactic Cesarean Section at Term?"[72]

What does research on friends' advice say? What does research say about what we can know about strings of events? I think now of Elena Ferrante's character Lila, who chastises neophyte novelist Lenù for her tendency to favor surface impressions, saying something like, Ugly things don't come out of nowhere, you immature cheeseball. Everything that happens has already been taking place for a long time.[73]

Yet, it can be difficult to draw the necessary distinctions. I am afraid and therefore I believe anything can take place. My fear encourages me. To be afraid is to believe that something is going to happen, and, in this case, "is going to" may mean "is predetermined to happen without my knowledge of this pre-determination." That something could happen—that what happens could be sudden—that I would not have known that the conditions for this something had been in effect for some time: this is what I fear.

Grantly Dick-Read doesn't want me to worry. Bodies have been giving birth since time immemorial! But he neglects the cost of malpractice insurance, the prevalence of so-called defensive medicine, the tyranny of the fetal heart monitor.[74] The penetration of the spinal epidural space. The insistence that this baby must be born NOW. He does not tell the story of the contemporary war against risk, nor the tale of the appearance of the ac-coucheur and the dollar signs, as we would put it today, in that person's eyes. He will only sell his ideas to me as lifestyle, not as history. There is a reason why his book remains in print.

In the Earth's Past trilogy, we learn that the dimensionality of matter itself has been, already, even before humans could fully conceive of this, weaponized.[75] War was, it turns out, always ubiquitous, always inevitable, even when we believed we lived in peace; war is, alas, of a part with the nature of reality itself—which is to say, expressly built into reality by our enemies, whom it is too late for us now to equal in their advanced technological construction of reality and hyperbolic fear or, in turn, destroy.

A diary entry:

> I am less than two weeks from the due date. "My" due date. The baby feels fine. I feel fine. It is hard to believe that this state will change—that there will be a transformation. What

is pregnancy like? I feel compelled to make some record of this time, as if I have done too little so far. But it isn't *like* anything, except in so far as it has made me psychologically more stable and rounder and to some extent more inclined to sleep. My eating patterns have not really changed. The swimmer wriggles inside me. He addresses me with his feet, with his small hands, with his right elbow, which sometimes comes into contact with my left hip. At night, I sometimes feel his head sinking within my pelvis. I imagine someone swimming when this happens. The swimmer casually deploys themselves into some tunnel or other aperture.

What no one told me about labor is that it is psychedelic. It is porous, vaporous. It is a cave. It is a deep, thick cloud; a mouth. My memory of being in labor during the birth of my son includes such thoughts as: *This is not really labor, this is not really happening, this is not happening to me, I am not going to give birth, I am not pregnant, I am not who I think I am, I am pretending to exist, I have never existed, knot, not, a line.* I'd think: *my pregnancy is something that I have mistakenly believed to be real and, therefore, being unreal, it cannot possibly result in birth. Too bad,* I'd think, *that I'm a fraud. Too bad everyone is going to be so disappointed. Too bad not and amn't. Ugh*—I'd collide with another contraction.

I was in despair for most of the three days it took but believed myself rational. I sat inside the rumbling void. Forgot about the world. Did not know the world. Did not read the news and hardly spoke and lay in bed or draped over the toilet. I did not know the world and had never known it, as I learned. I threw up everything, including water. This was my world. Vomiting and vomit. A dim fog. Around hour forty-five I remember thinking the following words (by then no longer a sentiment, rather something more objective), *It has been so long since I felt joy.*

And yet not a day passes that I do not long to go back there. It was the most informative three days of my life.

The feminist psychoanalyst Julia Kristeva has written about a kind of time related to the space-time of pregnancy and birth. She calls this space-time "women's time" in a famous essay of the same title. Perhaps this time (and its pursuant space), cocreated with a concept—*women*—is a time we could begin to view elegiacally and, therefore, optimistically. We could think about a specific time belonging to women, so called, even as we attempt to open this category. Women, in Kristeva's view, are humans who have long been excluded from the time of history, the time of linear, progressive events of consequence and material profit; relegated, instead, to the cyclical and allegedly nonprogressive eternity of reproduction and the "empty" space of their own bodies.[76] Certainly, the space-time of pregnancy and birth is a space-time that much of contemporary social life teaches us to fear and that, without quite knowing it, I feared and rejected. I fear it even now, although I am also actively engaged in attempting to adore its redemptive weirdness.

In another essay, related to a Marian view of the order of the world, "Stabat Mater," Kristeva writes,

> The weight of the "non-said" (*non-dit*) no doubt affects the mother's body first of all: no signifier can cover it completely, for the signifier is always meaning (*sens*), communication or structure, whereas a mother-woman is a rather strange "fold" (*pli*) which turns nature into culture, and the "speaking subject" (*le parlant*) into biology. Although it affects each woman's body, this heterogeneity, which cannot be subsumed by the signifier, literally explodes with pregnancy—the dividing line between nature and culture— and with the arrival of the child—which frees a woman from

uniqueness and gives her a chance, albeit not a certainty, of access to the other, to the ethical.[77]

In other words: pregnancy and birth are an affront to reason, logic, and sense. We don't have the words to speak of these events, but we absolutely must try. We must try because we must recreate the world in their image—if we seek an ethical world, a world beyond the simplistic call and response of threat of violence and the deterrence of this threat. One hardly needs to be "a woman" to want to risk this.

Also, this notion of being "free[d] . . . from uniqueness": I'm still pondering this. In this liberation, the border between self and other ceases to be clear cut, ceases to be—like "the dividing line between nature and culture"—singular, absolute, knowable, whole.

-¦-

It is true that gravidity and birth changed the nature of space for me.

After my son's birth, I started thinking about bad things. Some of these bad things were straightforward: they included falling down the stairs while holding the baby, accidentally dropping the baby, bumping the baby's head against a cabinet door or the edge of a table or a wall, spilling hot water on the baby. They included horrible things that had happened to babies (in general) during wars (in general), horrible things that people (in general) had done to babies for economic reasons as well as inexplicable reasons, the boundaries of cruelty and depravity. Sienna, the midwife I worked with in anticipation of a homebirth, had warned me about this possibility. Weeks before the baby was born we had discussed postpartum depression, about which I had some vague notion. I assumed it meant that you would not want to get out of bed and meanwhile your baby wailed.

Sienna corrected me.

It could be like that, she said, but the way it occurred for many women—"and men," she said, "or whoever, partners can experience it, too"—was through what she called intrusive thoughts.

Speaking of boundaries, this is actually the limit of what can be written down. I can't describe the things I thought to you. I can't describe them because I would have to choose—and the ways in which life has been extinguished from flesh before witnessing eyes and in private are too numerous to name in language. Something that birth taught me: Whatever can occur has already occurred. Whatever you can imagine, has. Although I am an atheist I can say, this is a fact resembling a god. It is deeply humbling.

Sometime after 1393, a partly literate, middle-class woman named Margery Kempe living in Norfolk, England, was visited by Jesus Christ.

Jesus drops in on Margery after the birth of her first child. During her pregnancy Margery had suffered from fevers and after her labor was seized by fear of death. In her *Book*, her postpartum tribulations are a time of visions: "develys" come to Margery with open mouths filled with waves of flame; they threaten her and pull at her body, seeming to be about to swallow her alive.[78] The devils also employ a treacherous, seductive language that compels Margery to slander all those she loves: "sche spak many a reprevows worde and many a schrewyd worde; sche knew no vertu ne goodnesse; sche desyryd all wykkydnesse."[79] Included in her desire for all wickedness is the wish to harm herself. She does so with her own fingernails, for she had "noon other instrumentys," as the scribe composing her account puts it.

Then, while Margery's human keepers have left her to her own devices, apparently restrained in bed, Jesus appears to her in "lyknesse of a man," clad in purple silk. He asks to know why she has forsaken him and asserts that he, for his part, has never forsaken her. He then rises into the "eyr" and hovers in place "that sche mygth wel beholdyn hym in the eyr tyl it was closyd ageyn," retreating from her into what we might nowadays describe as an interdimensional portal, almost certainly vulvar in shape.[80]

Margery is stabilized. She asks her husband for the keys to the buttery—the well-to-do medieval person's refrigerator—so that she can eat and drink "as sche had don beforn."[81]

Margery Kempe's *Book*, the earliest known autobiography in vernacular English, was rediscovered approximately six hundred years after this initial manifestation of the son of God to its author. A copy of the original made at some point in the fifteenth century was found in a home in Derbyshire; subsequently identified as Margery's account by the medievalist Hope Emily Allen; and, in 1940, published by Oxford University Press. The *Book* details Margery's struggle to separate from her husband, John (with whom she had thirteen additional children before, in 1431, reaching a financial settlement with him to coexist chastely); her pilgrimages in England and to Jerusalem, Rome, Compostela, and Wilsnack; and her long relationship with Jesus, whom she describes as "most bewtyuows."[82]

Today, Margery's persistent visions are sometimes explained as hallucinations associated with puerperal or postpartum psychosis.[83] There are a series of symptoms associated with this disorder, including delusions of bodily colonization or misidentification, delusions that one is dead or decaying (Cotard's delusion), delusions that one has changed bodily form, denial of birth itself, hallucinations, catatonic states, self-mutilation, and even flashes of genius.[84]

While I don't believe I was ever psychotic, the mentions of the fear of falling and of hovering bodies, Margery's concern that she will be consumed by the maws of demons that undulate

with gaseous, fiery forms, and the sight of Jesus floating conspicu-
ously in the air and then disappearing into a space that seems
smuggled up within space itself, a kind of doorless extent that
opens and then is "closyd ageyn," remind me vividly of psychic
states I experienced both during labor and shortly after having
given birth. And particularly in birth's aftermath: I can recall
telling Sienna that the modest two-floor house we were living in
was "too large" and that I was afraid of walking upstairs or down.
Sienna was concerned that I wasn't getting enough calories, and
this might have been true (she prescribed smoothies, which I
drank enthusiastically), but there was something more than low
blood sugar at work here. I was suddenly afraid of space itself. I
could all too easily float away or tumble into emptiness, as I perceived matters. I recall being amazed that people walk up and
down staircases *all the time*. I purchased a pair of slip-on sneakers with grippy soles, hoping these would inspire greater confidence. I sometimes had urgent thoughts about how I needed to
get away from my partner at all costs. I considered the bag that I
would pack and the hotel reservation I would make online. *If we
get away we will be totally safe*, I told myself. Never mind that I was
the owner of the house we were living in and that my partner
was working nonstop to care for me and our son. Meanwhile, I
could see through walls. I could see into the future and there was
nothing solid there.

One particularly agonizing afternoon I called a close friend.
"You need to get help," she said. And I did.

Where does the baby come from? Gametes give rise to a zygote,
or yoked cell, that gives rise to a blastocyst that will later form
an embryo, as well as the chorion and amnion surrounding this
embryo, that after nine weeks develops organs, becoming a
fetus. The baby, not yet baby, begins to enter space as a splitting
process.

A door opens in the air.

I recall the moment of implantation. I lay in bed and there was a distinct twinge. I could call it a "loud" twinge.

Something enters into relation, yet you are still only yourself.

The poet Toi Derricotte, writing in her autobiographical poem-essay *Natural Birth*, describes the moment of reckoning with this change in space and self, reckoning with it in the midst of birth:

> i
> grew deep
> in me
> like fist and i
> grew deep
> in me
> like death
>   and i
> grew deep
> in me
> like hiding in the sea and
> i was
> over me
> like
> sun and i
> was under
> me
> like sky and i
> could look
> into myself
> like one
> dark eye.[85]

The gestating, birthing body becomes a site of cosmic irony: nothing is hidden, yet what appears to be the case contrasts consequentially with what is the case. A pregnant person does not have another "person" inside them, yet a pregnant person has left personal singularity far behind.

Claire Denis's 2018 film *High Life,* which I watched while pregnant, is a sort of retelling of the tale of Lot's daughters. It puts actor Robert Pattinson into outer space as the father of an experimental child—a mysteriously gestated fetus—portraying the attempt to create a livable world under nearly unbearable circumstances.[86] The film's trailer, with its repetition of the child's footsteps on the floor of the spaceship and the baby's vocalization, "da-da," is chilling and, in fact, quite a bit scarier than the film itself, for these are uncanny moments of touching, of reaching toward consciousness. The soft, arch-less infant's foot finds a barrier. The infant seeks to be upright. To find the orientation, up. The vessel provides sustenance and shelter from the cold vacuum of space. The vessel also offers the possibility of orientation and not just in relation to walking. It is an organ that will supply images and ideology to the child's sensorium.

High Life is excruciating in its tenderness, in its treatment of vulnerability. It is in direct dialogue with Stanley Kubrick's *2001: A Space Odyssey.* To the spinning bone/phallus, Denis replies with an alternate ur-form: that of the curve. This curve is, on the one hand, the lens of the camera, but it is also the all-important membrane that makes possible the rise of life: it is the amniotic sac and the filtering placenta, the spiral of the glassy umbilical cord, the edge of the petri dish. And, as we come to see, it is the gleaming, energy-rich edge of the black hole. *High Life* has largely dispensed with phalluses, with the notable exception of a single stainless steel dildo—a curved dildo—attached to a mechanical horse in the communal shipboard "fuck box." (The spaceship's engineers were apparently most concerned with satisfying crewmembers' needs for deep vaginal penetration accompanied by powerful torque; the dildo's angle does not look ideal for anal play, but of course in outer space you'd improvise.) In *High Life*, in place of the potential for violence we associate with phallic things, is the enormous potential for loss we associate with unknowably vast expanses and mysterious thresholds that either reflect or absorb whatever meets them. In outer space there is risk of a kind of falling that is not possible on earth; a "height" and depth that do not exist in terrestrial contexts. One cannot meet the ground. One cannot really be buried, although that does not mean that at least one character, Tcherny, portrayed by André Lauren Benjamin (André 3000), does not try.

High Life's depiction of monumental and inhospitable curving distances brings home a larger question, the wisdom of living in space, along with the quality of life "up there." If all human civilization is, at the end of the day, an attempt to create a material reality that can support the thriving of a being that cannot hold up its own head during its first weeks of existence, then our ventures into space will require that we revisit this fundamental limiting condition, along with what people need to thrive beyond infancy. As geneticist Christopher E. Mason maintained in his recent polemic *The Next 500 Years: Engineering Life to Reach New Worlds* (2021), the inhospitality of the regions beyond Earth's atmosphere will necessitate genetically engineered embryos that will mature into genetically engineered crews and citizens, humans whose altered DNA will allow them to survive massive doses of radiation, among other environmental challenges.[87] Mason argues that we have a "*necessary*" moral duty to colonize space because to neglect to do so is to essentially murder ourselves, given we know that either we will destroy all human life on Earth through our own civilizational struggles or the sun will eventually die, taking our planet with it (should some other interplanetary catastrophe not transpire first).[88] "Humans alone possess an awareness of the possibility of our entire species' extinction and of the Earth's finite life span," Mason observes.[89] It is this exceptional self-knowledge that, in Mason's account, makes for a moral imperative: to leave Earth in order to preserve what is vulnerable. Konrad Szocik, a sociologist reviewing Mason's book in the journal *Science*, questioned "whether radically modified humans in remote space colonies will be truly happy."[90] To put this souci differently, it is far from clear that simply keeping entities nominally resembling humans alive would suffice to reproduce what we value about humanity. Maybe annihilation might be a more self-loving course—particularly if we believe that the putative high life will be without joy, silliness, or liberty.

Mason's eugenics is dependent on the technology of the exowomb—and here is where his predictions align with Denis's images. The fetuses of goats, mice, and lambs have all been gestated with limited success by researchers employing artificial wombs, and, as Mason notes, in 2014 a Swedish woman who had received a transplanted uterus from a postmenopausal friend was able to give birth to a healthy child after an IVF procedure.[91] But the exowomb is an ambiguous affordance: it has the potential to unmarry biological sex and current patriarchal divisions of labor, even as it might allocate all control over reproduction to institutions or the state, intensifying hierarchies and male control. In *High Life*, the ship-as-exowomb is controlled by Dibs, played by Juliet Binoche, a gifted scientist doing time for infanticide. Dibs refers to herself as a "witch," but for all her long dark hair and spooky attention to the potential life inside machines, she is little more than a flunky of the penal state that has supplied her with able bodies. Predictably, social order dissolves around her.

I wonder if Christopher E. Mason has watched *High Life*. If not, he probably should. The film perhaps suffered from ill timing. Given the more recent popularity of Elon Musk's forays into space colonization, Denis's film could now be better read as critique of the culture of penal slavery that might be necessary for humanity's rapid ascent to the stars. Upon the film's release, it was, for example, panned in *Artforum* as "a lugubrious sci-fi farrago" by a reviewer who seemed very worried that no one would notice that it "plunders the imagery of Andrei Tarkovsky's sci-fi classics."[92] (Naughty, thieving Denis! Stealing from dead masters although she certainly already has plenty of money!) Personally, I admire Denis for leveraging her success to enter a pricey imaginary dominated by male directors—narratives about intergalactic arms races in which technology functions seamlessly, lady bots in sexy uniforms are de rigueur, and mavericks win the day. Robert Pattinson's harried and taciturn space dad, a guy worn down by massive existential questions, along with years of imprisonment and boredom, is one of the more original studies of contemporary human psychology I have seen on a screen. Denis's is a cautionary and, to me, sadly familiar vision, despite the outer-space setting. *High Life* figures planetary dispossession well.

But when I rewatch Denis's film it also occurs to me that she has captured the vertigo I experienced in labor and the postpartum period, a different if related disturbance of the body I call home. It is difficult for me to say if this vertigo is a historical condition or a peculiarity of my own psychology. Perhaps it is a little of both. I find myself wondering: is the suicidal madness experienced by the crew not, whatever else it is, a kind of collective postpartum psychosis brought on by their pertinence to a constantly pregnant, repeatedly miscarrying, hormonally erratic body (i.e., their "mother" ship)? And maybe *High Life* isn't really a film about outer space. Or it is only slightly a film about outer space. Because it is mostly a film about pregnancy and the as-yet-unsevered connection between birth and a human future.

I remember when the waters broke. It was around 11:00 p.m. on a Tuesday night, the eighth of December, 2020. I was sitting on the couch downstairs with Peter, my partner, and as I was getting up I felt a wetness between my legs. I reached down and there was watery blood. This frightened me and so I photographed my hand using my phone and texted Sienna to ask her if what

I was seeing might be bloody show. "Hi," was her calm response and then yes, it might be. I think this was when there was a surge of liquid and I hobbled upstairs to the bathroom. Here I should mention that earlier in the evening I had taken it upon myself to try "exercises for labor induction"[93] after an ill-fated YouTube browse that had begun in the hopes of finding some stretching exercises—and then became more desperate once I read the strangely competitive comments section under the videos. People announced the progress of their pregnancies ("39 weeks and 2 days!!"). They expressed their fervent desire that the movements depicted would cause labor to begin soon if not immediately. They repeatedly employed the prayer hands emoji. Although my search had begun with the thought that some gentle stretches might be a nice thing at the end of this long day with my very large belly putting pressure on my back among other parts of me, I became a desperate thing. My due date three days off, I was now hell-bent on avoiding carrying past term. I squatted and lunged. I brought the birth ball down to the kitchen and bounced on it while we ate dinner. I kept bouncing and ate dessert. Later—briefly—I would blame my waters breaking on this instructional video (and perhaps I should leave my experience in the comments section there). However, everyone says labor cannot be started by so-called natural or nonmedical means until it is "ready" ("ready": this is to personify and accord it agency). But let's get back to the bathroom:

Peter and I have managed to place a phone call to Sienna. I am sitting on the toilet and my legs are shaking uncontrollably.

Peter says it is the chills.

Sienna says it is hormones.

I think it is a combination of the two.

We establish that my water has broken and that the blood we see is the result of membranes tearing. Sienna says to call her in the morning, or if/when things pick up. I put on a menstrual pad and get into bed.

I'm not sure if I ask Peter to sleep in the other room immediately, or if this comes later. I am sad. I maintain what you could call an open mind, but in some interior place I'm grieved that the waters have broken and I need to be alone. This isn't what I'd wanted and I know that it can make labor more difficult. If I fail to labor soon, I risk induction; infection is now also a concern. I begin listening to recordings of self-hypnosis scripts for active labor—in the dark, Bluetooth earbuds in. This does seem to cause contractions to come on. I sleep between them, but then I am up, sort of singing and howling as they overtake me. I think to myself, *Wow, this is not going to be easy.* I'm mildly impressed but too distracted by my own discomfort to reflect much on the intensity of the feelings coursing through my uterus and wringing out the muscles of my lower back. I sing "Nature Boy," by Nat King Cole, and all the parts of the German version of the Mack the Knife song by Bertolt Brecht and Kurt Weill that I can remember, "Und der Haifisch, der hat Zähne / und die trägt er im Gesicht! / Und Macheath, der hat ein Messer / doch das Messer sieht man nicht!" This somehow gets me through to the morning, when I throw up for the first time.

I text Sienna: *hey sienna. i just wanted to let you know things are going well. i've been having regular contractions all night but i slept a little. they're no more than 30 sec long right now and i'm going to keep dozing on and off as long as i can. they do feel strong though!! please let me know if you have any thoughts; feeling calm and amniotic fluid very clear (no color)*

I'm amazed now by the detail as well as the use of polite conventions in this writing. Labor was clearly not so strong at this point. It would take another day for me to text (on Thursday in the morning): *hi! still lying side. resting well but/and contractions mega strong when they do come*

Mysteriously, here I edit myself, appending: * on side

Was I afraid that Sienna might reject me during my labor? It was as if I believed, despite her decades of experience, that she had never before communicated with a woman who was in the process of giving birth and might criticize or be alarmed at the style in which I was communicating in my text messages. Looking back on this, I wonder at myself. I'm wondering, I think, at my own pessimism. It's a truly fantastical form of pessimism. Magic—magic pessimism. Magic doubt. I seem to know something I don't yet know I know.

I kept reading sci-fi throughout the pregnancy. I needed vaster distances and ever more unfamiliar forms of consciousness. It was intuitive, mostly. In part, I was pawing through paperbacks for reconfigurations of physical space and historical time that would somehow crystallize and miniaturize the era of the global pandemic, shrink it so it fit on the head of a pin. I never did manage that, but other things occurred.

Among my discoveries was Greg Egan's *Diaspora*, an antidote, avant la lettre, to *The Three-Body Problem*. First published in 1997, it is, to me, at least, a strikingly optimistic (maybe injudiciously so) expression of the possibilities inherent to increasingly pervasive and subtle technologies of external memory and virtually managed consciousness. It is also a tale of planetary apocalypse and its extraterrestrial aftermath. I read the novel with relief. It begins, appropriately enough, with a birth scene: a digital being who eventually names viself Yatima, after an orphaned lion cub ve observes in an educational simulation, is conceived and gestated by "non-sentient software" in the "conceptory" of Konishi polis, a sort of server farm buried beneath the Siberian tundra in the thirtieth century.[94] Egan expends some ten pages on description of Yatima's parthenogenic becoming; ve is a "psychoblast" or "embryonic mind" whose contours and particularities are elaborated by programs and subprograms within a digital womb.[95] Konishi is unusual in that it has invested in the maintenance of "ancient" autogenic protocols for the development of new citizens. Here, systems of consciousness are "grown together, interacting even as they were being formed," such that, much as "a budding flower's nondescript stem cells followed a self-laid pattern of chemical cues to differentiate into sepals or petals, stamens or carpels," so the digital mind seed is encouraged to "divide up space by marking it distinctively, then let the local markings inflect the unwinding of all further instructions."[96] Difference leads to complexity; divergence is key to growth. The opening of the novel is a showstopper.

As we read *Diaspora*, we learn that there are three distinct classes of beings associated with its future Earth: fleshers and dream apes, "biological descendants of *Homo sapiens*" who have chosen to retain their mortal embodied forms and reproduce by means of sex; gleisners or "conscious, flesher-shaped" robots who, although they are technically "conscious *software*," "attach great importance to being run on hardware which forces them to interact constantly with the physical world"; and, lastly, the primary protagonists of the novel, the contemplative polis citizens, conscious software in possession of "inalienable rights" that include "unimpeded access to public data" and "a pro rata share of processing power."[97] The fleshers and dream apes are, unfortunately, in a series of horrific scenes reminiscent of John Hersey's reporting on the 1945 detonation of the atomic bomb over Hiroshima, killed by an unexpected astrophysical event.

Desirous to understand the origins of this event, which even the advanced understanding of the polises could predict only with limited advance warning, a group of citizens and uploaded formerly human refugees journey to the far reaches of the universe, seeking out the Transmuters, a sentient race who have the power to manipulate subatomic particles and now dwell in a higher-dimensional vacuum beyond the cosmos.

Although space is not entirely hospitable to life in *Diaspora*, Egan seems convinced that any consciousness capable of governing dimensionality itself would have moved beyond aggression, mortality, along with related logics of scarcity, deterrence, and basic fear of the motivations of other forms of consciousness. As an artificial wormlike being called the Contingency Handler informs the diasporic citizens who discover traces of the long-since-departed Transmuters' movements, "'Bring your people through. They're welcome here. There's room enough for everyone.'"[98]

While I personally find *Diaspora* to be of greater interest than Liu's series, I see why it has not attained crossover status. In a sense, it is a tale of play-through, or reading-through, since almost everything that happens is the result of software running and there are few organic events, as such—although one of Egan's central proposals seems to be that there are reasons to see selves as selves, *period*, whether they are digital or organically embodied. *Diaspora* asks the reader to contemplate what they most value about embodiment, as well as why they have the tendency to view personal identity as fundamentally and authentically seated in flesh, given the limitations of so-called meat space, plus the infinity of our desires and dreams. Or course, things aren't trending in the direction Egan imagines. Much contemporary technology takes economic scarcity and social asymmetry not just as preconditions for its operation but as end goals. Yet Egan's unabashedly utopian vision remains relevant nearly three decades after the novel's first publication, in that he proposes concrete reasons to value life (a style of contemplation we are, as ever, in desperate need of). The possibility of intimacy turns out to be a reason to admire humanity, in that the "tradition" of intimacy among selves is one of the best things humans have been able to pass forward to the digital citizenry. Intimacy remains paramount, even in a posthuman society.[99] Digital selves love—romantically, but also philosophically. Digital selves love the future. Digital selves require a sense of world.

When one ponders existence in the terms Egan proposes in

Diaspora, the rage and hegemonic will to claim real space, real matter in *The Three-Body Problem* seem not just unlikely from a technological point of view but like a poorly worded cry for help. There is a woundedness to Liu's vision of the future, a dread that no matter what I do, it will not be enough to stop them, the others, the ones who know more than I do, the ones who were wounded before me and who now want to steal my life, the ones who are wounding me now. Although Liu's series ends with a vision of romantic love as a sort of reverse Eden,[100] much is left unresolved. Foremost among the loose strings is the matter of why an extraordinarily limited conception of embodiment and the nature of matter itself persists as an obsession for hyper-advanced societies operating on higher dimensional planes. Advances in technology seem to provoke few realizations about the nature of property, in-groups, bodies, or, again, the value of sentient life. The "aliens" kill. Why do they kill? Because they don't want to die. And they don't want to die because they view their own selves and civilization as unique, fundamentally finite, and irreplaceable—in other words, they have the mentalities of incest-addled Victorians, despite being countless millennia beyond the internal combustion engine.

Such a murderous other would be impossible in *Diaspora*. For in this conception of the intertwined futures of physics and computing, that which is authentic and unique has no future of any significance, given the instability of matter across huge timescales. The citizens don't want to kill aliens, they want to find them. They want someone to shed light on their own strange history. Even as largely immaterial beings, they retain a profound curiosity about what it is they stand on, what its deeper rules are.

Meanwhile, *Diaspora*'s "aliens" have no wish to kill the citizens. Why should they? Space is so big it is incomparable to space, as such.

-:-

The part I liked was pushing. It was also the part I disliked, and the part I had been waiting for. Did it feel as I had imagined it would feel? Possibly. In any case, it was the only part of labor that was recognizable. It was the only part (it is the only part) I can explain to you now: I can explain the feelings. I bore down and, miraculously, to my mind, the baby was caused to move.

It may also be that this was the period during labor when I indulged in the famous thought of the laboring person, *Why did I do this to myself?* The contractions churned through me. Each wave seemed to terminate in my lower back with a sort of explosion. It felt like being kicked in the head, but not in my head. I thought of Peter, who was standing about two feet away from me, alongside the hospital bed, because I had, at hour 52, been advised by Sienna that based on her understanding of what we could expect from the hospital, she would no longer recommend that I attempt to birth at home.[101] I mournfully consented to a transfer. I felt I had failed. I would have wept, but I knew I was in for hell, and so I did not cry or protest. It was important to conserve energy. We drove forty minutes on icy roads to a small rural hospital that had an attached birth center, and it was here that I thought, *I should not have had sex with him. I should*, I thought, *have understood that sex could lead to this. It could easily lead to this experience, and I never really believed it. I have mostly if not exclusively been having sex for fun and I would like to note to my past self that I was flirting with dynamite.* I yelp-grunted, "Please stop hovering!"

I went under again. "Nnnnnnnnnnnnnghhh," I intoned, bearing down.

I panted. The Pitocin made me feel like I was drowning. I did not like the Pitocin and I did not like the IV pinned into my right hand. I had been told that I could not sleep. I was desperate for sleep, it was all I wanted, but it was forbidden to me. This felt like gaslighting or torture. I was, meanwhile, naked and at war. Anyone in the room could contemplate my exposed asshole, should they be so moved.

I was also experiencing a confused and vivid form of déjà vu. OK, I was thinking, strangely matter-of-factly within the maelstrom, it's happening again. They're asking too much of you. You can't let them "put you in prison" (my thought at this time) "again" for crimes against "normalcy." So, some voice in me reflected, you're going to have to go to that deep place where something is saved, and you can eat this saved thing. You're allowed to use this now.

The baby descended. The first part of the difficulty with pushing was the feeling of the competition of the baby's head with other byways and entities in the lower part of my body. I can't tell you exactly what was squished or otherwise inconvenienced, but I do recall that even the feeling of resting was one of extreme fullness, of the bulbous, hard presence of the head, but perhaps this is an expanded memory of what was likely a rather brief period, the time when the head had traversed my pubic bone and was "resting" near its exit. I use quotation marks because this was not an example of rest but rather one of movement, of two steps forward and a step and a half back. I forced him forward, and he slid back.

In my now increasingly many-layered mind, I recall being disappointed—deflated, half-killed—that "we" were being let down by the social world, yet again, as I explained this to myself. But there was also an irascible part of this plural me who said, "FUCKING GET MAD, BITCH. You aren't even a woman, you are a spirit, and these sick clowns are trying to deny this. Go into the magic cave and eat the sacred cookie NOW."

Thus did I eat what I take to be a transhistorical cookie.

This was when I felt the burning. I had been waiting for it. I felt a certain concern in that I recognized that this sensation would become stronger before my work was done, and I wondered if I was going to enjoy that strengthening. In fact, I knew I was not going to enjoy it and part of me considered what I perceived as my hubris, thinking I was just going to get out of this predicament. I was going to be overwhelmed. (I needed to sleep, and they would not let me.) I despaired, but like a person who must jump because there are no other options, I raced forward, not wanting to wait to be pushed. And so I pushed. And pushed even when there was no contraction. I ignored the people telling me to wait, to wait for the contraction. And in this way, the baby was born. His head emerged fully and I did not know what to do.

"What do I do now?" I panted, surprised to be alive. I was now on the other side of the most physical pain I have ever felt.

Get his body out, someone may have said, and it slithered out of me almost without sensation.

I worked with a homebirth midwife, and I did give birth, although not at home. There are multiple ways this story could be told, but mostly I think it is a story about storytelling itself, learning another language for a thing that defies narrative, that appears only fitfully in most histories of the world.

Pain, as I saw it, would seek out its own metaphor, and so I needed to be prepared with a metaphor for it. I needed a narrative, a plan. But is *pain* even the right word? For the sensations of labor are not the sensations of burning one's hand on the stove, not the sensations of fractured limbs, paper cuts, root canals, or heartbreak.

Are you responsible for your own pain? Is anyone? Was I? How is pain social? Self-hypnosis was my mental discipline of choice, and two or three nights a week I sat in an alcove before dinner and listened to pirated MP3s a friend had shared with me on Google Drive.

But I can't tell you if I learned anything I used while I was in labor. That is what is so mysterious.

And there is also the question of pleasure: how pleasure does hold the world together for humans and how we experience it in small ways all the time, even in moments of extreme distress.

-:-

After the baby was born, I barely glanced at the placenta. It sat in what appeared to be a former yogurt container, a white plastic bucket. I could not remember who put it there. The baby still had his umbilical cord and I gazed at it in fascination. It was so perfect with its pink and gray twists. It seemed to be made of glass, colorful and eerily detailed, like the botanical models created by Leopold and Rudolf Blaschka for Harvard University in the late nineteenth century. This glossy cord, like the baby himself, had not existed and then had come to exist. The placenta, which was born quickly and simply after the baby with just a little push (it seemed to "surf" out of me), was praised by Susan, the birth center midwife. "What a beautiful placenta!" she said. When I looked at the placenta out of the corner of my eye in its yogurt container it was the darkest red. I felt for a moment as if I had achieved that fantasy we all entertain at one time or another of being able to meet ourselves. Even more strangely, I felt that I could not judge it. It looked back at me, although it had no eyes. It didn't have secrets, just a presence. It inspired curiosity. It knew more than I did and, meanwhile, it was an organ in a bucket. It had come from me and existed within me and had been the familiar of my child. It held my cells and held my son's cells. Now a nurse was offering to throw it out.

I told her we were going to take it home. I might have said, "I'm going to bury it," a notion I was inventing in that moment.

-:-

For me, labor had three bodies.

There was the life in the body that grew within me, and there was the body of the movement of labor, and there was my tiny actual body, somewhere. There was the body of the present, and there was the past, and from somewhere came a baby. There was what I felt, what I knew, and, then, whatever was the case.

They wouldn't come together. Still, it's not that they were incoherent.

There was my body, the body that would become the body of my son (the body that today is his body but that, then, was mine, was my body), and there was the phantasmagoric body of the state, the body of tort law, the body of insurance and certification, of statistics and generalization, of organizational protocols; the body of control. The body of the state touched me as language and it touched me in other ways. It was made of metal and plastic and various databases. It wanted me to shut up and push. It had always been there, this third body, but never before had I dwelled so intimately with it. Never before had the state wanted so much from me, and never before had it been so apparent to me, even as it crouched behind an elaborate scrim made out of discourse about the mitigation of risk.

I had sixty hours of back labor.[102] I was completely unprepared for this. My labor was far worse than I could have imagined, but somehow I was prepared for this. Something in me said: It's going to shake you, what this thing is. It's going to take you back to something, and you will believe that you cannot survive it. Know that you will believe that you cannot survive it. Accept that your experience will include the certainty that you will die. When you come to the point of believing that you cannot survive and are certain that you will die, this is when you must dig in, because this is the moment when you will know that it is your own. It is nobody's but your own. And you must answer it in these moments. You must say, "I am still here." You must say, "I am not dead." You must trust that you are strong enough to believe that you cannot survive. You must trust that you are strong enough to experience the certainty of death. You will doubt everything. You will doubt even that you are yourself. Be afraid if you like, it's a normal reaction, but also be aware that this is going to happen. You will lose everything. You will despair. You will be uncertain as to who experiences these things. But no matter what happens, remember that you are not required to give up. You can give up but you aren't required to; it's a subtle difference and one worth noting. You can keep going even if it seems futile and that will be the right thing to do. It will be all right to do ridiculous, seemingly futile things, things that will seem to make no sense in light of your own non-survival. For there is an ethics of your own body as it is in time that you may learn. There is an ethics of birthing. An ethics of futility and joy.

Prepare to love this foray into futility, for it is yours, too.

What part of my brain was it that spoke to me with these pre-monitions during my pregnancy? It was still me, but the voices floated toward me from a great distance. A messenger went to the outermost regions of what I understood as the edges of my-self and brought back these transmissions. They were difficult to decipher. They weren't written in language. They were moods, possibilities, shuffling movements of a kind of psychic air. They were hints—dare I say it—offered by ancestors, many of whom were not my own.

I operate under the assumption that everyone's experience of labor is different. And not only this: my midwife and various other birth workers I have met have, to a person, assured me that, in phenomenological and psychological terms, every labor is differ-ent. Every person's labor is different and each labor a person has (or will have) will be different from those that came before. This said, the *physiological* progression of labor is well known. It is no mystery. Nor are the algorithms used to determine interventions in a medical context fundamentally unknowable; rather, they are withheld.

Almost immediately after my son's emergence from my body, after his lanky, slick body was caught and passed up beneath me so that I could hold him and then turn over and bring him to my breast, and after a hovering pediatrician was shooed away, the attending birth center midwife and nurse and my own midwife began assuring me that my "next baby" would be born differently. "The next one will be so much easier!" I remember Susan exclaiming.

I said nothing in response to these, to me, curious comments. I wondered why everyone wanted me to have more kids.

It was, as everyone says, astounding: that our baby was born, that it was over. But this was my intellect assessing the situation. My intellect also deemed my labia fairly hurt. I asked a nurse if it was possible to have some ice.

She gave me a disposable diaper full of ice and I managed to sit in it. The birth center midwife, who had left the room for some reason, returned and told me that she needed to check to see if I required stitches. When she saw that I was already sitting on ice, she was annoyed. She told the nurse that she shouldn't have done that. Perhaps swelling was going to help her see what sort of state I was in. Perhaps an unswollen vulva that had suffered tearing was harder to stitch.

Susan peered up me. She was my great enemy. She prodded me dexterously.

"Please don't do that!" I said.

"Just some road rash."

"What?"

"You don't need stitches." The midwife explained that there

was a shallow vertical split in the interior of the right side of my labia but this wasn't something she could do anything about. "It will heal."

Because I was priding myself on my retained mental capacity in this moment, I proposed an analogy with the flesh of a person's mouth.

"Sure," she said.

-:-

Before becoming pregnant and then giving birth, I knew little about pregnancy, nothing about birth, little about babies. Looking back, I can see that my tendency was to idealize pregnancy, fear birth itself (which I considered an emergency and probable bloodbath), and avoid babies. In a way, pregnancy was for me much what I thought it would be: the pandemic limited my movements and so I was able to convince myself that the hormonal changes and relatively minor physical discomfort I felt were just that, minor. I was spacey, sometimes pleasantly so. I kept working. However, I was annoyed by the spaciness, by my frequent inability to "do another thing." I would sometimes go multiple hours at a time just looking into the air. The baby himself is another story and I can only touch on his ways and how I know him very briefly here. I will note that I have held him or worn him on my body as I was writing this essay (am holding him as I write), and so in that sense he is a part of it in more ways than one.

-:-

"I wonder why I have never seen a birth scene filmed from the woman's point of view," the artist Carmen Winant asks.[103]

I try to imagine what such a scene might look like. Were I the birthing person, we would see little of the room my body was in. It's not that I couldn't or didn't want to see this space; it's that this visual information hardly seemed to matter. What can I say about where I was? It was a realm of infinite dimensions, black or gray. Like a long beach at night. I wandered, scouring the sands. Waves rolled in. The sky trembled.

There is nothing for you in this place, someone noted, as if in voiceover. I did not understand, at the time, that this was a good thing. One hardly wants to be getting what one needs from the threshold of death, the upper regions of the underworld.

This isn't an analytic essay, but I would be remiss if I did not repeat one or two political points here: in the 1980s, there was a strain of liberationist thought that considered the desire to restrict abortion a displacement of apocalyptic fear.[104] Interesting that this "sick burn" has been forgotten so soon, for it is likely applicable to contemporary restrictions.

It is also worth noting that Justice Sandra Day O'Connor criticized the logic of the *Roe* decision because, as she wrote in 1983, it ties reproductive freedom to the notion that a fetus cannot survive outside the womb.[105] Yet, as science moves inexorably toward a point at which there will be no time during which a fetus cannot survive outside the womb—a time of fully capable exowombs—this logic of protection of rights on account of dependency will grow attenuated and illogical, is perhaps already becoming so. In one reading, these developments amount to a masterful wresting of reproductive power and fiat away from parents into the hands of institutions and the state. There are other possible readings; however, it now appears that we are living in the world in which the exowomb may serve as a sort of retroactive proof of fetal personhood, may be deployed as a technology that constructs our social reality in this way. And the coming colonization of space may be undertaken by a humanity composed of obscenely wealthy persons, along with other merely *person-like* beings, whose personhood is always in question and therefore fungible, whether they are pregnant or not.

I was scared to give birth and I believe that I was right to be scared, although not for the reasons I thought of at the time. I was scared to give birth because—as I explained this to myself—I was afraid of experiencing a complication and dying, and also I was scared to give birth because I was afraid of being in tremendous pain and being unable to obtain relief from that pain and then somehow going insane from the pain I was feeling and being stripped of my rights by doctors because of my pain-induced madness. I wondered if I might be cursed. I wondered if people might find this out about me if I were to give birth—that during the course of my attempt to give birth someone with more knowledge would have a light go on and say to themselves, "Oh yes, I see what's going on here! This is a cursed person!" I thought about the history of mental illness in my family, about the numerous estrangements.

It was very easy for me to become pregnant at age forty. Bizarrely easy, although as far as I knew I had never been pregnant before, a fact that had led me to believe that it was not possible for me to have children. I was afraid that, in my late engagement with human reproduction, I had done something fatal. I was afraid I had made a choice I could not now unmake and that I was entering into an interaction with social forces fundamentally inimical to me. I feared that my refusal to bear children at a "normal" age—indeed, when I was thirty-two, a gynecologist had, apropos of nothing, informed me that I should try to get pregnant "soon" because later "it gets hard to do"—was a refusal for which I would be punished. I was afraid that because my partner and I were not married and because I was planning to give our child my last name, tout court, without the usual consolation of either a hyphen or treating the paternal last name as a nonoptional "middle name," I would be subject to censure.

I was not wrong.

But I was also very wrong, because in my logic I blamed myself. I blamed myself out of ignorance. I knew some things about

birth. I was aware that since the seventeenth century if not before, male obstetricians had experimented with different means
of making birth "easier"—perhaps more for themselves than for
birthing people. I knew that J. Marion Sims, formerly the subject of a Central Park monument, had performed experimental
surgeries on enslaved women without anesthesia.[106] I had read
Silvia Federici's writing on witches.[107] I was aware of certain statistics. But I kept this array of information in a box. I read the
"left" books that were relatively easy to obtain and meanwhile
held out for a boring normalcy around birth. I listened to a brilliant podcast called *Birthful*. Still, I accused myself of being too
weird, of needlessly intellectualizing plain old life, of continuing
to suffer lazily from chronic anxiety I had already spent years
in therapy attempting to heal. Yet, the thing was, the pragmatic
task of getting care during pregnancy and the everyday practice of chatting with other people about their pregnancies and
births convinced me I needed to be more paranoid, rather than
less. Two things were happening: first, I was repeatedly shown
that I was more like other people than I had ever, ever imagined
I could viscerally feel I was (and I am grateful for this); two, I
found that, for me, pregnancy required a particular consideration or thought work and I didn't know exactly how to fulfill this
exigency. The question remains with me, the problem of bodies
and the time we need. Birth itself could not solve it.

This is the story of my birth, of my son's birth: I waited until I
was forty years and two months old to get pregnant, what I considered the absolute last possible moment. I knew I would be
able to become pregnant at this time yet I do not know why I
knew this. I worked with a homebirth midwife and I learned to
hypnotize myself before my labor. Except for my partner, the father of my son, there were no adult men in the room of the birth
center where our son was born. I never consulted with an obste-

trician regarding my pregnancy. I devoted considerable time
to my body during my pregnancy. I understood, I do not know
why, that labor would be a process of incremental, devilishly
slow progress. I knew I would labor for what seemed like forever
and indeed I did. I knew it would feel like vomiting. Vomiting for
three days straight, whole body perplexed. Again, I do not know
why I knew this. I knew I would stoically withstand what happened. I was determined. I wasn't sure if I would make it, if it
would go well, but I was betting on myself.

People take pride in different things. Sometimes I take pride
in my labor. And here I mean: the labor that led to a birth. But
I want to clarify that I take pride in this labor not because it is
something I did. Something I accomplished. I take pride in it
because it was something I was able to offer myself. I made the
choice to have it, the labor, along with my child. I gave that to
myself: I said, here, I want you to have this. I've been so stingy
in the past and I need to make amends. See how it goes. Find out.
Learn what it feels like to give birth. Receive this information.
Fuck the people who tell you you don't need it, that you can't have
it, that you can't handle it.

I held my own head in my hands as I pushed the baby out.
A voice in my mind said, *If it hurts this much, it means it is something you absolutely should not do.* And I said to this voice, *In this
instance, you are wrong.*

Sixty hours had passed since the water broke and I was completely alone with myself. I was conscious of the residue of what
other people had, over the course of my life, told me I should
not or could not or might reasonably be forbidden to do. Their
interdictions were present. No one except me wanted me to give
birth. No one else would condone it. I was unmarried and I was
old. No one except me would grant permission that this soul be
born. Countless presences hung back, observing this. They were
unreal people, as far as I could tell, bodiless ones from old, lost
worlds. They liked this sort of thing. They seemed amused that I

had come this far. As I walked into what I saw in my mind's eye as a wobbling yellow fire, a vaporous nest of light floating grotesquely above uncertain ground, I moved beyond comfort or pain. The tips of my fingers touched my face. The pain, like the sensation of the tips of my fingers on my face, was merely actual. I studied the sensation of the tips of my fingers pressed so gently against my face, gracing the skin of my forehead. I weighed the insignificance of this feeling, treated the mildness of it as a precious substance, turned it over, pondered it, even praised it. I felt the strangest love.

Whatever I was, person on all fours, head in their hands, the pain was like a word, merely descriptive. It was a veil made of the present, fundamentally not of the same category as my being, nor that of the child whose head rested palpably inside me, stretching my labia, an impossible and merely actual presence. It was, as I have just written, no more than actual, a function of the body in time. In the space of my mind's eye, alive, staring at this fact, I gasped in awe.

At this moment, my son was born.

Acknowledgments

To the people who variously read, edited, inspired, and fact-checked these essays; created this book; provided funding, childcare, new leads, and moral support—Alexander Chee, Chris Clemans, Percival Everett, Megan Ewing, Sarah Fan, Sienna Flanders, Emily Fox-Penner, Elaine Gan, Jay Garcia, Robert Glück, Graywolf Press, Yuka Igarashi, Jess Kimball, Shiv Kotecha, Chris Kraus, Wendy Lee, Claire Lehmann, Jonathan Lethem, Tan Lin, the Program in Literary Arts at Brown University (most especially: Gale Nelson and Matthew Shenoda), Maureen McLane, Nicholas Muellner and Catherine Taylor and the students at the MFA in Image-Text at Cornell University, Lara Mimosa Montes, Martha Ormiston, Jennifer Nelson, Kim Rosenfeld, Elana Rosenthal, Astrid Rotenbery, Susan Stewart, Peter Katz, Arabella Katz, Yves Ives—THANK YOU.

Notes

Of Unicorns

1. Pliny the Elder reports in the eighth book of his *Natural History*, "Hanc feram vivam negant capi," literally, "This wild beast alive they deny [that it can] be captured." John Bostock and Henry Thomas Riley translate, "This animal, it is said, cannot be taken alive," "Chap. 31.—The Terrestrial Animals of India," in *The Natural History of Pliny*, vol. 2 (London: H. G. Bohn, 1855), 281. I prefer a slightly different wording.

2. Hasbro's Transformers were "developed by Hasbro from a Japanese line of transforming robot toys manufactured by Takara"; Lincoln Geraghty, "Drawn to Television: American Animated SF Series of the 1980s," *Science Fiction Film and Television* 3, 2 (Autumn 2010): 288. These figurines were highly successful during the mid-1980s, and the company seemed to find the model of explicitly gendered toys combined with a related cartoon series effective where sales were concerned (see also the identity-shifting doll Jem and her associated television show, *Jem*). Hasbro's activities reflected the deregulation of children's television by the Reagan administration (Geraghty, 289), with a multiplicity of characters key to the corporation's gambit, i.e., repeat purchases entailed. The first My Little Ponies of 1982 were just six in number, although they multiplied rapidly. My Pretty Pony was, by contrast, a squat and resigned-looking hard plastic figurine about ten inches tall. It could wink only one eye.

3. Except for Twinkle-Eyed Ponies, whose eyes were made of a separate piece of faceted translucent plastic set within the pony's head. Twinkle-Eyed Ponies appeared in two sets in 1986 and 1987. I have dated the toys using a search of historical newspapers, usually with reference to Toys "R" Us ads from these two years. One ad of this type proclaims, "Eyes beam with all the colors of the rainbow! Combable [*sic*] hair, ribbon, more. Ages 3–up. 4[.]97 Each"; *Central New Jersey Home News*, January 28, 1987, 13. Heather DePonia dates these sets "1985–1986" and "1986–1987" in *The My Little Pony Collector's Inventory: A Complete Checklist of All US Ponies, Playsets and Accessories from 1981 to 1992* (Persippany, NJ: Priced Nostalgia Press, [2022]), 4, 38–40, 50.

4. The neoclassicism of "Pastoral Symphony" carries more than a trace of the United States' history of enslavement. It nods to the early nation's architectural styles and included racist depictions of two centaurette servants, edited out for the 1991 video release. See Paula Schwartz, "It's a Small World . . . And Not Always P.C.," *New York Times*, June 11, 1995, and Moya Luckett, "*Fantasia*: Cultural Constructions of Disney's 'Masterpiece,'" in *Disney Discourse: Producing the Magic Kingdom*, ed. Eric Smoodin (New York: Routledge, 1994), 235. If Hasbro did indeed

appropriate the look of Disney's ur-ponies (this is difficult to prove), the toy company resituated them in a less explicitly loaded, nonetheless European, realm.

5. Ridley Scott shot postproduction footage for a unicorn dream sequence for *Blade Runner* (1982), even before filming *Legend* (1985)—an example of the creature's odd resonance. The postproduction footage only appeared in the 1992 director's cut, yet the pointed use of the unicorn as a figure for replicant Rick Deckard's contested humanity helps to gloss the animal's symbolism and popularity during the period. As Scott has said, "I'd predetermined that that unicorn scene would be the strongest clue that Deckard, this hunter of replicants, might actually be an artificial human himself"; Paul M. Sammon, "Interview with Ridley Scott," in *Ridley Scott: Interviews*, ed. Laurence F. Knapp and Andrea F. Kulas (Jackson: University of Mississippi Press, 2005), 90.

6. The 1980s commercial in question is featured in the opening of Urban Outfitters' 2012 promotional documentary, *The World of Lisa Frank*.

7. Oberon Zell maintains in a short documentary about his life, *The Wizard of OZ* (2016), that the "unicorn" technique was derived from "the work of a veterinarian from the state of Maine in the 1930s who was doing research in horn development." This veterinarian was, in fact, the biologist William Franklin Dove, who published his research in 1935 as "The Physiology of Horn Growth: A Study of the Morphogenesis, the Interaction of Tissues, and the Evolutionary Processes of a Mendelian Recessive Character by Means of Transplantation of Tissues," *Journal of Experimental Zoology* 69, 3 (1935): 347–405. Dove created a unicorn bull.

8. On October 18, 1985, the *Chicago Tribune* reported that Ringling Bros. billed appearances by Lancelot as "The Living Unicorn"; Phil Vettel, "Telling the Living Truth about the Unicorn."

9. "Unicorn attends party at disco," *Park City Daily News*, April 19, 1985.

10. "U.S. Agency to Check A Purported Unicorn," United Press International, *New York Times*, April 9, 1985.

11. This quotation appears in Susan Heller Anderson and David W. Dunlap, "New York Day by Day: Unmasking the Unicorns," *New York Times*, April 11, 1985.

12. From 1988 to 1989, Hasbro introduced Loving Family Ponies, a set of parents with a child, and the next year introduced Pony Bride, who was not accompanied by a groom. These gestures toward heterosexuality and marriage nevertheless seem slight in the greater pantheon of pony figures. Although adult male ponies, Big Brother Ponies, were twice introduced, in 1986–1987 and 1987–1988, their relationships with the greater herd of apparently female ponies were not explicitly sexual. (Dating of toy ranges verified via historical newspaper searches; for example, on December 6, 1987, in the *Daily News* [New York], "A Grownup's Compleat Guide to Choosing Toys Sure to Please All Kids," Sherryl Connelly writes, "And now there are boy ponies, Big Brother Ponies [$5.69]"; see also DePonia, *My Little*

Pony Collector's Inventory, 4–5, 54, 72.) In one episode of the cartoon series, the first iterations of Big Brother Ponies (4-Speed, Quarterback, Salty, Slugger, Steamer, and Tex) eagerly return to Ponyland's Dream Valley, as if from time away at college? This is unclear. We never learn why they left nor why it matters that they are back. I regret, meanwhile, that I do not have time to treat the later-generation MLPs, along with the contemporary phenomenon of the 4chan-originating brony fandom and its relationship to sexuality and eroticism.

13. Here I have amalgamated various MLP advertisements available via YouTube .com.

14. Quoted in Lise Gotfredsen, *The Unicorn*, trans. Anne Born (New York: Abbeville Press, 1999), 16.

15. Chris Lavers, *The Natural History of Unicorns* (New York: William and Morrow, 2009), 226–32.

16. Lavers, 232.

17. Gotfredsen, *Unicorn*, 12.

18. Susan Bush, "Labeling the Creatures: Some Problems in Han and Six Dynasties Iconography," in *The Zoomorphic Imagination in Chinese Art and Culture*, ed. Jerome Silbergeld and Eugene Y. Wang (Honolulu: University of Hawai'i Press, 2016), 76–77.

19. Quoted in Odell Shepard, *The Lore of the Unicorn* (New York: Barnes & Noble, 1967 [1930]), 27–28. Ctesias's travelogue includes the crucial information that "the dust filed from [the unicorn's] horn is administered in a potion as a protection against deadly drugs."

20. Shepard, 34–40.

21. Shepard, 42–44.

22. Adolfo Salvatore Cavallo, *The Unicorn Tapestries at the Metropolitan Museum of Art* (New York: Metropolitan Museum of Art, 1998), 22. Shepard, *Lore of the Unicorn* (46), maintains that the term *Physiologus* never corresponded to a real person but was rather a textual convention used in early didactic Christian fables. These fables were later excerpted to focus on the animals themselves, rather than their relevance to scripture.

23. See, for example, the rendition of the hunt of the unicorn included in illuminations in the *Rothschild Canticles*, a fourteenth-century manuscript currently housed at Yale's Beinecke Library (MS 404, fol. 51r). Here a smiling nude lady skips joyfully toward an elated beige unicorn with a very big horn.

24. Margaret B. Freeman, *The Unicorn Tapestries* (New York: Metropolitan Museum of Art, 1976), 47. Cavallo, *Unicorn Tapestries* (29–30), notes the correspondence between the hunting imagery in the Cloisters tapestries and Gaston Phébus's *Livre de chasse* of the late fourteenth century.

25. "It has beneath its horn something as clear as glass, so that in it, a person can look at his own face, as if looking in a mirror"; Hildegard von Bingen, *Hildegard von Bingen's Physica: The Complete English Translation of Her Classic Work on Health and Healing*, trans. Priscilla Throop (Rochester, VT: Healing Arts Press, 1998), 210. In the original Latin there appears to be a bone. "Sub cornu autem suo os habet quod velut vitrum perspicuum est" ("Beneath its horn it has a bone that is as glass transparent"); von Bingen, *Physica: Liber Subtilitatum Divesarum Naturarum Creaturum*, ed. Reiner Hildebrandt and Thomas Gloning, vol. 1, *Text mit Berliner Fragment im Anhang* (Berlin: De Gruyter, 2010), 336. Lavers, *Natural History of Unicorns* (102), converts this "bone" into a piece of metal; I'm not sure why.

26. Cavallo, *Unicorn Tapestries*, 27. Michel Pastoureau and Élisabeth Delahaye, *Les Secrets de la licorne* (Paris: Réunion des musées nationaux, Grand Palais, 2013), 120.

27. Cora E. Lutz, "The American Unicorn," *Yale University Library Gazette* 53, 3 (January 1979): 135.

28. Quoted in Lutz, 138.

29. Quoted in Lavers, *Natural History of Unicorns*, 163–164.

30. For the relative popularity of the heraldic unicorn in the fourteenth and fifteenth centuries, see Pastoureau and Delahaye, *Secrets de la licorne*, 63–64.

31. M. P. Heide-Jørgensen, "Narwhal: *Monodon monoceros*," in *Encyclopedia of Marine Mammals*, ed. Bernd Würsig et al. (Amsterdam: Elsevier Science & Technology, 2017), 627–30.

32. In 1969, the New York Aquarium purchased a narwhal calf from Inuit hunters and flew it to the city; it died in captivity within a month. In 1970, the Vancouver Aquarium acquired three calves and two adult female narwhals. The calves died in less than a month. The adults died two months later. Blake Butler, "Tragic history of Vancouver Aquarium's narwhals is worth revisiting," *Vancouver Sun*, September 11, 2020.

33. Laura U. Marks, *Touch: Sensuous Theory and Multisensory Media* (Minneapolis: University of Minnesota Press, 2002), 3.

34. "The money necessary for this purchase has been given by Mr. John D. Rockefeller, Jr., and the amount paid in round figures is $600,000"; Joseph Breck, "The Acquisition of George Grey Barnard's Cloisters and Gothic Collections by the Metropolitan Museum of Art," *American Magazine of Art* 16, 8 (August 1925): 438. This sum apparently included purchase of the land the museum stood on.

35. The Cloisters opened in May 1938 (Freeman, *Unicorn Tapestries*, 227). Barnard passed away on April 24 of that year from a heart attack and so did not live to see the museum open to the public.

36. Cavallo, *Unicorn Tapestries*, 11. Cavallo notes that the hunters' "doublets, and hose, as well as their hair styles, and the snug bodices and high-hipped skirts

of the women's gowns, as well as the form of their headdresses" are additional giveaways. For a near-contemporary account of Spanish colonial genocide, see Bartolomé de las Casas, *A Short Account of the Destruction of the Indies*, ed. and trans. Nigel Griffin (New York: Penguin Books, 1992 [1542]).

37. Quoted in Freeman, *Unicorn Tapestries*, 220.

38. The tale of the loss and reclamation of the tapestries by the de La Rochefoucauld family is recounted in similar terms by both Freeman (223–24) and Cavallo, *Unicorn Tapestries* (14–17).

39. Cavallo, 17.

40. Cavallo, 17.

41. Freeman, *Unicorn Tapestries*, 227–28.

42. See Freeman's chapter, "The Hunt," 91–107.

43. Cavallo, *Unicorn Tapestries*, notes (11) that an exhibition of the *Hunt of the Unicorn* tapestries alongside the *Lady with the Unicorn* series in Paris in 1973 and '74 inspired new research by French scholars who subsequently suggested the *Hunt of the Unicorn* tapestries were not a unified, narrative set.

44. "There is a marked stylistic difference," Cavallo writes (34). He additionally reminds the reader of the vastness of our ignorance regarding these artworks: "We do not know how many episodes were originally represented in the Unicorn-as-Lover set nor how many pieces it comprised" (36). Barbara Drake Boehm, a curator emerita of the Cloisters, maintains that the seven tapestries "appear to be an ensemble," likely commissioned to celebrate a marriage. Conversation with the author, January 19, 2024. For an elaborate reiteration of undecidability, see Thomas P. Campbell, *Tapestry in the Renaissance: Art and Magnificence* (New York and New Haven: Metropolitan Museum of Art and Yale University Press, 2002), 70–79.

45. See, for example, Lavers's *Natural History of Unicorns* ("Iconographically the scenes all hang together," 84) or Francine Prose's essay of September 18, 2020, "What We Aren't Seeing," https://www.theparisreview.org/blog/2020/09/18/what-we-arent-seeing/.

46. Lavers (98) summarizes: "As far as the literary evidence allows us to discern, some Europeans in the twelfth century came to believe that the unicorn had medicinal powers. By the end of the fourteenth century the belief had become attached to alicorn and known to scholars, as had the idea that alicorn could detect toxic substances. Between the fifteenth and seventeenth centuries alicorn was regularly used by aristocrats, popes and other rich people as a guard against poisoners: it was widely thought that the material perspired in the presence of tainted food and drink, even though it didn't." Here some readers may begin to be reminded of philosopher Giorgio Agamban's theories of foundations of law in the figure of the *homo sacer*.

47. For more on the history of poisoning and the alicorn and languier, see Franck Collard, *Pouvoir et poison: Histoire d'un crime politique de l'Antiquité à nos jours* (Paris: Seuil, 2007), 154.

48. Shepard, *Lore of the Unicorn*, 186–87.

49. Shepard, 119–40.

50. Shepard, 20.

51. Quoted in Shepard, *Lore of the Unicorn*, 49.

52. The amatory wildness of the unicorn—who is customarily male despite the Arthurian narrative—is, further, transferable: In some illustrations and tapestries of the fifteenth century, the unicorn is accompanied not by a modest maid but by a seminude wild woman. She sports a jumpsuit of fur, hair, or leaves and contentedly strokes the unicorn's mane. She rides triumphantly on his back. Her small breasts are exposed. See multiple illustrations included in Pastoureau and Delahaye, *Secrets de la licorne*, 78–79.

53. Shepard, *Lore of the Unicorn*, 85–86.

54. Matti Megged writes, "But beneath all the various representations and interpretations we may conclude without doubt that the Unicorn was the most human of all mythical creatures. Its 'human' character could be expressed by different means: direct analogy between him and man, metaphorical affinity, hints of physical resemblance, allusions to similar destiny. In several cases we even find advice or instruction to human beings to regard the Unicorn as a paradigm for their behavior and destiny." *The Animal That Never Was* (New York: Lumen Books, 1992), 21.

55. See Wolfgang Palaver, "Mimetic Desire," in *René Girard's Mimetic Theory*, trans. Gabriel Borrud (East Lansing: Michigan State University Press, 2013), 33–134. Palaver (119–20) writes, "In the Girardian conception, the other's desire is . . . the model that designates the desirability of all objects." In part through selective readings by the technology investor Peter Thiel, Girard has recently become an object of right-wing enthusiasm.

56. "Like all primitive gods, the saint protects as long as he monopolizes and incarnates the plague"; René Girard, *The Scapegoat*, trans. Yvonne Freccero (Baltimore: Johns Hopkins University Press, 1989), 61.

57. Dominique Lestel, *L'animal est l'avenir de l'homme: Munitions pour ceux qui veulent (toujours) défendre les animaux* (Paris: Fayard, 2010), 29. Quoted in Deborah Bird Rose, *Shimmer: Flying Fox Exuberance in Worlds of Peril* (Edinburgh: Edinburgh University Press, 2022), 7.

58. Palaver, "Mimetic Desire," 184–87.

59. See, e.g., Andrew C. McKevitt, *Consuming Japan: Popular Culture and the Globalizing of 1980s America* (Chapel Hill: University of North Carolina Press, 2017).

60. There are so many examples of this trope that it is impossible to name them all. Some well-known European horror films make the connection between sanctified sacrifice and the genre of horror explicit (this sort of film is termed "folk horror"). See 1973's *The Wicker Man* or 2019's *Midsommar*.

61. Serres describes a "silent influence of the tactile," indicated by the unicorn as well as by the tapestry itself. Translation mine. *Les cinq sens* (Paris: Grasset, 1985), 60. The tapestry historian Heinrich Göbel also conjures images of this artform that are fleshly in nature. Of "the so-called contour-slits" he writes, in his characteristic looping style, "If for instance the lachrymal bag underneath the eye is to be accentuated, the weaver makes the perpendicular steps—when the tapestry is hung up the slits then appear horizontal—in the desired curve longer than usual, tiny crevices appear, which are widened by the weight of the tapestry and form a slight but clearly visible line"; *Tapestries of the Lowlands*, trans. Robert West (New York: Bretano's, 1924), 15.

62. Rainer Maria Rilke, *The Notebooks of Malte Laurids Brigge*, trans. Stephen Mitchell, intro. William H. Gass (New York: Vintage Books, 1990), 127, 130.

63. Anne Dufourmantelle, "Assiduity," in *In Praise of Risk*, trans. Stephen Miller (New York: Fordham University Press, 2009), 152.

64. See DePonia, *My Little Pony Collector's Inventory*, throughout.

65. This story is derived from a fragment by Aristotle. In this fragment, King Midas is on a hunting expedition and Silenus is the unexpected catch of the day. See Malcolm Davies, "Aristotle Fr. 44 Rose: Midas and Silenus," *Mnemosyne* 57, 6 (2004): 682–97. As this fragment is retold in *The Birth of Tragedy*, King Midas asks—as a sort of archaic stand-in for the more modern Nietzsche, who has in mind the ills of national and possibly global history—what is best for mankind, and Silenus's full advice is, "The very best thing is utterly beyond your reach: not to have been born, not to *be*, to be *nothing*. However, the second best thing for you is to die soon"; Friedrich Nietzsche, *The Birth of Tragedy and Other Writings*, ed. Raymond Geuss and Ronald Speirs, trans. Ronald Speirs (Cambridge: Cambridge University Press, 1999), 3. Silenus is a wild man of the forest. He is Dionysus's tutor and comes from a world previous to that of the god of wine. He is sometimes portrayed as part horse or goat, particularly as having the ears of a horse. He has knowledge of mysteries. Is he another unicorn?

An Image of My Name Enters America

1. Robert Glück, "My Margery, Margery's Bob," in *Margery Kempe* (New York: New York Review Books, 2020), 168.

2. Glück, 168.

3. Quoted in Lucy Ives, "Responding to Bloody Letters: A Note on Vividness," in *Exposé: Essays from the Expository Writing Program* (Harvard University, 1998–99), 60.

4. Unattributed sidebar, *Exposé*, 56.

5. Telnet is a client/server application first developed in 1969 and used as a messaging service at Harvard University, among other universities, at the end of the twentieth century.

6. Ives, "Responding to Bloody Letters," 56.

7. Dante Alighieri, *Inferno*, in *La Divina Commedia: Con note e con tre tavole schematiche*, ed. Guido Vitali (Livorno: Raffaello Giusti, 1915), 3.

8. My own translation of Alighieri's opening lines.

9. "The 'inculcation of home religion' was often proposed as 'the ultimate answer to matters in the public sphere,' including social homogeneity, political conflict, and the effects of the disestablishment of religion. Churchlike, mystical, and character-shaping, the home of midcentury American ideology reflected the era's millennialism, which stressed the endless perfectibility of social institutions through evangelism, imparted largely by women as agents of revival ministers." Patricia West, *Domesticating History: The Political Origins of America's House Museums* (Washington, DC: Smithsonian Institution Press, 1999), 1.

10. Quoted in Ives, "Responding to Bloody Letters," 56.

11. Gaston Bachelard, "Le monde comme caprice et miniature," in *Études* (Paris: Vrin, Bibliothèque des textes philosophiques, 1970), 27. My translation.

12. Virginia Woolf, "A Sketch of the Past," in *Moments of Being*, ed. Jeanne Schulkind (New York: Harcourt Brace, 1985), 65.

13. Colleen McDannell, *The Christian Home in Victorian America, 1840–1900* (Bloomington: Indiana University Press, 1986), 151. Quoted in West, *Domesticating History*, 1. "When white manhood suffrage detached property holding and home ownership from the right to vote, symbolic 'homes' found a still more important place in political rhetoric. A more inclusive and mobile electorate voted in record numbers in the 'log cabin' campaign of 1840, presumably expressing a belief in the influence of a virtuous native birthplace on male political character"; West, 3.

14. Jeffrey Trask, *Things American: Art Museums and Civic Culture in the Progressive Era* (Philadelphia: University of Pennsylvania Press, 2012), 153–54. A small note of clarification: a house museum is a space that was once inhabited; period rooms are constructed for the purpose of display and therefore have a fundamentally fictional cast.

15. Trask, 62.

16. Robert de Forest, "Address on the Opening of the American Wing of the Metropolitan Museum of Art," *Museum of Fine Arts Bulletin* 23, 135 (February 1925): 3. This quote specifically refers to a 1909 exhibition of American antiques that is described as a test case.

17. Antiques and period room panels were increasingly expensive as the interwar period wore on. The American Wing's curators searched widely, and the boom in antiques in the Northeast meant that it was often necessary to look elsewhere in the country for more affordable items. Trask writes in *Things American*, "For many individual families, selling a room from an old plantation house provided descendants the possibility of saving a house from foreclosure. Ironically, the Old Dominion, birthplace of the preservation movement, ultimately served as the Metropolitan's best resource for elite period rooms" (164).

18. This fireplace is listed in the Met's collection as *Fireplace wall paneling from the John Hewlett House*. It is dated 1740–60, with the provenance: "Mrs. Robert W. de Forest, New York, until 1910."

19. Trask, *Things American*, 181.

20. Frances Yates, *The Art of Memory*, in *Selected Works*, vol. 3 (London: Routledge, 1999 [1966]), 3.

21. See accounts in Joshua Foer, *Moonwalking with Einstein: The Art and Science of Remembering Everything* (New York: Penguin, 2011).

22. My grandfather's passenger number, by means of which his record of entry at Ellis Island can be searched, was 105138060455. Although the letters that make up his name are partly hand-written and not clearly legible, his name was registered as "John Ivas," according to Ellis Island's contemporary database (i.e., his record can also be searched using this name, and not the name "John Ives," which was his name at the time of his death). My grandfather traveled on the SS *Aquitania*, which sailed from Southampton, England, and arrived on April 30, 1921. His name is located on line 013 of the manifest, and he traveled with his mother, Maryam Ivas. My grandfather's age is listed as "9y." He traveled in steerage. His passage was paid for by his mother.

23. "United States Census, 1940," entry for John Ives and Stella Ives, recorded at 68-28 Yonkers City Ward 4 (Area 3), St. John's and Mary Randall Memorial Home for Aged Women, Salvation Army Men's Club. My grandfather's date of birth is listed as 1911, congruent with his age at the time of the 1921 ship's manifest, and in 1940 he lives with my great-grandmother, whose name is now "Mary Ives" and who is a widow (my great-grandfather Elia, who preceded his family members in the United States, died in 1930). Also in the household are my grandmother Stella, John's wife; my aunt, Barbara; and my father, Garrison. My father's age (in fact almost two years at this time) is incorrectly recorded as "0." John and Mary's place of birth is "Persia." Everyone listed in this record is now deceased, except for my father.

Ruth Kambar writes, "The Assyrian community of Yonkers, descendants of the ancient Assyrians of Mesopotamia, initially emigrated from eastern Turkey and northern Iran, particularly from the Urmia region, between the late 1800s and the early 1900s prior to and during World War I." The current Assyrian flag is "closely tied to Yonkers; in 1974, the Assyrian Universal Alliance voted in Yonkers to approve the flag as a symbol of the homeland and the indigenous people of Iraq"; *Assyrians of Yonkers* (Charleston, SC: Arcadia Publishing, 2019), 7.

24. Nicholas Orme, "Of St Iia or Ia <or Hia>, Commonly Called St Iies & St Iues," in *Nicholas Roscarrock's "Lives of the Saints": Cornwall and Devon* (Rochester, NY, and Suffolk, UK: Boydell & Brewer, Devon and Cornwall Record Society, 1992), 78.

25. Elizabeth Rees, "IA," in *An Essential Guide to Celtic Sites and Their Saints* (London: Burns & Oates, 2003), 215.

26. "Ives, St.," in *A Topographical Dictionary of England*, ed. Samuel Lewis (London, 1831), 469. Lewis (470) notes a lesser-known parish of St. Ives near Huntingdon, so named for "St. Ivo or Ives, a Persian archbishop, who traveled in England as a Christian missionary, and died about 600." Ivo's connection to Persia is, however, apparently spurious; see Cyril Hart, "Eadnoth 1 of Ramsey and Dorchester," in *The Danelaw* (London: Hambledon Press, 1964), 613–23.

27. Patrick Hanks, "Ives," in *Dictionary of American Family Names* (Oxford, UK: Oxford University Press, 2003), 1499.

28. Contemporary yew species are "all thought to come from one ancestor, *Paleotaxus redivida*, which grew on the landmass before it separated into continents. An example of this was preserved on a Triassic Age fossil laid down 200,000,000 years ago. A later fossil of yew was found, of *Taxus jurassica*, 140,000,000 years ago." Robert Bevan-Jones, *The Ancient Yew: A History of Taxus Baccata*, 3rd ed. (Oxford, UK: Oxbow Books, 2017), 2.

29. Bevan-Jones, 8, 10–11.

30. Yggdrasill is often understood to be an ash tree, but there are at least two reasons to doubt this interpretation: first, Yggdrasil is described as coniferous in the *Völuspá* in the *Poetic Edda*; second, its name may contain the word *yew* ("*yggia* from **igwja*," meaning "'yew-tree,'" combined with "*drasill* from **dher-* 'support,'" giving "'yew-pillar'"). "From Läffler to de Vries it has been assumed that [Yggdrasill] was a yew tree (*taxus baccata*), on the one hand because of the expression *barr* whereby a conifer must be meant, on the other hand because Tacitus mentions that the Celts worshipped such a tree. In spite of this, there is naturally no reason to 'refute' the concepts given in the *Edda* with regard to which type of tree Yggdrasill is." Rudolf Simek, *Dictionary of Northern Mythology*, trans. Angela Hall (Suffolk, UK: D. S. Brewer, 2007), 375–76.

31. Bevan-Jones, *Ancient Yew*, 150.

32. Hermione Lee, *Virginia Woolf* (London: Chatto & Windus, 1996), 21–23.

33. Lee, 81.

34. See Marion Dell and Marion Whybrow, *Virginia Woolf and Vanessa Bell: Remembering St Ives* (Padstow, UK: Tabb House, 2003).

35. James F. Peltz, "Formula for Success: In a Rough Market, St. Ives, a Maker of Beauty Products, Milks Its Swiss Connections," *Los Angeles Times*, August 4, 1987.

36. After offering a reply to the question "Where Can I Buy St. Ives Skin Care Product?," the St. Ives FAQ page of August 2023 turns to the matter of "Does St. Ives Have Microbeads in Their Products?" The site states: "The presence of plastics in the marine environment is an important issue. Unilever stopped using plastic scrub beads in 2014 in response to concerns about microplastics in oceans and lakes. We had formerly used them in some of our exfoliating products. We now use alternative exfoliating ingredients, such as apricot kernels, cornmeal, ground pumice, silica and walnut shells, enabling people to feel confident that the Unilever face and body washes they use do not contribute to the accumulation of microplastics in the world's oceans." https://www.stives.com/faq-st-ives.

37. Henri Bergson, *Matter and Memory*, trans. N. M. Paul and W. S. Palmer (New York: Zone Books, 2005 [1911]), 135.

38. Bergson, 140.

39. The word was *Assyrian*.

40. Quoted in Wanda M. Corn, *The Great American Thing: Modern Art and National Identity, 1915–1935* (Berkeley: University of California Press, 2001), 311.

41. The Emergency Quota Act of 1921 made use of the 1910 census. As Mae M. Ngai writes, "Although the quotas reduced southern and eastern European immigration by 20 percent from prewar levels, nativists believed it was still unacceptably high. They argued for a 2-percent quota based on the 1890 census." Ngai describes the use of the 1890 census as "crudely discriminatory." Mae M. Ngai, *Impossible Subjects: Illegal Aliens and the Making of Modern America* (Princeton: Princeton University Press, 2004), 21.

42. Ngai, 24.

43. For quota numbers associated with the act, see Ngai, 28–29. These quotas were not implemented until 1929.

44. Ngai, 23.

45. Madison Grant, "The Passing of the Great Race," *Geographical Review* 2, 5 (November 1916): 356.

46. Grant, 360.

47. Grant claims that the subordination of Black Americans is crucial to the nation's health. Madison Grant, *The Passing of the Great Race, or The Racial Basis of European History* (New York: Charles Scribner's Sons, 1916), 78.

48. "What the Melting Pot actually does in practice, can be seen in Mexico, where the absorption of the blood of the original Spanish conquerors by the native Indian population has produced the racial mixture which we call Mexican, and

which is now engaged in demonstrating its incapacity for self-government. The world has seen many such mixtures of races, and the character of a mongrel race is only just beginning to be understood at its true value"; Grant, *Passing*, 15.

49. For Grant's list of living Nordics ("men of Nordic blood to-day"), see Grant, 170.

50. For a discussion of the ornate European mythologies tied to the term *master* in antebellum discourse, see Ritchie Devon Watson, Jr., *Normans and Saxons: Southern Race Mythology and the Intellectual History of the American Civil War* (Baton Rouge: Louisiana State University Press, 2008). See also Grant, *Passing*, 78, 125, 187.

51. Jonathan Spiro, *Defending the Master Race: Conservation, Eugenics, and the Legacy of Madison Grant* (Lebanon, NH: University Press of New England, 2008), 357.

52. "STRIKERS BATTLE IN DENVER STREETS; RIOT IN ILLINOIS; One Killed, 30 Hurt in Colorado City When Strikebreakers Operate Cars. MOB THREATENS CITY HALL Plant of Denver Post Wrecked—Strikebreakers Take Refuge in the Cathedral. CALL TROOPS IN ILLINOIS Mob Seizes West Frankfort in War on Foreigners—Three Dead, 40 Injured—Houses Set Afire. Mob Beats Strikebreakers. Shots Fired in the Outbreak. Chief Armstrong Injured. STRIKERS BATTLE IN DENVER STREETS MOB SEIZES TOWN, THREATENS FOREIGNERS Appeal to Gov. Lowden for Troops at West Frankfort, Ill.—Three Killed, 40 Hurt," *New York Times*, August 6, 1920.

53. Simmons and his followers used highly paid recruiters to market their enterprise to millions. David E. Kyvig, *Daily Life in the United States, 1920–1940: How Americans Lived Through the "Roaring Twenties" and the Great Depression* (Chicago: Ivan R. Dee, 2004), 166–67.

54. The witticism "Klanbake," used to refer to the 1924 Democratic Convention, is the innovation of a *New York Daily News* columnist who also deployed the terms *klanvention* and *klandidate*; Joseph A. Cowan, "Pat's Swig Peps His Patter," *New York Daily News*, June 25, 1924. Although the Klan was present in both political parties of the 1920s and both parties' constituencies have changed in the intervening century, in 2017 and beyond the term *Klanbake* has circulated online as part of a series of memes portraying the contemporary Democratic Party as uniquely racist and hypocritical. See Jennifer Mendelsohn and Peter A. Shulman, "How Social Media Spread a Historical Lie: A Mix of Journalistic Mistakes and Partisan Hackery Advanced a Pernicious Lie about Democrats and the Klan," *Washington Post*, March 15, 2018.

55. This took place on August 8, 1925. Lorraine Boissoneault, "Eleven Times When Americans Have Marched in Protest on Washington: Revisiting Some of the Country's Most Memorable Uses of the Right to Assemble," *Smithsonian Magazine*, January 17, 2017.

56. All three cases are discussed in Matthew Frye Jacobson, *Whiteness of a Different Color: European Immigrants and the Alchemy of Race* (Cambridge, MA: Harvard University Press, 1998), 236, 240.

57. See the SS *Aquitania* manifest described in note 21.

58. "United States Census, 1940," entry for John Ives and Stella Ives.

59. Hsuan L. Hsu writes that olfaction is "a sense fraught with uncertainty and ambiguity insofar as it blends representational and material modes of communication"; *The Smell of Risk: Environmental Disparities and Olfactory Aesthetics* (New York: New York University Press, 2020), 19.

60. Wolfgang Ernst, *Stirrings in the Archives: Order from Disorder*, trans. Adam Siegel (Lanham, MD: Rowman and Littlefield, 2015), 92. Here Ernst quotes Christoph Drösser, "Ein verhängnisvolles Erbe," *Die Zeit*, June 23, 1995.

61. For discussion of this aspect of Ernst's thought and what Ernst terms "time-critically-generated time," see Mark B. N. Hansen, "Medium-Oriented Ontology," *ELH* 83, 2 (2016): 383–86.

62. "The 'right to be forgotten' reflects the claim of an individual to have certain data deleted so that third persons can no longer trace them. Therefore, the right to be forgotten is based on the autonomy of an individual becoming a rightholder in respect of personal information on a time scale; the longer the origin of the information goes back, the more likely personal interests prevail over public interests." Rolf H. Weber, "The Right to Be Forgotten: More Than a Pandora's Box?" *Journal of Intellectual Property, Information Technology and E-Commerce Law* 2 (2011): 121.

63. In other words, "the requirement that digital signal processing occur within strict time windows"; Hansen, "Medium-Oriented Ontology," 383.

64. Woolf, "Sketch of the Past," 65.

65. "Flowers, unlike the faces of human beings, appear to be the perfect size for imagining. . . . When a poet describes a flower, even (I think) when a poet merely names a flower, it is offered as something which, after a brief stop in front of the face, can immediately pass through the resisting bone and lodge itself and light up the inside of the brain." Later, describing the productive "substitution of the muscular glide of the eye for the gliding motion of the body," Scarry settles briefly on "Heathcliff's reaching arm and fist that clenches and unclenches air," as an example of vivacious, substantive movement in the novel *Wuthering Heights*. I doubt she intends that her reader connect these two passages. Elaine Scarry, *Dreaming by the Book* (New York: Farrar, Straus and Giroux, 1999), 46–47 and 148.

66. Ives, "Responding to Bloody Letters," 56–57.

67. This sentence was likely uttered as a part of Adolf Hitler's August 22, 1939, Obersalzberg Speech. The speech exists in three extant textual versions today and was a subject of debate during the Nuremberg Trials. At present, there is scholarly consensus regarding the accuracy of the version of the speech that contains this sentence, although dissenters remain. Historian Margaret Anderson, for one, writes that "we have no reason to doubt the remark is genuine." Margaret Lavinia Anderson, "Who Still Talked about the Extermination of the Armenians?," in *A Question of Genocide: Armenians and Turks at the End of the Ottoman Empire*,

ed. Ronald Grigor Suny, Fatma Müge Göçek, and Norman M. Naimark (Oxford, UK: Oxford University Press, 2011), 199.

68. Ives, "Responding to Bloody Letters," 58.

69. Quoted in Ives. The quoted poem is Siamanto, "The Dance," in *Bloody News from My Friend: Poems by Siamanto*, trans. Peter Balakian and Nevart Yaghlian (Detroit: Wayne State University Press, 1996), 41–44.

70. Anahit Khosroeva, "The Ottoman Genocide of the Assyrians in Persia," in *The Assyrian Genocide: Cultural and Political Legacies*, ed. Hannibal Travis (New York: Routledge, 2018), 137–57. Khosroeva makes use of eyewitness accounts taken from the Armenian newspaper *Mshak* 59 (March 19, 1915).

71. SS *Aquitania* manifest, April 30, 1921, line 013. Here, in the column corresponding to the prompt, "Whether going to join a relative or friend; and if so, what relative or friend, and his name and complete address," we see "Father: Ne[illegible] [I/E]was." At the time of his death, my great-grandfather was known as "Elia Ives."

72. My great-grandfather was, in fact, dead at the time of my father's birth. My great-grandmother died in 1957, when my father was nineteen or twenty. As I understand, her language was the Urmi dialect of Sūret.

73. Rosmarie Waldrop translates these sentences, "'Do not worry about your trace. You are the only one who cannot erase it.'" Edmond Jabès, *The Book of Resemblances*, 3, *The Ineffaceable, The Unperceived*, trans. Rosmarie Waldrop (Hanover: Wesleyan University Press and University Press of New England, 1991), 89.

74. The translation of the passage concerning the rabbi who takes "an assumed name" is Waldrop's (89). The French original concludes, "Et il avait ajouté à l'intention de reb Samhob, son maître vénéré qui, pour se faire oublier de tous, s'était réfugié, sous un nom d'emprunt, dans une petite localité en bordure du désert, où nul n'aurait songé à le trouver: 'Ne te soucie pas de la trace. Tu es seul à ne pouvoir l'effacer.'" Jabès, *Le livre des ressemblances*, 3, *L'ineffaçable, L'inaperçu* (Paris: Gallimard, 1980), 109.

75. Galit Atlas, "A Tale of Two Twins," Couch, *New York Times*, April 11, 2015. This column is accompanied by an illustration by Daehyun Kim, depicting a young person who is constructing a tent-like image of themselves using sticks and a thin textile.

76. Ives, "Responding to Bloody Letters," 59–60. Here I quote Les Murray, *Fredy Neptune* (New York: Farrar, Straus and Giroux, 1999), 5.

Earliness, or Romance

1. "Love is the enemy of memory. But this is a paradox. For love is a much memorialized, mourned, and fetishized feeling that invests institutions of intimacy such as the couple and the family with the power to organize life and the memory

of life across generations and millennia, nations and worlds." Lauren Berlant, *The Female Complaint: The Unfinished Business of Sentimentality in American Culture* (Durham: Duke University Press, 2008), 169.

2. In 1929, Benét would win the Pulitzer Prize for his long poem *John Brown's Body*, a history of the Civil War in verse. Another of Benét's poems furnishes the phrase, "Bury my heart at Wounded Knee," which subsequently appeared as the title of Dee Brown's best-selling 1970 history of the genocide of Native Americans.

3. In late 1953, in listings for minor parts in the cast, the film still went by the title *A Bride for Seven Brothers*. See, e.g., "Hoofer's Bonanza," *Hollywood Reporter* 127, 14 (December 4, 1953), 6. For an exact account of the title change, see Thomas S. Hischak, *Musicals in Film: A Guide to the Genre* (Santa Barbara: Greenwood, 2016), 236.

4. Stephen Vincent Benét, "The Sobbin' Women," in *Thirteen O'Clock: Stories of Several Worlds* (New York: Farrar & Rinehart, 1937), 144–46.

5. The legend of the Rape of the Sabine Women is recounted by Cicero, Livy, Dionysius of Halicarnassus, Ovid, and Plutarch. Milly is probably in possession of Plutarch's *Lives of the Noble Greeks and Romans*, and we can suppose that this is the version of the story the brothers learn. The section on the Sabines occurs in the "Life of Romulus." For a discussion of nationalism and various versions of the story, see Catherine Connors, "The Sobbin' Women: Romulus, Plutarch, and Stephen Vincent Benét," *Illinois Classical Studies*, 38 (2013). 127–48.

6. Benét, "The Sobbin' Women," 151.

7. Benét, 144.

8. Benét, 149.

9. Benét, 138.

10. Regarding landownership in early Oregon, see David Alan Johnson, *Founding the Far West: California, Oregon, and Nevada, 1840–1890* (Berkeley: University of California Press, 1992), 44.

11. For further information on Oregon's Black exclusion laws, particularly "Peter Burnett's lash law," see Thomas C. McClintock, "James Saules, Peter Burnett, and the Oregon Black Exclusion Law of June 1844," *Pacific Northwest Quarterly* 86, 3 (1995): 121–30, and R. Gregory Nokes, "Appendix C. Oregon's Exclusion Act and Lash Law, June 18, 1844," in *The Troubled Life of Peter Burnett* (Corvalis: Oregon State University Press, 2018), 219–20.

12. "At present all is confusion, uncertainty and panic," wrote Thomas Jefferson in late June 1819. A boom in prices for agricultural goods, combined with reckless lending and liberal terms for land sales, led to a bubble that burst when inflationary trends within North America became exposed to deflationary trends worldwide. The Panic of 1819 is sometimes described as the original Great Depression. William H. Crawford, secretary of the treasury at the time, noted that there were in previous history few recorded examples of "distress so general and so severe."

The amount of currency in circulation dropped from over $100 million to $45 million. Debtors' prisons and almshouses filled. The first positive rate of unemployment in the nation's history inhered, with fifty thousand people unemployed by October of 1819 in Baltimore, Philadelphia, and New York. Effects dragged on until 1823. Numerous foreclosures and commercial property liquidations accompanied a wave of migration west. Thomas Jefferson in a letter to Richard Rush, June 22, 1819, founders.archives.gov/documents/Jefferson/03-14-02-0411. George Dangerfield, *The Era of Good Feelings* (New York: Harcourt Brace, 1952), 176, 179. Andrew H. Browning, *The Panic of 1819: The First Great Depression* (Columbia: University of Missouri Press, 2019), 182, 185. Robert V. Remini, "Texas Must be Ours," *American Heritage* 37, 2 (February 1986).

13. The Pontipee family "were all high-colored and dark-haired—handsome with a wilderness handsomeness—and when you got them all together, they looked more like a tribe or a nation than an ordinary family. I don't know how they gave folks that feeling, but they did. Yes, even the baby, when the town women tried to handle him. He was a fine, healthy baby, but they said it was like trying to pet a young raccoon"; Benét, "The Sobbin' Women," 138.

14. Daniel Immerwahr, *How to Hide an Empire: A History of the Greater United States* (New York: Farrar, Straus and Giroux, 2019), 33–34.

15. I saw the original off-Broadway version of *Hedwig and the Angry Inch* in 1998 in New York City. My ticket was a high school graduation gift from Albertine, an individual who appears later in this essay.

16. The speech of Aristophanes takes place from roughly 189c to 193e. See Plato, *Symposium*, trans., intro., and notes Alexander Nehamas and Paul Woodruff (Indianapolis: Hackett, 1989), 25–31.

17. Diotima's speech is indirectly related by Socrates, roughly 203b–212b; Plato, 48–60.

18. Singer (19) notes that the term *courtly love* does not originate in the Middle Ages but was rather coined in the late nineteenth century by the scholar Gaston Paris. Singer also observes that "sexual love between men and women is *in itself* something splendid, an ideal worth striving for. This may not seem revolutionary, but in fact it is a radical conception that few thinkers in Europe had seriously entertained before the eleventh century"; "The Concept of Courtly Love," in *The Nature of Love*, vol. 2, *Courtly and Romantic* (Chicago: University of Chicago Press, 2009 [1966–87]), 23.

19. Marina Warner, *Alone of All Her Sex: The Myth and Cult of the Virgin Mary* (Oxford, UK: Oxford University Press, 2013 [1976]), 152–153.

20. Singer, "Introduction: Concepts of Love in the West," in *Nature of Love*, 10.

21. "In *Love's Labour's Lost* ideal love is thus transmuted into marital love, and this remains constant throughout the succeeding plays"; Singer, "William Shakespeare: Philosopher of Love," in *Nature of Love*, 211.

22. See Sigmund Freud's *Three Essays on the Theory of Sexuality* (1905).

23. "A woman's education must therefore be planned in relation to man. To be pleasing in his sight, to win his respect and love, to train him in childhood, to tend him in manhood, to counsel and console, to make his life pleasant and happy, these are the duties of woman for all time, and this is what she should be taught while she is young. The further we depart from this principle, the further we shall be from our goal, and all our precepts will fail to secure her happiness or our own." Jean-Jacques Rousseau, "Sophy, or Woman," in *Émile, or On Education*, trans. Barbara Foxley (London: J. M. Dent & Sons; Toronto: E. P. Dutton, 1911), 328.

24. The mention of these albums occurs in the sixth chapter of *Madame Bovary, or Morals of the Province*. As Carol Rifelj writes, "Keepsakes were annual gift publications combining literary selections with illustrations. Published in the 1830s and 40s, they were usually Christmas or New Year's gifts for women or young girls"; "'Ces tableaux du monde': Keepsakes in *Madame Bovary*," *Nineteenth-Century French Studies* 25, 3–4 (Spring–Summer 1997): 360.

25. Freud writes about love as a kind of "refinding": "The finding of an [love] object is in fact a refinding of it"; Sigmund Freud, "Transformations of Puberty," in *Three Essays on the Theory of Sexuality*, trans. and ed. James Strachey, intro. Steven Marcus (New York: Basic Books, 1975 [1905]), 88. In the mode of attachment, love is indirectly instigated by the prohibition of incest, and the similarity between the prohibited object of love (a parent) is usually unknown to the lover. There is also the mode of narcissism, of finding oneself in another. To read liberally here: various events and influences gather within the tent of "refinding."

26. Robert C. Solomon and Kathleen M. Higgins, introduction to *The Philosophy of (Erotic) Love* (Lawrence: University Press of Kansas, 1991), 7.

27. In-text translation mine. "Love is to give what one does not have to someone who does not want it"; Jacques Lacan, *The Seminar of Jacques Lacan XII: Crucial Problems for Psychoanalysis, 1964–65*, trans. Cormac Gallagher (London: Karnac, 2002), 191. Lacan repeats the phrase "L'amour, c'est donner ce qu'on n'a pas" in multiple places, sometimes to refer to the way in which psychoanalysis is an act, on the part of the analyst, of giving that which the analyst does not possess (see also *Le transfert* [Paris: Seuil, 1991], 147).

28. Adam Phillips, "On Love," in *On Flirtation* (Cambridge, MA: Harvard University Press, 1994), 39.

29. See Freud, *Three Essays on the Theory of Sexuality*. Donald Winnicott, in a gentler and more pragmatic interpretation of this process, famously maintained that "There is no such thing as a baby. . . . A baby cannot exist alone, but is essentially part of a relationship"; *The Child, the Family, the Outside World* (Oxford, UK: Penguin Books, 1964), 88. Winnicott points to the nursing couple and the presence of an adult body always in proximity to the infant's body. Versions of this view are held by many infant researchers. See W. Zhang, Q. Pan, and B. Guo,

"The Significance of Infant Research for Psychoanalysis," *Humanities and Social Sciences Communications* 9, 194 (2022): 1–8.

30. ". . . held tightly by some prop, human or artificial (what, in France, we call a *trotte-bébé* [a sort of walker])"; Lacan, "The Mirror Stage as Formative of the *I* Function as Revealed in Psychoanalytic Experience," in *Écrits: The First Complete Edition in English*, trans. Bruce Fink, Héloïse Fink, and Russell Grigg (New York: W. W. Norton, 2006), 76. It is worth noting that Lacan's understanding of the time-line of child development seems shaky at best and his observations work a bit better as poetic thumbnails, in my opinion.

31. For the effects on the self of this process and its possible relationship to inter-generational transmission of patterns of abuse, see Winnicott's theory of com-pliance: "Compliance" by "the infant is the earliest stage of the False Self, and belongs to the mother's inability to sense her infant's needs"; "Ego Distortion in Terms of True and False Self," in *The Maturational Processes and the Facilitating Environment* (New York: International Universities Press, 1965), 145. Winnicott claims that compliance with harmful behavior can become a template for later patterns of action, conceptions of the self, and views of the world.

32. One of Luhmann's contemporary claims to fame is as a productivity inno-vator. He is legendary for his *Zettelkasten* method, which he allegedly used to write books that made him an authority in the field of media studies, despite limited time. The 1969 lecture, written for a seminar Luhmann gave at Bielefeld University, has been published as *Love: A Sketch*, ed. André Kieserling, trans. Kathleen Cross (Cambridge, UK: Polity Press, 2010). This lecture precedes Luhmann's more complex, communication-theory-driven book, *Liebe als Passion*, published in the early 1980s. The 1969 text is a sociology of love, although clearly linked to the later study.

33. "Love operates according to the counter-condition that the individuality of the experiencing person is . . . turned into the very point of reference. . . . Because the person I love sees, feels and judges things in a particular way, their world-view is also convincing for me"; Luhmann, *Love*, 12.

34. Niklas Luhmann, *Love as Passion: The Codification of Intimacy*, trans. Jeremy Gaines and Doris L. Jones (Stanford: Stanford University Press, 1998). See, in par-ticular, "The Evolution of the Semantics of Love," 41–47.

35. "Rather, it is individuality, one of the most concrete characteristics of man, that now becomes the most general. What had in past times to be viewed as highly con-tingent must accordingly now be conceived of as a necessity and characterized by its reference to the world. Yet, this new concept, this definition of the individual as *uniquely constituting the world*, suspends the notion of individual as *nature* that was valid until approximately 1800"; Luhmann, *Love as Passion*, 181.

36. Simone de Beauvoir, *The Second Sex*, trans. and ed. H. M. Parshley (New York: Vintage Books, 1989 [1952]), 644.

37. Shulamith Firestone, *The Dialectic of Sex: The Case for a Feminist Revolution* (New York: Morrow, 1970), 84. On these matters, see also Sophie Lewis's recent work.

38. Philip Slater, *The Pursuit of Loneliness: American Culture at the Breaking Point* (Boston: Beacon Press, 1970), 87.

39. Slater, 88.

40. Lauren Berlant, *Cruel Optimism* (Durham: Duke University Press, 2011), 24.

41. In a three-volume history of American sentimentality—*The Anatomy of National Fantasy* (1991), *The Queen of America Goes to Washington City* (1997), and *The Female Complaint* (2008)—Berlant sought a vocabulary to describe fantasies they saw as key to public life.

42. Lauren Berlant, *The Anatomy of National Fantasy: Hawthorne, Utopia, and Everyday Life* (Chicago: University of Chicago Press, 1991), 28.

43. Lauren Berlant, *The Queen of America Goes to Washington City: Essays on Sex and Citizenship* (Durham, NC: Duke University Press, 1997), 3.

44. Berlant, *Female Complaint*, 169.

45. Slater, *Pursuit of Loneliness*, 88.

46. Berlant, *Desire/Love* (Brooklyn, NY: punctum books, 2012), 71–72.

47. bell hooks, *All About Love: New Visions* (New York: William and Morrow, 2000), xxviii. hooks's remarks on these matters are worth quoting in full: "This despair about love is coupled with a callous cynicism that frowns upon any suggestion that love is as important as work, as crucial to our survival as a nation as the drive to succeed. Awesomely, our nation, like no other in the world, is a culture driven by the quest to love (it's the theme of our movies, music, literature) even as it offers so little opportunity for us to understand love's meaning or to know how to realize love in word and deed."

48. hooks, 6.

49. hooks, 185.

50. "MILLS ANNA B," New Jersey State Archives, Trenton; Marriage Indexes; Index Type: Bride; Year Range: 1915–1919; Surname Range: M–M.

51. Mary Rawlings and Benjamin Butts were married in Fort Dodge, Iowa, on Christmas Day in 1906. Iowa Department of Public Health, Iowa Marriage Records, 1880–1945; Textual Records; State Historical Society of Iowa, Des Moines.

52. The 1900 United States Federal Census records "Frank Butts" as living with his wife, "Grace Butts," and their son, "Chester," in Philadelphia, where Frank is "Choir Master." They have been married for thirteen years, as they report. Bessie Aileen, born in 1888, would have been twelve at this time, although she is not recorded in this census.

53. 1910 United State Federal Census, Census Place: Manhattan Ward 12, New York; roll: T624_1026; Page: 7b; Enumeration District: 0680; FHL microfilm: 1375039.

54. *New York Observer and Chronicle* 89, 16 (October 20, 1910), 507.

55. *New York Times*, September 14, 1912, 13.

56. According to the 1915 New Jersey State Census, Benjamin Franklin and Mary Emma are living in Haworth. She is a "Housewife." He is an "Evangelist." State Census of New Jersey, 1915; New Jersey State Archive; Trenton; reference number: L-04; film number: 5. By the time of the 1920 Federal Census, Benjamin Franklin, still living in Haworth, is married to Anna Butts and self-describes as a "Clergyman." Anna's occupation is "None." They do not live at the same address as Mary Emma and Benjamin Franklin did. 1920 United States Federal Census; census place: Haworth, Bergen; roll: T625_1017; page: 13B; enumeration district: 13.

57. *San Francisco Examiner,* May 28, 1927, 16.

58. In 1930, Benjamin Franklin, Onna, and their three children live in Las Cruces, New Mexico. 1930 United States Federal Census; census place: Las Cruces, Dona Aña; page: 4A; enumeration district: 0005; FHL microfilm: 2341129.

59. https://hymnary.org/tune/im_a_little_daisy_butts. The Reverend Butts was born in either 1866 or 1867, based on various documents. Other information here may be spurious.

60. "Delegates to C.E. Meeting Return Home," *Madera Mercury* 93, July 11, 1923.

61. See https://www.findagrave.com/memorial/134660932/benjamin-franklin-butts.

62. See https://www.findagrave.com/user/profile/47930139, accessed November 15, 2023.

63. Toni Morrison, *The Bluest Eye: A Novel* (New York: Knopf, 2007 [1970]), 122. The other most destructive idea is "physical beauty."

64. Ruth B. Bottigheimer, "From Gold to Guilt: The Forces Which Reshaped *Grimms' Tales*," in *The Brothers Grimm and Folktale*, ed. James M. McGlathery (Champaign: University of Illinois Press, 1988), 200, 195.

65. Bottigheimer, 195–96.

66. See G. Sperati, "Amputation of the Nose throughout History," *Acta Otorhino-laryngologica Italica* 29, 1 (February 2009): 44–50.

67. R. Philip Bouchard, *You Have Died of Dysentery: The Creation of The Oregon Trail—the Iconic Educational Game of the 1980s* (self-published ebook, 2016).

68. A. Aron, E. Melinat, E. N. Aron, R. Darrin Vallone, and R. J. Bator, "The Experimental Generation of Interpersonal Closeness: A Procedure and Some Preliminary Findings," *Personality and Social Psychology Bulletin* 23, 4 (April 1997): 363–77.

69. For example, "When did you last cry in front of another person? By yourself?" Or, "If you were to die this evening with no opportunity to communicate with anyone, what would you most regret not having told someone? Why haven't you told them yet?" "The 36 Questions That Lead to Love," Modern Love, *New York Times*, January 9, 2015.

70. Mandy Len Catron, "To Fall in Love with Anyone, Do This," Modern Love, *New York Times*, January 9, 2015.

71. Note that the staring portion of the procedure was not included in the 1997 paper and never published, although it was apparently part of the team's research in 1991.

72. Catron, "To Fall in Love with Anyone."

73. One exception to the paper's general reticence regarding romantic love itself is a brief note stating that after an initial trial in 1991 one pair married: "Encouraged by high postexperiment ratings of closeness and anecdotal reports of the impact of the experience over the next few months (including one pair who married!) we adapted this task." Aron et al., "Experimental Generation," 364.

74. Kathaleen Boche, "Hatchets and Hairbrushes: Dance, Gender, and Improvisational Ingenuity in Cold War Western Musicals," in *The Oxford Handbook of Dance and the Popular Screen*, ed. Melissa Blanco Borelli (New York: Oxford University Press, 2014), 339.

75. Michael Kidd, interviewed in *Sobbin' Women: The Making of "Seven Brides for Seven Brothers,"* directed by Scott Benson (1997).

76. Julie Newmar, interviewed in *Sobbin' Women*.

77. "However graceful, the potential sexual innuendo of the 'Lonesome Polecat' number was not lost on the Production Code Administration (PCA). The context of the number hints at sexual frustration and masturbation, while the line, 'A man can't sleep when he sleeps with sheep' suggested much more. PCA censor Joseph I. Breen warned the filmmakers, 'Great care will be needed with the scene with the sheep, to avoid any objectionable inference. We do not need to remind you that there are some extremely offensive jokes about men and sheep, and if this particular phrase of your song is to be approvable, it will have to avoid this danger. Specifically, we suggest not having the sheep leaning against the men, or anything of that sort." Kathaleen Boche, "Dancing Americana: Choreographing Visions of American Identity from the Stage to the Screen, 1936–1958" (PhD diss., Florida State University, 2014), 152.

78. A 1998 landmark study of some 9,500 respondents conducted by the Centers for Disease Control and Prevention and Kaiser Permanente found that more than half had experienced childhood abuse or "household dysfunction," and that these experiences appear to be related to health issues in adulthood and death. Vincent J. Felitti et al., "Relationship of Childhood Abuse and Household

Dysfunction to Many of the Leading Causes of Death in Adults: The Adverse Childhood Experiences (ACE) Study," *American Journal of Preventive Medicine* 14, 4 (1998): 245–58.

79. Genesis 32:24, King James Bible Online, 2023 [1769], https://www.kingjames bibleonline.org/.

80. Here I indicate both the seventeenth-century fairy tale written by Charles Perrault and the trippy 1970 Catherine Deneuve vehicle, *Peau d'âne*.

81. The roughness (intimacy) of this list has been preserved.

The End

1. Barbara Johnson, "Opening Remarks," in *The Critical Difference: Essays in the Contemporary Rhetoric of Reading* (Baltimore: Johns Hopkins University Press, 1982 [1980]), xii.

2. Ronald Sullivan, "Tornado Tears Through Berkshires, Killing 3 in an Auto," *New York Times*, May 30, 1995.

3. The story of the cornstalk impaling a car radiator, which may, of course, be apocryphal, is associated with a tornado of November 16, 2015, in Pampa, Texas (see https://weather.com/storms/tornado/news/strange-tornado-damage-photos). Strange events, such as the plucking of feathers from chickens otherwise left unharmed, are sometimes known as "freaks of the storm" or "tornado oddities." Near Great Bend, Kansas, an "iron water hydrant was supposedly found full of splinters," writes Thomas P. Grazulis of a 1915 storm in *The Tornado: Nature's Ultimate Windstorm* (Norman: University of Oklahoma Press, 2001), 16. Such spooky occurrences, often the subject of local lore, seem associated with low atmospheric pressure or the action of high winds but may have other causes. Chickens are thought to molt spontaneously in fear, for example. See also Randy Cerveny and Joseph T. Schaefer, "Tornado Oddities," *Weatherwise* 55, 4 (2002): 20–27.

4. This phrase is George Oppen's. "Of Being Numerous," in *New Collected Poems*, ed. Michael Davidson, preface by Eliot Weinberger (New York: New Directions, 2008), 167.

5. This generic illustration of Saussure's dyadic or binary sign shows a linguistic sound-image (this is less a sound-in-itself than a recommendation for a sound, a sound recognizable by convention) and a concept, combined. It is notable that, although I as a college sophomore confusedly believed that Saussure's diagram depicted a word, this is not the case—indeed, Saussure sees the sound-image itself as "a word," while the sign as a whole indicates something larger and implicates the senses. Saussure additionally does not believe that a sign is the same thing as a sentence. So, what is a sign? Saussure seems concerned that signs may not be recognizable at all, in themselves. "Language then has the strange, striking characteristic of not having entities that are perceptible at the outset and

yet of not permitting us to doubt that they exist and that their functioning constitutes it," we learn. Saussure insists that context alone allows us to recognize linguistic elements (phonemes, concepts) and use them over and over; they occupy constant places in a given system, and this is how we know them. We know them through their differences, not through their positive content. He famously describes a train that arrives at a station at a certain time of day: "We feel that it is the same train each day, yet everything—the locomotive, coaches, personnel—is probably different." Ferdinand de Saussure, *Course in General Linguistics*, trans. Wade Baskin, ed. Perry Meisel and Haun Saussy (New York: Columbia University Press, 2011), 67, 107, 108.

6. Johnson still holds this title.

7. Maria Baghramian contends that such thinkers as Claude Lévi-Strauss, Jacques Derrida, Michel Foucault, and Jean-François Lyotard, following Friedrich Nietzsche and Ferdinand de Saussure, "attempt to show that all systematic thought and metaphysical system-building involves hierarchical presuppositions, which once laid bare, undermine themselves or deconstruct"; *Relativism* (London: Routledge, 2004), 105. In this intellectual milieu, assertions of truth are understood as the creations of various interested parties; it is perhaps less that truth, as such, does not exist than that its use and legibility are limited or situational, rather than transcendent. See also Lucy Ives, "After the Afterlife of Theory," *The Baffler* 39, May 2018.

8. Here I indicate "the linguistic turn," a historical catchall used to describe transformations in philosophy during the twentieth century. Ludwig Wittgenstein's focus on language games and logic, as opposed to description of concepts, is thought to have inaugurated the contemporary anglophone discipline of analytic philosophy. In literary and social scientific fields, the linguistic theory of Ferdinand de Saussure promoted a view of knowledge in which linguistic systems dominate concepts, as such.

9. See such belated postmortems as Bob Harris's brief rant for the *New York Times*, June 30, 2008, "Isn't It Ironic? Probably Not."

10. See Lee Konstantinou, "Introduction. The Character of Irony," in *Cool Characters: Irony and American Fiction* (Cambridge, MA: Harvard University Press, 2016), 1–48.

11. Bio-power is a "set of mechanisms through which the basic biological features of the human species became the object of a political strategy"; Michel Foucault, *Security, Territory, Population: Lectures at the Collège de France, 1977–78*, ed. Michel Senellart, trans. Graham Burchell (New York: Palgrave Macmillan, 2007), 1.

12. Richard Rorty, *Contingency, Irony, and Solidarity* (Cambridge, UK: Cambridge University Press, 1989), 73.

13. Rorty, xv.

14. Rorty, 8.

15. Barbara Johnson, "Anthropomorphism in Lyric and Law," *Yale Journal of Law & the Humanities* 10, 2 (1998): 556. This essay is also included in *Persons and Things* (Cambridge, MA: Harvard University Press, 2008), 188–207.

16. To give a bit of context for my use of this term: the philosopher Pierre Hadot, using an alternate spelling, conceives of *askesis* as a spiritual and intellectual exercise in which the individual "re-places himself within the perspective of the Whole"; *Philosophy as a Way of Life: Spiritual Exercises from Socrates to Foucault*, ed. and intro. Arnold I. Davidson, trans. Michael Chase (Malden, MA: Blackwell, 1995), 82.

17. See Laura Swan, "Euphrosyne of Alexandria," in *The Forgotten Desert Mothers: Sayings, Lives, and Stories of Early Christian Women* (Mahwah, NJ: Paulist Press, 2001), 83–84. Use of the name "Smaragdus" is recounted in Johann Peter Kirsch, "St. Euphrosyne," in *The Catholic Encyclopedia*, ed. Charles G. Herberman et al. (New York: Encyclopedia Press, 1909), 11.

18. John R. Hall, *Apocalypse: From Antiquity to the Empire of Modernity* (Cambridge, UK: Polity Press), 147.

19. Quoted in Hall, 148.

20. Hall, 148.

21. In the New Testament, the eschatological task of the risen Christ is to initiate the last judgment and gather the just into the resurrection, which will also constitute the end of history. Ann Lee, who was believed by her followers to be the parousia of Christ in female form, advised renunciation of worldly encumbrances and embrace of celibacy. Her sect's name was related to "a belief in the power of the eschatological Spirit shaking the age in preparation for the millennium," and before they fled England the Shakers regularly engaged in "'Sabbath-breaking,' noisily interrupting the formal worship of churches in order to denounce every institutional religious organization as belonging to Antichrist, and to announce the nearness of the new age to be inaugurated at Christ's Second Coming." As the second appearance of Christ, Ann Lee was herself "the Shaker apocalypse," the ultimate unveiling, and she labored as an "eschatological mother" to bring forth "the children of the New Creation"; Kathleen Deignan, *Christ Spirit: The Eschatology of Shaker Christianity*, ATLA Monograph Series 29 (Metuchen, NJ: American Theological Library Association, 1992), 32–33, 36, 49, 54.

22. As Anne V. Wilson and Silvia Bellezza write, "Our data revealed that minimalist influencers and enthusiasts carry an air of virtuousness and moral superiority in eschewing rampant capitalism and offer opportunities for reinvention and self-fulfillment through minimalism"; "Consumer Minimalism," *Journal of Consumer Research* 48, 5 (2022): 801. The recently shuttered luxury-goods emporium, Tiina the Store, was a prime example of minimalist, Shaker-esque aesthetics in an aspirational space. In an interview about her decision to close her business, Tiina Laakkonen explained that when she opened her store the uber-wealthy who were her customers had "nowhere . . . to shop" in their search for

logo-free, transcendently high-quality goods. Guy Trebay, "Farewell to a Store That Was Gap for Billionaires," *New York Times*, August 10, 2023. Such accounts of consumer minimalism suggest that the contemporary aesthetic is tied to sophistication, worldliness, and the simultaneous rejection of such qualities in multiple, sometimes contradictory ways, and that a form of separatism is important to its pursuit. Given the climate crisis, the notion of an end of the world spurring minimalist tastes would seem relevant here, too, although, of course, it is difficult to say how "sustainable" consumer minimalism is.

23. In some descriptions, Ann Lee seems to view the apocalypse as personal, rather than historical, in nature. "She told them there would never be a universal day of judgment for all mankind. Salvation is not an event, said Mother Ann. It is a quiet transformation that takes place within an individual who has entered wholly into the life of the spirit. For that person, the 'world' and all its desires have come to an end, and the Millennium has begun"; Nardi Reeder Campion, *Ann the Word: The Life of Mother Ann Lee, Founder of the Shakers* (Boston: Little, Brown, 1976), 84.

24. Miller wrote of his war experiences in a newspaper article published after the "Great Disappointment": "It seemed to me that the Supreme Being must have watched over the interests of this country in an especial manner, and delivered us from the hands of our enemies"; "Mr. Miller's Apology and Defence," *Advent Herald and Morning Watch* 10, 1 (August 13, 1845), 1. See this "Apology" for other details of his life.

25. The time period given here is "2300 days." Miller records his interpretations of biblical chronology in his "Apology," 1–2.

26. "At one point perhaps as many as fifty thousand of these Adventists scattered over New England and western New York as an integral part of the millennial ethos of the late 1830s and early 1840s"; Jonathan M. Butler, "Adventism and the American Experience," in *The Rise of Adventism: Religion and Society in Mid-Nineteenth-Century America*, ed. Edwin S. Gaustad (New York: Harper & Row, 1974), 175.

27. See https://www.jw.org/en/library/books/2022-Service-Year-Report-of-Jehovahs -Witnesses-Worldwide/2022-Grand-Totals//, and *2023 Statistical Report*, new series, vol. 5, Seventh-day Adventist Church, https://documents.adventistarchives.org /Statistics/ASR/ASR2023A.pdf.

28. The deaths are enumerated in the US Department of Justice's "Report to the Deputy Attorney General on the Events at Waco, Texas: The Aftermath of the April 19 Fire" (1993). This report is no longer available on the DoJ's website but has been archived at https://web.archive.org/web/20170511015809/https: /www.justice.gov/publications/waco/report-deputy-attorney-general-events -waco-texas-aftermath-april-19-fire.

29. McVeigh spoke to "Southern Methodist University student journalist Michelle Rauch outside Koresh's Waco compound in April '93, before the ATF siege"; Brian

Morton, "The Guns of Spring," *Baltimore City Paper*, April 15, 2009. This interview was "a big break" for the FBI, once Rauch realized the connection three years after the fact. Richard A. Serrano, *One of Ours: Timothy McVeigh and the Oklahoma City Bombing* (New York: W. W. Norton, 1998), 69.

30. See, e.g., McVeigh's obsession with FBI sharpshooter Lon Horiuchi, who shot Vicki Weaver at the Ruby Ridge standoff in Boundary County, Idaho, while she was holding her ten-month-old child. As at Waco, military tactics were used against heavily armed citizens who were, significantly, embedded with family. James Michael Martinez, *Terrorist Attacks on American Soil: From the Civil War Era to the Present* (Lanham, MD: Rowman & Littlefield, 2012), 288–91.

31. McVeigh spoke to Rauch about his military service and understanding of federal officers' twisted desire to "play with their toys paid for by government money," including Bradley tanks; Serrano, *One of Ours*, 70.

32. Quoted in Barry J. Balleck, *Allegiance to Liberty: The Changing Face of Patriots, Militias, and Political Violence in America* (Santa Barbara: Praeger, 2014), 171. Serrano (78) contends that this was a friendship breakup letter.

33. Lou Michel and Dan Herbeck, *American Terrorist: Timothy McVeigh & the Oklahoma City Bombing* (New York: HarperCollins, 2001), 283.

34. Martha Himmelfarb, *The Apocalypse: A Brief History* (West Sussex, UK: Wiley-Blackwell, 2010), 1.

35. Cynthia L. Haven, *Evolution of Desire: A Life of René Girard* (Ypsilanti: Michigan State University Press, 2018), 131, 136.

36. Jacques Lacan, "Of Structure as an Inmixing of an Otherness Prerequisite to Any Subject Whatever," "Discussion," in *The Structuralist Controversy: The Languages of Criticism and the Sciences of Man*, ed. Richard Macksey and Eugenio Donato (Baltimore: Johns Hopkins University Press, 1972 [1970]), 195.

37. Haven, *Evolution of Desire*, 123, 132.

38. Élisabeth Roudinesco, *Jacques Lacan & Co.: A History of Psychoanalysis in France, 1925–1985*, vol. 2 (Chicago: University of Chicago Press, 1990), 410, cited in Haven, 130–131.

39. Roland Barthes, "To Write: An Intransitive Verb?" "Discussion: Barthes-Todorov," in Macksey and Donato, *The Structuralist Controversy*, 150.

40. The speaker was Georges Poulet. Haven, *Evolution of Desire*, 138.

41. This opinion was offered by Neville Dyson-Hudson in a talk titled "Structure and Infrastructure in Primitive Society: Lévi-Strauss and Radcliffe-Brown"; Haven, 223. In her article, which by and large praises Lévi-Strauss's intellect, Susan Sontag makes such remarks as, "Anthropology is necrology. 'Let's go and study the primitives,' say Lévi-Strauss and his pupils, 'before they disappear,'" and "Anthropology has always struggled with an intense, fascinated repulsion to-

wards its subject"; "A Hero of Our Time," *New York Review of Books* 1, 7 (November 28, 1963), 6–8.

42. "Only a subject can understand a meaning; conversely, every phenomenon of meaning implies a subject"; Jacques Lacan, "Aggressivity in Psychoanalysis," in *Écrits: A Selection*, trans. Alan Sheridan (London: Tavistock, 1977 [1966]), 9.

43. Until a remark by Elana Rosenthal, who kindly fact-checked this essay, I believed that my note on Ruscha's text was in error. I wrote, "Note that I do not think that the artist Ed Ruscha ever wrote such a book and I believe that here I was referring to Edward Tufte's book, *The Visual Display of Quantitative Information*, but this is just a guess." However, Rosenthal was able to locate Ruscha's narrative, "The Information Man," which Ruscha wrote by hand in 1971 in a journal. In his story, Ruscha imagines that a character who knows everything about everyone says things to him like "'You have not said the word "yours" for 12 minutes,'" and, helpfully, can tell Ruscha what has happened to all the copies of his limited-edition photobooks. I'm amazed that in the early 2000s I had knowledge of this ultrarare text. Where on earth did I hear about it—and did I eventually read it? See *Ed Ruscha / Now Then: A Retrospective*, ed. Christophe Cherix with Ana Torok and Kiko Aebi (New York: Museum of Modern Art, 2023), 8–10.

44. I have not been able to confirm the accuracy of all these quotations.

45. Arthur Hobson Quinn, *Edgar Allan Poe: A Critical Biography* (Baltimore: Johns Hopkins University Press, 1998 [1941]), 639–43.

46. The theory of Poe's death by cooping has been variously promoted and disputed. It was first put forth in 1872 by R. H. Stoddard, a New York–based writer and editor, in *Harper's Magazine*. Stoddard wrote that Poe was "seized by the lawless agents of some political club," although as John Evangelist Walsh notes, there is "a troubling lack of support for the unusual claim"; *Midnight Dreary: The Mysterious Death of Edgar Allan Poe* (New York: St. Martin's Minotaur, 2000 [1998]), 53. Quinn, *Edgar Allan Poe* (639), criticizes descriptions in which Poe is "drugged, taken from one polling place to another." However, he speculates that cooping may have been so well known in Poe's day that mentions of death as associated with this practice in contemporary journalism would have been deemed "unnecessary."

47. It is not, in fact, clear when Poe might have contracted rabies, if he did, and this could have occurred as early as a year before his death. See Associated Press, "Poe's Death Is Rewritten as a Case of Rabies, Not Telltale Alcohol," *New York Times*, September 15, 1996.

48. Eiros and Charmion are not these two dead people's earthly names; rather, they've been rechristened posthumously and bear the names of a pair of servants who apparently worked for Cleopatra, if we believe Plutarch. Poe's education in the classics emerges in an odd way here, inflecting the story with droopy arabesques and spellings reminiscent of ancient or Eastern languages transliterated into English—the Edenic realm the two spirits inhabit is, for example, called "Aidenn," presumably after the Arabic. The effects of authenticity, such as they

are, that the story trades in thus include an air of mystical neoclassicism also on display in the weirdest of Poe's poems, such as "Ulalume," where pseudo-archaic language can start, paradoxically, to feel futuristic. Edgar Allan Poe, "The Conversation of Eiros and Charmion," in *The Complete Stories*, intro. John Seelye, Everyman's Library no. 99 (New York: Knopf, 1992 [1839]), 393–99.

49. "This analysis through repetition is to become, in Lacan's ingenious reading, no less than an *allegory of psychoanalysis*. The intervention of Dupin, who restores the letter to the Queen, is thus compared, in Lacan's interpretation, to the intervention of the analyst, who rids the patient of the symptom. The analyst's effectiveness, however, does not spring from his intellectual strength but—insists Lacan—from his position in the (repetitive) structure. By virtue of his occupying the third position—that is, the *locus* of the unconscious of the subject as a place of substitution of letter for letter (of signifier for signifier)—the analyst, through transference, allows at once for a repetition of the trauma, and for a symbolic substitution, and thus effects the drama's denouement." Shoshana Felman, "On Reading Poetry: Reflections on the Limits and Possibilities of Psychoanalytical Approaches," in *The Purloined Poe: Lacan, Derrida, and Psychoanalytic Reading*, ed. John P. Muller and William J. Richardson (Baltimore: Johns Hopkins University Press, 1987), 147.

50. Anne Dufourmantelle relates a story of an analyst who is distracted by a "beautiful pigeon at [his] window" and therefore does not hear what his patient is saying at a crucial moment. In spite of—or perhaps because of—this, the patient is apparently cured and never returns. The content of what was spoken was less important than the act (here, of speaking freely). Dufourmantelle, "At the Risk of Passion," in *In Praise of Risk*, trans. Stephen Miller (New York: Fordham University Press, 2009), 19–20.

51. Barbara Johnson, "The Frame of Reference: Poe, Lacan, Derrida," in Muller and Richardson, *The Purloined Poe*, 242. I quote this republication of the essay, as opposed to the version included in *The Critical Difference*, because it constitutes a particular artifact in my encounter with Johnson.

52. Johnson, "Frame of Reference," 247. "To be fooled by a text implies that the text is not constative but performative, and that the reader is in fact one of its effects. The text's 'truth' puts the status of the reader in question, 'performs' him as its 'address.'"

53. Johnson, "The Frame of Reference," 250. Derrida's concept of *différance* refers to the nonidentity of written language with that which it represents (at literal figurative, and aural levels), as well as language's ability to be meaningful only through its difference from itself (rather than by way of fixed referential capacity or other unchanging feature). In this essay, Johnson repeatedly uses the English word *difference* when writing about Derrida's interpretation of the Poe story.

54. Johnson, "Anthropomorphism in Lyric and Law," 573.

55. Miguel de Cervantes Saavedra, "The Glass Graduate," in *Exemplary Stories*, trans. C. A. Jones (London: Penguin Books, 1972 [1613]), 121–46.

56. "Cases were concentrated among the wealthy and educated classes of men. . . . Sufferers were observed to be normal in every respect, bar the belief that they had turned to glass. As a result, they could function relatively well, albeit remaining anxious in case anyone came too close and risked shattering their fragile limbs"; Victoria Shepherd, *A History of Delusions: The Glass King, a Substitute Husband and a Walking Corpse* (London: Oneworld Publications, 2022), 165.

57. Shepherd (164) excerpts the account of a witnessing "member of the order of St Denis," sometimes known as Michel Pintoin or the Monk of St Denis, author of the *Chronique du Religieux de Saint-Denys, contenant le regne de Charles VI de 1380 à 1422.*

58. Quoted in Shepherd, 166.

59. Quoted in Shepherd, 166.

60. "Key Features That Define the Psychotic Disorders," in *Diagnostic and Statistical Manual of Mental Disorders*, Fifth Edition, Text Revision (DSM-5-TR), consulted via DSM Library, Psychiatry Online, https://doi.org/10.1176/appi.books .9780890425787.x02_Schizophrenia_Spectrum.

61. This novel begins with the promising sentence, "Last December a woman entered my apartment who looked exactly like my wife"; Rivka Galchen, *Atmospheric Disturbances: A Novel* (New York: Farrar, Straus and Giroux, 2008), 3.

62. Here Hirstein is writing about confabulation, a form of imaginative speech associated with memory disorders, but I think his formulation works well in relation to delusion more generally. It is, at any rate, descriptive of states of mind I have experienced. William Hirstein, *Brain Fiction: Self-Deception and the Riddle of Confabulation* (Cambridge, MA: MIT Press, 2006), 4.

63. "Dissociative Disorders," in *Diagnostic and Statistical Manual of Mental Disorders*.

64. https://en.wikipedia.org/wiki/Depersonalization-derealization_disorder, accessed variously in August 2023.

65. Per the DSM-V, "Onset can range from extremely sudden to gradual"; "Dissociative Disorders," in *Diagnostic and Statistical Manual of Mental Disorders*.

66. The DSM-V does not discuss this symptom. A tool known as the "Dissociative Experiences Scale," developed by Eve Bernstein-Carlson and Frank Putnam, includes twenty-eight questions, five of which are believed to correlate specifically with depersonalization-derealization disorder. Question 11 is among these: "Some people have the experience of looking in a mirror and not recognizing themselves. Select the number to show what percentage of the time this happens to you. (0% Never, 100% Always) 0% 10% 20% 30% 40% 50% 60% 70% 80% 90% 100%"; http://traumadissociation.com/des. For a longer discussion of the DES and depersonalization/derealization, see Daphne Simeon and Jeffrey

Abugel, *Feeling Unreal: Depersonalization and the Loss of the Self* (New York: Oxford University Press, 2023 [2006]), 44–45. A patient's anamnesis quoted by Simeon and Abugel (50) reads, "I look in the mirror to try to re-center myself but I still feel like I'm in the Twilight Zone. Like a zombie, like the living dead. Am I really me? My thoughts about the depersonalization lead me on a perpetual tortured journey of questions without answers." Another (51): "I cannot feel sex. I touch my body, pinch it, rub it, to feel something. I look at my hands and wonder if they're mine; they look bigger, or smaller, or just strange. Sometimes when I'm very stressed my body gets lighter and lighter and I almost float away. It's like I leave my body entirely. Food tastes very bland, and sometimes I forget that I am thirsty. My voice sounds strange, like when I used to listen to recordings of myself. I see myself from the outside, like I'm looking at a mirror, yet when I look in the mirror it's not me that I see."

67. Per the DSM-V, "The mean age at onset of depersonalization/derealization disorder is 16 years, although the disorder can start in early or middle childhood; a minority cannot recall ever not having had the symptoms. Less than 20% of individuals experience onset after age 20 years and only 5% after age 25 years"; "Dissociative Disorders," in *Diagnostic and Statistical Manual of Mental Disorders*. Given the duration of my so-called episode, my case could be considered "extreme."

68. "Délire de negation," quoted in Shepherd, *History of Delusion*, 255. I should note that current descriptions of depersonalization/derealization disorder often include feelings of being dead, as in note 65. "The word *feel* is also fraught with its own mysteries. A person may suffer immensely from lack of feeling when hypoemotionality and numbing comprise one of their core depersonalization symptoms, yet suffering itself is a feeling—a negative one, a pained state of mind. But suffering alone is a very constricted emotional world, and some people with dpdr describe feeling nothing at all, like a full automaton—the 'living dead'"; Simeon and Abugel, *Feeling Unreal*, 44. The condition is full of contradiction; one does not feel (that one exists), yet one is in anguish. As a recent multiauthor paper has it, despersonalization/derealization disorder "causes immense distress"; J. R. Büetiger et al., "Trapped in a Glass Bell Jar: Neural Correlates of Depersonalization and Derealization in Subjects at Clinical High-Risk of Psychosis and Depersonalization–Derealization Disorder," *Frontiers in Psychiatry* 11 (September 2020): 1.

69. Matthew Ratcliffe, *Feelings of Being: Phenomenology, Psychiatry and the Sense of Reality* (Oxford, UK: Oxford University Press, 2008), 167.

70. Garry Young, *Philosophical Psychopathology: Philosophy without Thought Experiments* (London and New York: Palgrave Macmillan, 2013), 154. Young cites G. Conchiglia, G. Della Rocca, and D. Grossi's paper, "When the Body Image Becomes 'Empty': Cotard's Delusion in a Demented Patient," *Acta Neuropsychiatrica* 20, 5 (October 2008): 283–84.

71. I believe my memory is of the Mystery Spot of Santa Cruz, California, where in 1939 a man named George Prather created a tourist attraction that still exists.

Here visitors may experience distorted perceptions of scale and the illusion of the nonpertinence of the force of gravity.

72. Rorty, *Contingency, Irony, and Solidarity*, 84.

73. Rorty, xv.

74. See Guiseppe Ballacci, "Richard Rorty's Unfulfilled Humanism and the Public/Private Divide," *Review of Politics* 79, 3 (Summer 2017): 427–50.

75. See Francis Fukuyama's *The End of History and the Last Man* (New York: Free Press, 1992). The book was based on a 1989 essay and discusses liberal democracy as the final form of human self-governance. Although the events of September 11, 2001, are often portrayed as effectively disproving Fukuyama's central thesis—namely, that violent conflict would be replaced by technocratic control as the driving force behind human events as the twenty-first century dawned—Fukuyama's observations about the rise of administrative means of securing power seem relevant to the world of the 2020s, even if we disagree with his conclusions regarding the significance of this rise.

76. Johnson, introduction to *A World of Difference* (Baltimore: Johns Hopkins University Press, 1987), 2.

77. https://www.youtube.com/watch?v=9L-Md6QLTmE&ab_channel =ChuckHenebry. The quotations within this paragraph are taken from the video, rather than the article's text.

78. Johnson, "Anthropomorphism in Lyric and Law," 560.

79. Mitt Romney might have benefited from a read of Johnson's essay before he informed a heckler at the Iowa State Fair in August 2011 that "corporations are people." See Philip Rucker, "Mitt Romney Says 'Corporations Are People,'" *Washington Post*, August 11, 2011.

80. For more on these matters, see Johnson's extraordinary article, "Apostrophe, Animation, and Abortion," *Diacritics* 16, 1 (Spring 1986): 28–47. Here (35) Johnson writes, "There is politics precisely because there is undecidability."

81. Edward W. Said, "Abecedarium Culturae: Structuralism, Absence, Writing," *TriQuarterly* 20 (Winter 1971): 54.

82. Said, 68.

83. Said, 67.

84. Edward W. Said, *The World, the Text, and the Critic* (Cambridge, MA: Harvard University Press, 1983), 291–92.

85. Said, 292.

86. Said, 290.

87. John Guillory, *Cultural Capital: The Problem of Literary Canon Formation* (Chicago: University of Chicago Press, 1993), 154.

88. Amy Hungerford, *Postmodern Belief: American Literature and Religion since 1960* (Princeton, NJ: Princeton University Press, 2010), 19.

89. https://www.merriam-webster.com/dictionary/world.

90. The particle-pollution high on Wednesday, June 7, 2023, was 460 micrograms per cubic meter, according to a graphic published by the *New York Times* on June 9, 2023, https://www.nytimes.com/interactive/2023/06/08/upshot/new-york -city-smoke.html.

91. Postmortems of New York City mayor Eric Adams's response to the climate emergency found that his administration acted too slowly to warn residents; see Michael Gold's reporting in "Mayor's Response to Wildfire Smoke Was Sluggish, New York Officials Say," *New York Times*, July 11, 2023. In a *Wirecutter* update published in the online *New York Times* on June 7, 2023, Tim Heffernan and Ellen Airhart authored a list of recommendations for air purifiers, along with a DIY hack involving a filter, tape, and a box fan, titled "How Can I Clear My Home of Wildfire Smoke?" https://www.nytimes.com/wirecutter/blog/air-purifier-wildfire-smoke/.

92. Paul de Man describes reading as "a negative process in which the grammatical cognition is undone" owing to the "tropological dimension of language," which tends to displace the order of grammar, particularly in literary writing. "The Resistance to Theory," in *The Resistance to Theory*, foreword Wlad Godzich (Minneapolis: University of Minnesota Press, 1986), 17.

93. As per the DSM-V on depersonalization/derealization: "*Cognitive disconnection schemata* reflect defectiveness and emotional inhibition and subsume themes of abuse, neglect, and deprivation. *Overconnection schemata* involve impaired autonomy with themes of dependency, vulnerability, and incompetence. . . . There is a clear association between the disorder and childhood interpersonal traumas in a substantial portion of individuals. . . . In particular, emotional abuse and emotional neglect have been most strongly and consistently associated with the disorder. Other stressors can include physical abuse; witnessing domestic violence; growing up with a seriously impaired, mentally ill parent." Simeon and Abugel, *Feeling Unreal* (104), "*Emotional abuse* alone stood out as the one more specific type of maltreatment intimately related to DDD."

The Three-Body Problem

1. Julia Kristeva, "Women's Time," trans. Alice Jardine and Harry Blake, *Signs* 7, 1 (Autumn 1981): 33. This essay was subsequently republished in *The Kristeva Reader*, ed. Toril Moi (New York: Columbia University Press, 1986), 187–213.

2. Luke 2:7, King James Bible Online, 2023 [1769], https://www.kingjamesbible online.org/.

3. As of May 2018, Facebook and Instagram began to permit so-called graphic images of birth, in which genitals are visible. Writer, doula, and registered nurse Katie Vigos created a Change.org campaign to bring about this transformation;

see her Empowered Birth Project, https://www.instagram.com/empoweredbirth
project. In an article on Vigos's work, Allison Yarrow writes, "Even in 2018, most
pregnant women have no idea what childbirth entails—because they've never
seen it"; "The Childbirth Photos Instagram Didn't Want You to See," *Harper's
Bazaar*, May 11, 2018. It is worth noting that the Instagram Community Guidelines
page was only changed to reflect this policy and explicitly permit depictions of
birth three years after this was announced, in March 2021, and that before this,
in February 2021, images depicting mastectomy and breastfeeding were con-
spicuously greenlighted, although images of birth went unmentioned until a
month later.

4. This situation of simultaneous surplus and scarcity reminds me of a linguistic predicament author Samuel R. Delany describes: "What makes statements
like 'Blacks are lazy and shiftless,' 'Women are lousy drivers,' or 'Homosexuals
are emotionally unstable,' racist, sexist, or homophobic is . . . the vast statistical preponderance of these particular statements in the general range of utter-
ances of most people most of the time"; *Of Solids and Surds: Notes for Noël Sturgeon,
Marilyn Hacker, Josh Lukin, Mia Wolff, Bill Stribling, and Bob White*, 2020 Windham-
Campbell Lecture (New Haven, CT: Yale University Press, 2020), 21. This is to say
that although alternative, positive images of birth exist in contemporary media,
these remain comparatively few and therefore may not impact most Americans'
understanding of birth.

5. See numerous articles on the same topic, such as the unattributed "Netflix
Faces Call to Rethink Liu Cixin Adaptation after His Uighur Comments," pub-
lished in the *Guardian* on September 25, 2020. A little less than a year earlier,
Jiayang Fan had published an excellent profile in the June 24, 2019, issue of the
New Yorker, "The War of the Worlds," in which she describes Liu's position via the
following exchange:

> When I brought up the mass internment of Muslim Uighurs—around a
> million are now in reëducation camps in the northwestern province of
> Xinjiang—he trotted out the familiar arguments of government-controlled
> media: "Would you rather that they be hacking away at bodies at train
> stations and schools in terrorist attacks? If anything, the government is
> helping their economy and trying to lift them out of poverty." The answer
> duplicated government propaganda so exactly that I couldn't help asking
> Liu if he ever thought he might have been brainwashed. "I know what you
> are thinking," he told me with weary clarity. "What about individual lib-
> erty and freedom of governance?" He sighed, as if exhausted by a debate
> going on in his head. "But that's not what Chinese people care about. For
> ordinary folks, it's the cost of health care, real-estate prices, their chil-
> dren's education. Not democracy."

While Fan does not explicitly connect the views expressed here with Trisolaran
policies, she does move quickly in her text to the moment in the novels in which
the Trisolarans "intern" humans in Australia, perhaps inviting comparison.

6. President Obama told Michiko Kakutani, "The scope of it was immense. So that was fun to read, partly because my day-to-day problems with Congress seem fairly petty—not something to worry about. Aliens are about to invade," unattributed; "Transcript: President Obama on What Books Mean to Him," *New York Times*, January 16, 2017.

7. See Roberto Guidetti and Nadja Møberg, "Environmental Adaptations: Encystment and Cyclomorphosis," in *Water Bears: The Biology of Tardigrades*, ed. Ralph O. Schill (Cham, Switzerland: Springer Switzerland, 2018), 249–72; Ralph O. Schill and Stephen Hengherr, "Environmental Adaptations: Dessication Tolerance" (273–94); Steffen Hengherr and Ralph O. Schill, "Environmental Adaptations: Cryobiosis" (295–310); and K. Ingemar Jönsson et al., "Environmental Adaptations: Radiation Tolerance" (311–30).

8. The Trisolarans use their advanced understanding of physics to create a machine called a "sophon," a quantum computer built into the extra dimensions of a proton. "Unfolding" the extra dimensions and inscribing them with circuits, the Trisolarans convert the subatomic particle into a device they can control and communicate with, and which can travel at the speed of light, reaching Earth before they themselves do. Once on Earth, sophons spy on humans and scramble particle accelerators. As one Trisolaran explains, "A sophon can take the place of a target particle and accept the collision. . . . After a sophon is struck, it can deliberately give out wrong and chaotic results. Thus, even if the actual target particle is occasionally struck, Earth physicists will not be able to tell the correct result from the numerous erroneous results." This disinformative activity regarding "the deep structure of matter" makes it impossible for humans to perform physics experiments that would permit them to become the military equals of the Trisolarans before the extraterrestrials arrive. Liu Cixin, *The Three-Body Problem*, trans. Ken Liu (New York: Tor Books, 2014), 378.

9. Dick-Read describes the Fear-Tension-Pain Syndrome at length: "Inhibitory muscle fibres of the uterus are amongst those which are stimulated by the general reaction of the sympathetic nervous system," and "Fear produces within the uterus excessive tension which causes pain and is rightly interpreted as such by the integrating nuclei of the thalamic area. Fear induces restriction of the circulation of the blood through the uterus thereby limiting in many ways the efficiency of the mechanism of parturition, adding to its discomforts the exquisite muscle tenderness of ischaemia"; Grantly Dick-Read, *Childbirth without Fear: The Principles and Practice of Natural Childbirth* (London: Pinter & Martin, 2004 [1942]), 45, 47. I am not a neurologist, but I have to say that the sixty hours of labor I experienced were most uncomfortable in areas other than my uterus.

10. Ornella Moscucci, "Holistic Obstetrics: The Origins of 'Natural Childbirth' in Britain," *Postgraduate Medical Journal* 79, 929 (March 2003): 168–73. Moscucci (171) quotes from a 1944 edition of Dick-Read's publication *Motherhood in the Postwar World*. See also Donald Caton, "Who Said Childbirth Is Natural? The Medical Mission of Grantly Dick-Read," *Anesthesiology* 84, 4 (April 1996): 955–64. Adrienne

Rich is in dialogue with Dick-Read throughout her chapter on "Alienated Labor" (156–85) in *Of Woman Born: Motherhood as Experience and Institution* (New York: W. W. Norton, 1976). She identifies his "essentially patriarchal" (171) attitude during her own exploration of North American norms. Rich does not elaborate on the role of episiotomy.

11. Here I refer to the cover of Pinter & Martin's second edition of 2013.

12. In Elizabeth G. Raymond and David A. Grimes, "The Comparative Safety of Legal Induced Abortion and Childbirth in the United States," *Obstetrics and Gynecology* 119 (February 2012): 215–19, which covers the period 1998–2005, the maternal mortality rate is listed as 8.8 per 100,000 live births. Since this time, the abortion fatality rate has remained steady, but the maternal mortality rate has gone up dramatically; as of 2019 it was 20.1, approximately *thirty times* the abortion fatality rate from 2019 (about 0.63). See https://www.cdc.gov/mmwr/volumes/70 /ss/ss7009a1.htm and https://www.cdc.gov/nchs/data/hestat/maternal-mortality -2021/E-Stat-Maternal-Mortality-Rates-H.pdf.

13. This artwork is reproduced in Harold Speert, "Obstetrical-Gynaecological Eponyms: James Young Simpson and His Obstetric Forceps," *British Journal of Obstetrics and Gynaecology* 64 (1957): 746, with the following caption: "Ancient marble bas-relief depicting a birth scene. The accoucheur, in the centre, holds a pair of obstetric forceps aloft in his right hand. This marble tablet, measuring 74x55cm., was discovered in the early twentieth century in the vicinity of Rome. The attire and furnishings in the scene date it in the second or third century A.D."

14. James Owen Drife, "The Start of Life: A History of Obstetrics," *Postgrad Medical Journal* 78, 919 (May 2002): 311.

15. "The instruments themselves were always carried in a gilded chest and revealed once the woman had been blindfolded. The birth subsequently took place under blankets with only the Chamberlens in attendance of the patient. It was through these elaborate measures that the Chamberlens were able to keep the secret of forceps for nearly a century"; S. Sheikh, I. Ganesaratnam, and H. Jan, "The Birth of Forceps," *Journal of the Royal Society of Medicine Short Reports* 4, 7 (July 2013): 2. "They are said to have arrived at the house of the woman to be delivered in a special carriage. They were accompanied by a huge wooden box adorned with gilded carvings. It always took two of them to carry the box and everyone was led to believe that it contained some massive and highly complicated machine. The labouring woman was blindfold (*sic*) lest she should see the 'secret.' Only the Chamberlens were allowed in the locked lying-in room, from which the terrified relatives heard peculiar noises, ringing bells, and other sinister sounds as the 'secret' went to work"; Peter M. Dunn, "The Chamberlen Family (1560–1728) and Obstetric Forceps," *Archives of Disease in Childhood* 81, 3 (November 1999): 232–33. For further detail on the mysterious Chamberlens, see James Hobson Aveling, *The Chamberlens and the Midwifery Forceps: Memorials of the Family and an Essay on the Invention of the Instrument* (London: J. & A. Churchill, 1882).

16. The term *accoucheur* was used to distinguish male practitioners from mid-wives, given that the term "man-midwife" was sometimes used pejoratively, with overtones of gender trespass. The later eighteenth century was a time of a (cur-rently) much studied and debated "war" between female midwives and men who presented themselves as scientifically trained experts in birth and anatomy. Lisa Forman Cody argues that "obstetricians could only triumph once the fundamen-tal intellectual and emotional connection between midwives and maternity was ruptured, as it largely was from the early eighteenth century onward," owing, as Cody notes, to the reframing of pregnancy and birth as appropriate subjects of Enlightenment science. See Cody, "The Politics of Reproduction: From Midwives' Alternative Public Sphere to the Public Spectacle of Man-Midwifery," *Eighteenth-Century Studies* 32, 4 (Summer 1999): 479–80. Note that although Cody uses the term *obstetrician*, it would not have been in use by those who would describe themselves as such until after 1826, as per Merriam-Webster online, https://www .merriam-webster.com/dictionary/obstetrician. See pro-*accoucheur* accounts in Roy Porter, "A Touch of Danger: The Man-Midwife as Sexual Predator," in *Sexual Underworlds of the Enlightenment*, ed. G. S. Rousseau and Roy Porter, 206–32 (Chapel Hill: University of North Carolina Press, 1988 [1987]), and Adrian Wilson, *The Making of Man-Midwifery in England, 1660–1770* (Cambridge, MA: Harvard University Press, 1995). For another take on this language, fiction is quite helpful: "For all these reasons, private and publick, put together,—my father was for hav-ing the man-midwife by all means,—my mother, by no means." We see this usage in Laurence Sterne's *The Life and Opinions of Tristram Shandy, Gentleman*, which began its serial publication in 1759. In this narrative, a "thin, upright, motherly, notable, good old body of a midwife" is preferred by the protagonist's mother, who "was absolutely determined to trust her life, and mine with it, into no soul's hand but this old woman's only." The protagonist's father, meanwhile, prefers a male "operator." Laurence Sterne, *The Life and Opinions of Tristram Shandy* (London: Penguin Books, 2003 [1759–67]), 45, 12, 41, 45. Lastly, Ornella Moscucci's *The Science of Woman: Gynaecology and Gender in England, 1800–1929* (Cambridge, UK: Cambridge University Press, 1990) provides a definitive counter-history.

17. William Smellie, a Scottish, London-practicing man-midwife of the mid-eighteenth century, innovated the forceps by means of blades covered in leather and, later, a thinner material. Lard apparently eased insertion and helped to pre-vent transmission of sexually transmitted infections, Sheikh et al., "The Birth of Forceps," 2.

18. "Some recommend an instrument to perforate the skull, with double points curved and joined together; which, when pushed into the foramen, are separated, and take hold on the inside; but as the opening with the scissors and introducing the blunt hook as above, will answer the same end, it is needless to multiply in-struments, especially as this method is not so certain as the following," explains Smellie in *A Treatise on the Theory and Practice of Midwifery* (1752–64), an extremely detailed—and the first known—description of the trained use of forceps. Here I quote from the first volume (346) of an 1876 edition (London: The New Sydenham

Society) of this apparently canonical three-volume compendium edited and annotated by an obstetrician named Alfred H. McClintock (1821[22?]–1881).

19. The crochet is described in detail and lavishly illustrated in Alban Doran, "A Demonstration of Some Eighteenth Century Obstetric Forceps," *Proceedings of the Royal Society of Medicine* 6 (May 1913): 54–76.

20. Ian D. Graham, "The Episiotomy Crusade" (PhD diss., McGill University, 1994), 1. "During the 1800s and early 1900s, American and British physicians seldom performed the operation" (3).

21. "Vacuum extraction is a type of operative vaginal delivery using ventouse that aids the descent of the fetal head along the pelvic curve and ultimately assists the delivery of the fetus. Overall, the incidence of operative vaginal delivery in different countries ranges from 10% to 15%. Vacuum delivery has become more popular over the past few decades owing to reduced maternal morbidity compared to forceps delivery"; J. C. Malavika and Neharika Malhotra, "Ventouse Delivery," in *Labor and Delivery: An Updated Guide*, ed. Ruchika Garg (Singapore: Springer Singapore, 2023), 479.

22. Cesareans were successfully performed in Uganda long before this was possible in the West. Peter Dunn, "Robert Felkin MD (1853–1926) and Cesarean Delivery in Central Africa (1879)," *Archives of Disease in Childhood* 80, 3 (May 1999): 250–51. For accounts of pre-nineteenth-century cesareans in Europe, see Michael J. O'Dowd and Elliot E. Philipp, "Caesarean Section," in *The History of Obstetrics and Gynaecology* (New York: Parthenon Publishing, 1994), 160.

23. DeLee's "paper and what it advocates is regarded by obstetricians and social scientists alike as the cornerstone of modern obstetric practice"; Graham, "Episiotomy Crusade," 67. See also Dorothy C. Wertz and Richard C. Wertz, *Lying In: A History of Childbirth in America* (New Haven, CT: Yale University Press, 1989 [1977]), 141–43. Wertz and Wertz (143) write, "By the 1930s [DeLee's] routine was normative in many hospitals, for his rationale to prevent tears seemed reasonable: Many women delivering in hospitals *were* experiencing tears. But obstetricians did not ask whether tears resulted from the failings of nature or from hospital practices, which often immobilized a woman on her back with legs raised in stirrups."

24. Joseph Bolivar DeLee, "The Prophylactic Forceps Operation," *American Journal of Obstetrics and Gynecology* 1 (1920): 33–44, and *Transactions of the American Gynecological Society* 45 (1920): 66–83. These two texts differ very slightly throughout. "Essentially, the prophylactic forceps operation consisted of giving morphine and scopolamine (an amnesiac) during the first stage of labor, putting the mother to sleep with ether after the fetal head passed the cervix, performing a mediolateral episiotomy, extracting the infant with forceps, injecting ergot and pituitrin to contract the uterus and prevent postpartum hemorrhage, manually extracting the placenta, repairing the episiotomy incision, and administering more morphine and scopolamine to abolish, as much as possible, the memory of labor"; Graham, "Episiotomy Crusade."

25. DeLee, "The Prophylactic Forceps Operation," *American Journal*, 42; *Transactions of the American Gynecological Society*, 74.

26. DeLee, 41 and 72. Regarding the pitchfork metaphor: "If a woman falls on a pitchfork, and drives the handle through her perineum, we call that pathologic-abnormal, but if a large baby is driven through the pelvic floor, we say that it is natural, and therefore normal" (40, 71).

27. "Primary union is the rule and examination later shows that virginal conditions are usually restored"; DeLee, 39, 71.

28. "In skillful hands the danger is *nil*. . . . As yet, no mother or baby has died; there has been no case of infection or cerebral hemorrhage. The babies have thriven, the mothers have not shown the exhaustion and anemia of former days. The restoration of the parturient canal has been always perfect—indeed, too nearly perfect"; DeLee, 44, 77. It is worth noting that DeLee does not recommend his operation for everyone (it is unnecessary for multiparae with large pelvises) and states that only the highly trained should practice it, but of course these cautions seem minor in the face of his bombastic enthusiasm for the surgery.

29. DeLee, 34, 66. There are no references to be found in either version of DeLee's paper.

30. See the discussion sections that follow both publications of DeLee's paper.

31. Barbara Katz Rothman, "Laboring Then: The Political History of Maternity Care in the United States," in *Laboring On: Birth in Transition in the United States*, ed. Wendy Simonds, Barbara Katz Rothman, and Bari Meltzer Norman (New York: Routledge, 2006), 15.

32. See Bruce Bellingham and Mary Pugh Mathis, "Race, Citizenship, and the Bio-politics of the Maternalist Welfare State: 'Traditional' Midwifery in the American South under the Sheppard-Towner Act, 1921–29," *Social Politics* 1, 2 (Summer 1994): 157–89.

33. "Of all the lay midwives practicing in America during the early twentieth century, it was the granny midwife who was most affected by changes in medicine and state regulations. It was she who had the most to lose with the movement from folklore to forceps, asafoetida to anesthesia, home to hospital, licensing from God to licensing by the State. . . . The granny midwife's very body, the physical body of an elderly, black woman, was seen as unclean and deviant. Additionally, the material culture with which the granny midwife had practiced her craft, most notably her midwife's bag, became a trickster's bag for subversive practices"; Valerie Lee, *Granny Midwives and Black Women Writers: Double-Dutched Readings* (New York: Routledge, 1996), 17. Dramatic decreases in the number of births attended by granny midwives by the late 1940s in Georgia, for example, were seen as a success of nurse-midwife training programs; see Joyce B. Thompson and Helen Varney Burst, *A History of Midwifery in the United States: The Midwife Said*

Fear Not (New York: Springer, 2015), 95. A *Jackson Advocate* article of January 27, 1951, announced, "Negro Nurses Wipe Out Midwifery in Memphis Area," 4. See also Alicia D. Bonaparte, "The Persecution and Prosecution of Granny Midwives in South Carolina, 1900–1940" (PhD diss., Vanderbilt University, 2007).

34. Graham, "Episiotomy Crusade," 80.

35. Antiseptic methods became widespread after the publication of Joseph Lister's paper "On the Antiseptic Principle of the Practice of Surgery," in *The Lancet* 90, 2299 (September 21, 1867): 353–56. In spite of these advances, puerperal fever continued to ravage lying-in hospitals and maternity wards, with physicians who had examined corpses touching the bodies of birthing people without taking any hygienic steps and subsequent surgical interventions into birth similarly encouraging infection, until the introduction of sulfa drugs in 1937; see Irvine Loudon, "The American Lying-In Hospital," in *Death in Childbirth: An International Study of Maternal Care and Maternal Mortality, 1800–1950* (Oxford, UK: Oxford University Press, 1992), 330–32. "Topical hemostatic agents in the modern surgical era can be traced to 1909, when [Salo] Bergel first discussed the use of topical fibrin for hemostasis"; Chandru P. Sundaram and Alison C. Keenan, "Evolution of Hemostatic Agents in Surgical Practice," *Indian Journal of Urology* 26, 3 (July 2010): 375. George W. Crile performed the first successful direct blood transfusion in 1906; see N. Nathoo, F. K. Lautzenheiser, and G. Barnett, "The First Direct Blood Transfusion: The Forgotten Legacy of George W. Crile," *Operative Neurosurgery* 64, 3 (March 2009): 20–27. The WHO's recommendation of a 10–15 percent cesarean rate, necessary to reduce maternal mortality, is discussed later in this essay.

36. Matthew L. Edwards and Anwar D. Jackson, "The Historical Development of Obstetric Anesthesia and Its Contributions to Perinatology," *American Journal of Perinatology* 34, 3 (2017): 211–12. Accoucheur John Snow gave chloroform to Queen Victoria during the birth of Prince Leopold; Speert, "Obstetrical-Gynaecological Eponyms," 748.

37. Bethany Johnson and Margaret Quinlan, "Technical versus Public Spheres: A Feminist Analysis of Women's Rhetoric in the Twilight Sleep Debates of 1914–1916," *Health Communication* 30, 11 (October 2014): 1076–88.

38. Judith Walzer Leavitt, "Birthing and Anesthesia: The Debate over Twilight Sleep," in "Women: Sex and Sexuality, Part 2," *Signs* 6, 1 (Autumn 1980): 147–64.

39. "Women hailed Twilight Sleep as a triumph of technology"; Donald Caton, *What a Blessing She Had Chloroform: The Medical and Social Response to the Pain of Childbirth from 1800 to the Present* (New Haven: Yale University Press, 1999), 132–33. Caton (130) quotes a passage from Edith Wharton's 1927 novel, *Twilight Sleep*, in which "all that was so easily managed nowadays."

40. "By 1950 obstetric anesthesia was in vogue with both physicians and the public," Caton, 200. But, as we may surmise, anesthesia was not a solitary intervention. As one obstetrician noted, "The introduction of Nembutal into obstetric practice and the rapid improvement of anesthetic technics further increased

the use of outlet forceps with episiotomy"; Donald A. Dallas, "The Routine Use of Episiotomy with a Description of the Continuous Knotless Repair," *Western Journal of Surgery, Obstetrics and Gynecology* 61 (January 1953): 29.

41. "The first professional criticism of episiotomy appeared between 1975 and 1983 in the UK and the USA," write C. Clesse, J. Lighezzolo-Alnot, S. De Laverge, S. Hamlin, and M. Scheffler in "Socio-historical Evolution of the Episiotomy Practice: A Literature Review," *Women & Health* 59, 7 (2019): 766. There were, however, occasional critical articles published before this time, such as Channing W. Barrett's "Errors and Evils of Episiotomy," *American Journal of Surgery* 76 (1948): 284–85. As Clesse et al. note (765), wider popular questioning of routine episiotomy began with "lay publications." Boston Women's Health Collective's *Our Bodies, Ourselves* (New York: Simon & Schuster, 1973), for example, "strongly condemned the practice." Results of the first randomized controlled trials—showing that the results of routine episiotomy were contrary to those that had been touted since the publication of DeLee's paper—appeared in 1984: R. F Harrison, M. Brennan, P. M. North, J. V. Reed, and E. A. Wickham, "Is Routine Episiotomy Necessary?" *British Medical Journal*, Clinical Research ed., 288, 6435 (June 30, 1984): 1971–75; J. Sleep et al., "West Berkshire Perineal Management Trial," *British Medical Journal*, Clinical Research ed., 289, 6445 (September 8, 1984): 587–90.

42. See Jacqueline H. Wolf, *Deliver Me from Pain: Anesthesia and Birth in America* (Baltimore: Johns Hopkins University Press, 2009), 151–58. "Women were taught to request politely that only leg and not hand restraints be used"; Rothman, "Laboring Then," 26.

43. For Apgar's achievements, see Caton, *What a Blessing*, 201–6. Nancy Stoller Shaw, *Forced Labor: Maternity Care in the United States* (New York: Pergamon Press, 1974), 74.

44. American College of Obstetricians-Gynecologists, "Episiotomy: Clinical Management Guidelines for Obstetrician-Gynecologists," *ACOG Practice Bulletin* 71 (April 2006): 957–62.

45. Theresa Morris, *Cut It Out: The C-Section Epidemic in America* (New York: New York University Press, 2013), 70–76. Morris discusses the interrelated roles of electronic fetal monitors, epidurals, and Pitocin in the production of cesarean procedures. She writes (71), "[Pitocin] has become an intervention used to help women achieve vaginal birth in the face of other interventions, a practice that is indicative of the medicalized environment women face when giving birth in the contemporary United States. Because patience and waiting for a vaginal birth is not always the plan, Pitocin seems to be a created necessity. . . . Researchers find that women who have epidurals and receive a low dose of Pitocin to augment labor . . . have an increased risk of c-section." Morris found that increased risk of cesarean was related to refusal on the part of nurse practitioners to up Pitocin levels to generate delivery due to protocols; Morris (73) recalls, "This might explain the most common response I heard to what physicians do when

a nurse will not carry out an order to give a woman Pitocin or to increase the dose of Pitocin, a response that I, perhaps naively, found shocking the first time I heard it—physicians 'give up' and perform c-sections they feel are unnecessary." Or, as another physician tells Morris (76), "'There is really no pressure whatsoever to keep your c-section rate low.'" Morris's findings differ from the causality discussed in the 2008 documentary *The Business of Being Born*, where the use of Pitocin itself is linked to fetal distress.

46. Morris, *Cut It Out*, 14.

47. It is additionally worth noting that numerous review papers rate the quality of evidence regarding the outcomes of elective cesarean as low to moderate. The American College of Obstetricians and Gynecologists cautions, "Cesarean delivery on maternal request is not a well-recognized clinical entity" (e73) and "With the exception of three outcome variables with moderate-quality evidence (maternal hemorrhage, maternal length of stay, and neonatal respiratory morbidity), all remaining outcome assessments . . . were based on weak evidence. This significantly limits the reliability of judgments regarding whether an outcome measure favors either cesarean delivery on maternal request or planned vaginal delivery" (e74). It may be that there is no current obstetrical environment in which it is possible to make decisions on these matters under conditions of reliable probabilities. See Committee on Obstetric Practice, "ACOG Committee Opinion: Cesarean Delivery on Maternal Request," *Obstetrics & Gynecology* 133, 1 (January 2019): e73–e77.

48. From a medical point of view, the rise of fetal personhood may begin as early as the eighteenth century, when man-midwives' concern for neonate health seems figured by detailed illustrations published in professional manuals; see Josephine M. Lloyd, "The 'Languid Child' and the Eighteenth-Century Man-Midwife," *Bulletin of the History of Medicine* 75, 4 (Winter 2001): 641–79. Certainly, DeLee was very concerned about squished heads in the early twentieth century. Legally speaking, fetal rights in the United States are a post–World War II development; see Cynthia R. Daniels, "Fetal Animation: The Political and Cultural Emergence of Fetal Rights," in *At Women's Expense: State Power and the Politics of Fetal Rights* (Cambridge, MA: Harvard University Press, 1993), 9–30. For tort regimes' effects on obstetrics, see Louise Marie Roth, *The Business of Birth: Malpractice and Maternity Care in the United States* (New York: New York University Press, 2021), 62–65. Roth (70) contends that in obstetric care uncertainty has been "reclassify[ied]" as risk, with the result that "maternity care providers usually exaggerate the threat and overestimate the risk of a bad birth outcome because the downside of a birth injury or death is much larger than the upside of a normal birth."

49. Morris, *Cut It Out*, writes (150), "It is clear that informed consent in maternity care is lacking, and this observation is supported by much research." Roth (193) describes the obstetric practice of "'playing the dead baby card'" to enforce

compliance. Anecdotally speaking, of the dozen or so people—mostly friends and colleagues—whom I have encountered in the past two years who experienced an unplanned cesarean and who told me their story, no one has said they understood what was happening to them in the moment, nor what their options were.

50. Natalie Fixmer-Oraiz, *Homeland Maternity: U.S. Security Culture and the New Reproductive Regime* (Urbana: University of Illinois Press, 2019), 7.

51. For example, "Women of reproductive age who are American Indian and Alaska Native are 2.6 times as likely as white women to live under conditions that create problems during and after pregnancy"; Sema Sgaier and Jordan Downey, "What We See in the Shameful Trends on U.S. Maternal Health," op-ed, *New York Times*, November 17, 2021. The C-section rate is also highest for Black women; see Morris, *Cut It Out*, 185n82. For examples of selective and severe punishments, see Jia Tolentino's reporting in the July 4, 2022, issue of the *New Yorker*, "The Post-Roe Era." Fixmer-Oraiz, writing in 2019, names the cases of multiple women who were "deprived of fundamental human rights in the name of fetal health and protection" (2): Tamara Loertscher, Rinat Dray, Marlise Muñoz, Purvi Patel.

52. "Some of these practices persisted into the 1980s, for example, routine perineal shave, 'poodle cut,' or clip; routine enema; routine strapping down of hands and legs"; Thompson and Varney Burst, *History of Midwifery in the United States*, 95.

53. Rachel Cusk, *Kudos: A Novel* (New York: Farrar, Straus and Giroux, 2018), 59.

54. Liu, *Death's End*, trans. Ken Liu (New York: Tor Books, 2016 [2010]), 145.

55. Liu, 474.

56. The accuracy of ultrasound dating has been called into question, although studies continue to find that it is more accurate than using the date of the last menstrual period. Given that the ultrasound moved my due date forward, I could have been identified as carrying "past term" sooner (and, therefore, as a candidate for induction); as it turned out, this was not relevant for my pregnancy. For discussion of (in)accuracies of the dating scan, see Marsden Wagner, *Born in the USA: How a Broken Maternity System Must Be Fixed to Put Women and Children First* (Berkeley: University of California Press, 2006), 40. Wagner, despite his own apprehension regarding ultrasound dating, cites a Norwegian study that concluded ultrasound-predicted dates are indeed more accurate; see Bjørn Backe and Jakob Nakling, "Term Prediction in Routine Ultrasound Practice," *Acta Obstetrica et Gynecologica Scandinavica* 73, 2 (February 1994): 113–18. The first study "to prospectively investigate the impact of biological variation in ovulation and implantation timing on [gestational age] assessment in natural conception" was published in 2012 and found that fetal age is determined by a combination of ovulation and implantation timing; see A. A. Mahendru, A. Daemen, T. R. Everett, I. B. Wilkinson, C. M. McEniery, Y. Abdullah, D. Timmerman, T. Bourne, and C. C. Lees, "Impact of Ovulation and Implantation Timing on First-Trimester Crown-Rump Length and Gestational Age," *Ultrasound in Obstetrics and Gynecology* 46, 6 (2012): 630–35.

57. Rosalind Pollack Petchesky, "Fetal Images: The Power of Visual Culture in the Politics of Reproduction," *Feminist Studies* 13, 2 (Summer 1987): 276. The sonic weapon of current municipal choice is the LRAD, or long-range acoustic device, which police may use to broadcast instructions or emit physically distressing sound. See such reporting as Lee Fang, "Acoustic Cannon Sales to Police Surge after Black Lives Matter Protests," *The Intercept*, August 14, 2015.

58. Petchesky, 270.

59. Petchesky, 270.

60. Petchesky, 270.

61. Zoë Sofia, "Exterminating Fetuses: Abortion, Disarmament, and the Sexo-Semiotics of Extraterrestrialism," *Diacritics* 14, 2 (Summer 1984): 54.

62. In other words, it's easy to dream that the ultrasound image alarms us because the fetus is "alone"; harder to notice that the ultrasound image is a by-product of the death-oriented military-industrial complex.

63. Upon reading this section of the essay, the friend in question wrote, "Lol did I say that? I feel like I remember saying something like: you're lucky they were honest with you and told you what they intended to do. Most hospital midwifery practices don't tell you that they are going to coerce you into induction at 39 weeks. . . . I also think I said something about how hospitals use the words 'birth center' to describe the regular L&D ward because it's a good branding move but has nothing to do with promoting or practicing physiological birth."

64. F. Ramalheira and M. Conde Moreno, "Sharing Is Caring: A Review on Oxytocin Role in Human Behaviour and Clinical Implications," *European Psychiatry* 65, 1 (June 2022): 735.

65. "United States . . . has the highest maternal mortality rate in the industrialized world"; Emily Baumgaertner, "For Black Mothers, Birthing Centers, Once a Refuge, Become a Battleground," *New York Times*, September 30, 2023.

66. Most research on increased risk of uterine rupture is in the case of VBAC; see H. Zhang, H. Liu, S. Luo, and W. Gu, "Oxytocin Use in Trial of Labor after Cesarean and Its Relationship with Risk of Uterine Rupture in Women with One Previous Cesarean Section: A Meta-Analysis of Observational Studies," *BMC Pregnancy and Childbirth* 21, 11 (2021). Uterine rupture without a history of cesarian is rarer, but oxytocin may increase risk; see I. Al-Zirqi, A. K. Daltveit, L. Forsén, B. Stray-Pedersen, and S. Vangen, "Risk Factors for Complete Uterine Rupture," *American Journal of Obstetrics and Gynecology* 216, 2 (February 2017): 165.e1–165.e8. Older studies have shown a connection between oxytocin and elevated bilirubin, but there is not a consensus on the clinical significance; see S. S. Patil, Manjunatha S., Veen H. C., and V. Wali, "Oxytocin Induced Neonatal Hyperbilirubinemia," *Journal of Evidence-Based Medicine and Healthcare* 2, 21 (May 25, 2015): 3098–102. Oxytocin administration during labor appears to be an independent risk factor

for severe postpartum hemorrhage; see J. Belghiti, G. Kayem, C. Dupont, R.-C. Rudigoz, M.-H. Bouvier-Colle, and C. Deneux-Tharaux, "Oxytocin during Labour and Risk of Severe Postpartum Haemorrhage: A Population-Based, Cohort-Nested Case-Control Study," *BMJ Open* 1, 2 (December 21, 2011). Belghiti et al. note that "obstetric haemorrhage remains one of the leading causes of maternal mortality in developed countries, accounting for 10%–30% of direct maternal deaths in countries with maternal death enquiries. It is also a major component of severe maternal morbidity."

67. "Speeding up labor with Pitocin induction has been shown to carry the risk of overly rapid uterine contractions, which can mean insufficient oxygen for the baby and brain damage"; Marsden Wagner, *Born in the USA*, 7. According to the ARRIVE study conducted in 2018 (William A. Grobman et al., "Labor Induction versus Expectant Management in Low-Risk Nulliparous Women," *New England Journal of Medicine* 379, 6 [August 9, 2018]: 513–23), inducing low-risk primaparae with accurately estimated due dates at thirty-nine weeks could lower their chance of receiving a cesarean. This said, the providers participating in the study knew they were being observed and the relationship between induction and C-section monitored, and in an environment in which this is not the case, it is unclear if lower cesarean rates would inhere.

68. Wagner, *Born in the USA*, 132.

69. Wagner, 38.

70. Clarel Antoine and Bruce K. Young, "Cesarean Section One Hundred Years 1920–2020: The Good, the Bad and the Ugly," *Journal of Perinatal Medicine* 49, 1 (2020): 7.

71. "Epidemiologic studies showed that the practice of episiotomy (for primiparous and multiparous women) decreased from 84 percent in 1950 to 67.9 percent in 1960 and to 63.9 percent in 1980"; Clesse et al., "Socio-historical Evolution of the Episiotomy Practice," 764.

72. George B. Feldman and Jennie A. Freiman, "Prophylactic Cesarean Section at Term?" *New England Journal of Medicine* 312, 19 (May 9, 1985): 1267. Tellingly, this article begins with a description of a malpractice suit brought by a "40-year-old nullipara with an uncomplicated antepartum course."

73. Elena Ferrante, *Those Who Leave and Those Who Stay*, trans. Ann Goldstein (New York: Europa Editions, 2014), 274. Lila says that "the disgusting face of things alone was not enough for writing a novel," suggesting that the present is a mere "mask" that the novelist's "imagination" must plumb.

74. "Thomas Sartwelle, an American trial lawyer specializing in birth injury, blames the monitor for what he terms a 'phenomenon previously unseen in medicine's long history . . . defensive medicine.' He contends that the seemingly irrefutable record of fetal distress provided by monitor strips was responsible for the excessive damage awards issued by juries beginning in the mid-1980s. The

judgments, he writes, 'not only substantially altered medical practice but medical ethics as well. Physicians' response to the rising claims was abandonment of the venerable "first do no harm" principle, replacing it with the expedient self-serving ethics of "do whatever is necessary to keep trial lawyers at bay." 'Although Sartwelle defines the rising number of cesareans as 'harm,' most physicians have not"; Jacqueline H. Wolf, *Cesarean Section: An American History of Risk, Technology, and Consequence* (Baltimore: Johns Hopkins University Press, 2018), 153.

75. See the discussion of the structure of sophons in note 8. Additionally, by the final novel in the series, we understand that some sentient beings can reduce the dimensions of a given area of space by technological means, such that any being surviving in an n-dimensional space may be destroyed by the conversion of that space to n-minus-one dimensions. The "Zero-Homers" or "Resetters," for example, want to lower the universe to zero dimensions to perform a "reset"; Liu, *Death's End*, 562.

76. "'Father's time, mother's species,' as Joyce put it; and, indeed, when evoking the name and destiny of women, one thinks more of the *space* generating and forming the human species than of *time*, becoming, or history"; Kristeva, "Women's Time," 15.

77. Kristeva, "Stabat Mater," trans. Arthur Goldhammer, in "The Female Body in Western Culture: Semiotic Perspectives," *Poetics Today* 6, 1–2, (1985): 149. Republished in Moi, *The Kristeva Reader*, 160–86.

78. Margery Kempe, *The Book of Margery Kempe*, ed. Lynn Staley (Kalamazoo, MI: Medieval Institute Publications, 1996), line 151.

79. Kempe, 157.

80. Kempe, 23, 176.

81. Kempe, 179.

82. Kempe, 170.

83. "Persistent hallucinatory and delusory revelation, neuropsychiatric or socio-cultural, empowered Kempe's then unconventional independence and indomitable vocation, through sexual temptations, confrontations, trials and pilgrimages, in England and to Jerusalem, Rome, Compostela and Wilsnack"; Greg Wilkinson, "Margery Kempe: Puerperal Psychosis, Mysticism, and the First Autobiography in English," *British Journal of Psychiatry* 215, 6 (November 2019): 725.

84. "Early or prodromal symptoms of postpartum psychosis include insomnia, mood fluctuation, and irritability, with emergence of mania, depression, or a mixed state. Although rapid mood fluctuations are a hallmark of the disease, women suffering from postpartum psychosis often have symptoms that are atypical in patients with bipolar disorder. For example, mood-incongruent delusions are common and often related to the theme of childbirth. Disorganized, unusual behavior and obsessive thoughts regarding the newborn frequently

occur. Postpartum psychosis is notable for its delirium-like appearance, with cognitive symptoms such as disorientation, confusion, derealization, and depersonalization"; V. Bergink, N. Rasgon, and K. L. Wisner, "Postpartum Psychosis: Madness, Mania, and Melancholia in Motherhood," *American Journal of Psychiatry* 173, 12 (December 2016): 1180. "Confusion and perplexity are common symptoms of the disorder.... There is a lack of consensus about the type and duration of symptoms"; V. Sharma, D. Mazmanian, L. Palagini, and A. Bramante, "Postpartum Psychosis: Revisiting the Phenomenology, Nosology, and Treatment," *Journal of Affective Disorders Reports* 10 (December 2022): 2.

85. Toi Derricotte, *Natural Birth* (Trumansburg, NY: Crossing Press, 1983), 42.

86. Because we see shots of a Draeger 8000 SC incubator and there are no images of the sorts of exowomb technologies that have been used to grow lambs and mice, but we also see no images of birth itself, the manner in which this child is gestated and born is debatable. In any case, physiological birth is not practiced aboard this craft.

87. Is it worth asking if architectural and technological solutions could be found within "the next 500 years" before we need to switch up all our DNA?

88. Christopher E. Mason, *The Next 500 Years: Engineering Life to Reach New Worlds* (Cambridge, MA: MIT Press, 2021), xi.

89. Mason, xi.

90. Konrad Szocik, "The Biologically Optimized Spacefarer," *Nature* 372, 6541 (April 30, 2021): 469.

91. Mason, *The Next 500 Years*, 92.

92. James Quandt, "Lost in Space," *Artforum* 57, 8 (April 2019): 59.

93. These were my search terms.

94. Greg Egan, *Diaspora: A Novel* (New York: Night Shade Books, 2015 [1998]), 5. "Konishi polis itself was buried two hundred meters beneath the Siberian tundra" (10).

95. Egan, 8.

96. Egan, 9.

97. Egan, "Glossary," 323.

98. Egan, 300. The Contingency Handler was created by a society other than the Transmuters.

99. Different polises have different norms of intimacy. In C-Z we witness this exchange between two citizens: "Gabriel pressed his hand inside ver again, deeper this time; pulses of warmth spread out from the center of vis torso. Blanca turned toward him and stroked his back, reaching for the place where the fur became,

if he chose, almost unbearably sensitive. . . . The two of them were not slavishly embodied; harm remained impossible, coercion remained impossible"; Egan, 149.

100. At the close of *Death's End* (585), Cheng Xin and Guan Yifan, two survivors of the annihilation of humanity, experience vast expanses of time and space together and eventually begin a life in an artificial universe called Universe 647. Later, they leave this artificial universe, hoping to be part of what comes next.

101. By Sienna's account, she prefers to bring birthing people whose labors are not, in her estimation, progressing effectively into the hospital "in good shape," given her understanding of what may take place there. We might say that her care is indirectly informed by the relationship to risk prevalent in the hospital model of birth. She carries liability insurance and is licensed as a CPM (Certified Professional Midwife) by the state of Vermont. Conversation with the author, December 1, 2023.

102. As Sienna reports, my son was fully posterior when he emerged, meaning that his head was facing the front of my body. This presentation makes labor, particularly the pushing stage, more difficult than anterior positioning. Sienna says that when she and Susan saw this, their mutual reaction was surprise that I had managed to birth him vaginally after such a long labor. Conversation of December 1, 2023.

103. Carmen Winant, *My Birth* (Ithaca, NY: Image Text Ithaca/SPBH Editions, 2018), unpaginated. Winant has collected images of people giving birth and displayed them en masse, also publishing an artist's book including photographs of her mother giving birth, along with other women birthing. Before I gave birth, I found the images Winant assembled unnerving. After giving birth, looking over *My Birth*, I wished that it were more explicit.

104. See Sofia, "Exterminating Fetuses," for example.

105. In her dissenting opinion in *City of Akron v. Akron Center for Reproductive Health,* Justice O'Connor argued that *Roe v. Wade* was "on a collision course with itself" because technology was pushing the point of viability indefinitely backward. In *Roe* the court had defined "viability" as the point at which the fetus is "potentially able to live outside the mother's womb, albeit with artificial aid." After that point, the state could restrict abortion except when bringing the fetus to term would jeopardize the woman's life or health. See https://www.law .cornell.edu/supremecourt/text/462/416.

106. See Durrenda Ojanuga, "The Medical Ethics of the 'Father of Gynaecology,' Dr. J. Marion Sims," *Journal of Medical Ethics* 19, 1 (March 1993): 28–31.

107. See Silvia Federici, *Caliban and the Witch: Women, the Body, and Primitive Accumulation* (Brooklyn, NY: Autonomedia, 2004) and *Witches, Witch-Hunting, and Women* (Oakland, CA: PM Press, 2018).

Lucy Ives is the author of three novels: *Impossible Views of the World*; *Loudermilk: Or, The Real Poet; Or, The Origin of the World*; and *Life Is Everywhere*. Her writing has appeared in *Artforum, Harper's,* the *Paris Review,* and *Vogue*. She is the 2023–25 Bonderman Assistant Professor of the Practice in Literary Arts at Brown University.

Graywolf Press publishes risk-taking, visionary writers who transform culture through literature. As a nonprofit organization, Graywolf relies on the generous support of its donors to bring books like this one into the world.

This publication is made possible, in part, by the voters of Minnesota through a Minnesota State Arts Board Operating Support grant, thanks to a legislative appropriation from the arts and cultural heritage fund. Significant support has also been provided by other generous contributions from foundations, corporations, and individuals. To these supporters we offer our heartfelt thanks.

To learn more about Graywolf's books and authors or make a tax-deductible donation, please visit www.graywolfpress.org.

The text of *An Image of My Name Enters America* is set in Source Serif Pro. Book design by Ann Sudmeier. Composition by Bookmobile Design & Digital Publisher Services, Minneapolis, Minnesota. Manufactured by Sheridan on acid-free, 30 percent postconsumer wastepaper.